8.55

THE LOEB CLASSICAL LIBRARY

FOUNDED BY JAMES LOEB, LL.D.

EDITED BY

E. H. WARMINGTON, M.A., F.R.HIST.SOC.

FORMER EDITORS

†T. E. PAGE, C.H., LITT.D. †E. CAPPS, PH.D., LL.D.
†W. H. D. ROUSE, LITT.D. †L. A. POST, L.H.D.

SENECA

X

NATURALES QUAESTIONES

II

SENECA

IN TEN VOLUMES

X

NATURALES QUAESTIONES

II

WITH AN ENGLISH TRANSLATION BY

THOMAS H. CORCORAN, Ph.D.

PROFESSOR OF CLASSICS, TUFTS UNIVERSITY

CAMBRIDGE, MASSACHUSETTS

HARVARD UNIVERSITY PRESS

LONDON

WILLIAM HEINEMANN LTD

MCMLXXII

American ISBN 0-674-99503-1
British ISBN 0 434 99457 X

Printed in Great Britain

CONTENTS

BOOK IVA

THE NILE

LIBER QUARTUS A[1]

DE NILO[2]

Praefatio 1. Delectat te, quemadmodum scribis, Lucili virorum optime, Sicilia et officium procurationis otiosae,[3] delectabitque, si continere id intra fines suos volueris nec efficere imperium quod est procuratio. Facturum hoc te non dubito; scio quam sis ambitioni alienus, quam familiaris otio et litteris. Turbam rerum hominumque desiderent qui se pati nesciunt; tibi tecum optime convenit.

2. Nec est mirum paucis istud contingere: imperiosi[4] nobis ac molesti sumus; modo amore nostri, modo taedio laboramus; infelicem animum nunc superbia inflamus, nunc cupiditate distendimus; alias voluptate lassamus, alias sollicitudine exurimus; quod est miserrimum, numquam sumus singuli. Necesse est itaque assidua sit in tam magno vitiorum contubernio rixa.

---

[1] *l. octavus* EK[2]T; *liber septimus* Ex; *l. decimus* HG; *l. secundus* Diels, Gercke; [*Liber Quartus A*] *Liber Octavus* Oltramare.

[2] Gercke, Oltramare; *De Nili incremento* E.

[3] *negotiosae* Gercke.

2

BOOK IVA

THE NILE

PREFACE 1. To judge from what you write, my excellent Lucilius, you like Sicily and your office of governor with its leisure time. You will continue to be pleased if you are willing to keep all this within its own limits and not try to turn what is only an administrative office into supreme power. I have no doubt that you will act properly. I know how uninterested you are in ambition, how devoted you are to leisure and letters. Let those who do not know how to tolerate themselves search for the hustle of people and events. You find the best company in yourself.

2. It is not surprising that this happens to so few people. We are demanding and troublesome to ourselves. We suffer at times from self-love, at times from self-weariness. Now we inflate our unhappy soul with pride, now we torture it with desire. Sometimes we relax it with indulgence, sometimes we burn it up with anxiety; and what is most pitiful of all: we are never alone with ourselves. Inevitably, there is continuous strife among such a great co-habitation of vices.

---

[4] Erasmus, Oltramare, Alexander; *imperio si* HPZG; *superiorum* Gercke.

3. Fac ergo, mi Lucili, quod facere consuesti; a turba te, quantum potes, separa, ne adulatoribus latus praebeas. Artifices sunt ad captandos superiores; par illis, etiamsi bene caveris, non eris. Sed, mihi crede, proditioni, si capieris,[1] ipse te trades. 4. Habent hoc in se naturale blanditiae: etiam cum reiciuntur placent. Saepe exclusae novissime recipiuntur; hoc enim ipsum imputant quod repelluntur, et subigi ne contumelia quidem possunt. Incredibile est quod dicturus sum, sed tamen verum: ea maxime quisque patet, qua petitur. Fortasse enim ideo, quia patet, petitur.[2] 5. Sic ergo formare ut scias non posse te consequi ut sis impenetrabilis;[3] cum omnia caveris, per ornamenta ferieris.[4] Alius adulatione clam utetur, parce; alius ex aperto, palam, rusticitate simulata, quasi simplicitas illa, non ars sit. Plancus, artifex ante Villeium [5] maximus, aiebat non esse occulte nec ex dissimulato blandiendum. " Perit," inquit, " procari, si latet." 6. Plurimum adulator, cum deprehensus est, proficit; plus etiamnunc, si obiurgatus est, si erubuit. Futuros multos

---

[1] *si patueris* Garrod.
[2] Alexander agrees with Axelson in deleting *fortasse . . . petitur.*
[3] *ne si is penetrabilis* Z.
[4] Oltramare; *fieris* Z; *fiet* most MSS., Gercke.
[5] *Villeium* HP Oltramare; *villeum* G; *Vitellium* Z; *Suillium* Gercke.

---

[1] This Villeius is unknown. One manuscript has " Vitellius," who could be the Emperor Vitellius' father, a notorious

3. Therefore, my Lucilius, act just as you usually do. Keep yourself separated from the crowd as much as possible and expose no side of yourself to flatterers. They are clever experts at taking over their superiors. Even if you are well on guard you will be no match for them. But, believe me, if you are taken in by them you will be handing yourself over to betrayal. 4. Flattery has in it this natural appeal: even when it is rejected it is pleasing. Often refused it is finally accepted; for flattery considers it a merit even to be repulsed and cannot be subdued even by insults. What I am about to say is incredible, but none the less true: the side where a man especially exposes himself to flattery is the side on which he is attacked. Perhaps he is attacked for this very reason, because he is exposed. 5. Thus, resign yourself to realizing that you cannot manage to be invulnerable. When you have taken every precaution you will be struck right through your guard. One man will use flattery secretly, sparingly; another openly, obviously, with pretended roughness, as though it were naïveté, not artfulness. Plancus, the greatest flattery-artist before Villeius,[1] used to say that flattery must not be concealed or dissembled. " When you pay court,"[2] he said, " your effort is lost if it is not recognized." 6. A flatterer accomplishes most when he is detected; even more if he is rebuked, if he blushes. Bear in mind that in your

flatterer of Gaius, Claudius, and others (Tacitus *Ann.* 6.32; Suetonius *Vitell.* 2). However, as Oltramare says, all the other manuscripts are evidence against changing the spelling from Villeius. Munatius Plancus was consul in A.D. 13.

[2] The verb *procari* is difficult; cf. Oltramare in *R. Phil.* 1921, p. 32.

in persona tua Plancos cogita, et hoc non esse remedium tanti mali, nolle laudari. Crispus Passienus, quo ego nil cognovi subtilius in omnibus quidem rebus, maxime in distinguendis et curandis [1] vitiis, saepe dicebat adulationi nos [2] non claudere ostium, sed operire, et quidem sic quemadmodum opponi amicae solet, quae, si impulit, grata est; gratior, si effregit.

7. Demetrium egregium virum memini dicere cuidam libertino potenti facilem sibi esse ad divitias viam, quo die paenituisset bonae mentis. "Nec invidebo," inquit, "vobis hac arte, sed docebo eos quibus quaesito opus est quemadmodum non dubiam fortunam maris, non emendi vendendique litem subeant, non incertam fidem ruris, incertiorem fori temptent, quemadmodum non solum facili sed etiam hilari via pecuniam faciant gaudentesque despolient. 8. Te," inquit, "longiorem Fido Annaeo [3] iurabo et Apollonio pycte, quamvis staturam habeas pitheci

---

[1] *enarrandis* Z; *et curandis* omitted in E.
[2] Muret, Gercke, Oltramare; *adulationibus* HPZE.
[3] Gercke, Oltramare; *anne eo* G; *an me* (or *meo*) *eo* HP; *Ammeeo* Z.

---

[1] [Or "a (notable) person like yourself will raise up many a Plancus."—E.H.W.]
[2] Crispus Passienus was married to Domitia, Nero's aunt,

personal life in public there will be many a Plancus.[1]
To be unwilling to accept praise is no remedy against
this great evil. I never knew anyone more shrewd
in all matters indeed than Crispus Passienus,[2] and especially in identifying and treating character faults.
He often used to say that we do not slam the door on
flattery, we only close it gently, the way a door is
usually closed on a mistress. If she shoves against
it we are pleased, more pleased if she breaks it
down.

7. I remember hearing Demetrius,[3] a distinguished
man, tell a certain powerful freedman that he, too,
had an easy road to riches on the day he regretted his
high principles. " I will not begrudge any of you
from learning this skill," he said, " and I will teach
any of you who considers profit a necessity how to
make money, not by entering upon the dubious risks
of the sea, nor the competition of buying and selling,
nor by attempting the uncertain reliability of
farming or the still more uncertain prospect of the
forum, but by an easy and enjoyable method that robs
happy victims. 8. I will swear," he said, " that you
are taller than Fidus Annaeus [4] and Apollonius,[5]
the boxer, even though you have the stature of a
little monkey matched with a giant Thracian gladia-

then to Agrippina, Nero's mother. He was a friend of Seneca's
father.

[3] Demetrius the Cynic was a friend of Seneca. He lived to
be criticized under Domitian for defending a man who was
clearly guilty (Tacitus *Hist.* 4.40).

[4] The conjecture of Gercke and Oltramare of Annaeo for
the MSS.'s readings leads Oltramare to suggest that Fidus
Annaeus was a freedman of Seneca.

[5] This Apollonius is unknown.

cum [1] Thraece compositi. Hominem quidem non esse ullum liberaliorem non mentiar, cum possis videri omnibus donasse quicquid dereliquisti."

9. Ita est, mi [2] Iunior; quo apertior est adulatio, quo improbior, quo magis frontem suam perfricuit, cecidit alienam, hoc citius expugnat. Eo enim iam dementiae venimus ut [3] qui parce adulatur pro maligno sit.

10. Solebam [4] tibi dicere Gallionem, fratrem meum quem nemo non parum amat, etiam qui amare plus non potest, alia [5] vitia non nosse, hoc eum odisse. Ab omni illum parte temptasti. Ingenium suspicere coepisti omnium maximum et dignissimum quod consecrari mallet quam conteri; pedes abstulit.

[1] *pitheci cum* Kroll, Gercke, Alexander; *Thraecis cum* Lips; *thecisum* HZG; † *Thecisum* Oltramare; *thetisum* P.
[2] *mihi* FJOT.
[3] *ut . . . sit* Gercke, Oltramare for *quod . . . fit* HPZG.
[4] *solebant ibi* P.
[5] Gercke, Oltramare for *talia* HPZG.

---

[1] A " Thracian " gladiator was armed with a *sica*, dagger, national weapon of the Thracians; such gladiators would generally be matched against each other. There is no evidence that a gladiator was ever pitted against an ape (*pithecus*). However, as Alexander points out, Kroll's *pitheci* could mean a monkey (as in Plautus *Miles G.* 989 *pithecium*). And *compositi* can mean " compared " rather than " paired " or " matched." [If here in Seneca *pitheci* is right (and it is very doubtful) it does not matter what sort of primate mammal is meant. But usually a *Thr(a)ex* was pitted against another

tor.[1] In fact, I will not lie when I say no one is more generous than you—since you can be considered to have given to everybody what you have let them keep."

9. So it is, my dear Junior. The more open flattery is, the more shameless it is, the more it rubs the blush from its own face, and the more it shocks other faces to a blush, the more quickly it wins. For now we have come to such madness that whoever uses flattery sparingly is considered stingy.

10. I am used to telling you that my brother Gallio [2]—who is not loved as much as he deserves even by those whose love for him could not be greater—does not know other vices, hates flattery. You might try him on every side.[3] You might proceed to look up to his intelligence as the greatest of all and very deserving of his preference that it be ranked among the gods instead of being malignantly crushed. He would dodge the trip-up.[4] You might proceed to

Thr(a)ex. So I am inclined to agree with Lips's emendation *Thraecis cum*, with the implication not that any person in this context in Seneca is undersized but that he is of average height whereas Fidus and Apollonius were tall. Otherwise we ought to conclude that *thecisum*, as a corruption arising from *thraece* which follows, has irretrievably ousted what Seneca wrote here.—E.H.W.]

[2] Seneca's elder brother, Annaeus Novatus, as governor of Achaia refused to take action on complaints against Paul's preaching (*Acts* 18.12–17). He was adopted by his father's friend, the famous orator Junius Gallio.

[3] Throughout the rest of Sections 10, 11, 12 Seneca treats Lucilius' attempts to flatter Gallio, and the results, as past facts. In English it sounds better when treated as hypothetical.

[4] A metaphor from wrestling.

SENECA

Frugalitatem laudare coepisti, quae sic a nostris [1] moribus [2] resiluit ut illos nec habere, nec damnare videatur; prima statim verba praecidit. 11. Coepisti mirari comitatem et incompositam suavitatem, quae illos quoque quos transit abducit, gratuitum etiam in obvios meritum; nemo enim mortalium uni tam dulcis est quam hic omnibus, cum interim tanta naturalis boni vis est, uti artem simulationemque non redoleat; [3] nemo non imputari sibi bonitatem publicam patitur; hoc quoque loco blanditiis tuis restitit, ut exclamares invenisse te inexpugnabilem virum adversus insidias, quas nemo non in sinum recipit. 12. Eo quidem magis hanc eius prudentiam et in evitando inevitabili malo pertinaciam te suspicere confessus es, quia speraveras posse apertis auribus recipi, quamvis blanda diceres, quia vera dicebas. Sed eo magis intellexit obstandum; semper enim falsis † a vero petitur veri auctoritas.[4] Nolo tamen displiceas tibi, quasi male egeris mimum [5] et quasi ille aliquid iocorum aut doli suspicatus sit; non deprehendit te sed reppulit.

---

[1] *nostris* Z Oltramare; *nobis* most MSS.; *novis* Haase.

[2] Haase, Oltramare, Alexander; *morsibus* Z; *moribus* omitted in most MSS.

[3] *uti . . . redoleat* Haase for *ubi . . . redolet* MSS. Oltramare; *ut . . . redoleat* Fortunatus.

[4] Oltramare; *a vero petitur veritas* HG; *a vero veritas petitur* Alexander; *a vero petitura veri* (and beginning of next line) *ritas* Z; *a vero petitur auctoritas* Gercke; Warmington suggests *enim ⟨in⟩ falsis*, with deletion of *a vero* or else with *auctoritas* instead of *veritas*.

[5] *nimium* PG; *in unum* (or *in imum*) ZLO.

praise his frugality, which so recoils from our manners
that it seems neither to possess them nor to condemn
them. He immediately cuts short the first words.
11. You might proceed to admire his ability to get
along with other people and his unaffectedly pleasant
personality which charms even those it pays no special
attention to, a free benefit even for those who happen
to meet him. No other human being is so charming
to just one person as he is to all people. At the
same time the power of his natural goodness is so
great that it has no odour of artifice or dissimulation.
No human being, you might say, would refuse to
have himself credited with a goodness that applies
to the entire community. At this point, too, he
would resist your flattery; so you might exclaim
you had found a man impervious to deceptions which
anyone else would accept wholeheartedly. 12. You
might confess that you admire all the more this
common sense of his and persistence in avoiding an
inevitable evil, because you would express the
hope that however much alluring flattery you spoke,
it could be accepted with open ears because you
spoke the truth. Yet he would realize all the more
that you must be resisted; for, when falsehood is
presumably involved, the authority of truth is always
sought for by a true man.[1] None the less, I do not
want you to be displeased with yourself, as though
you would act your role poorly and Gallio would
suspect some joke or trick. He would not unmask
you, but he would reject you.

---

[1] The reading and meaning of the whole sentence are not
clear.

13. Ad hoc exemplar componere. Cum quis ad te adulator accesserit, dicito: " Vis tu ista verba, quae iam ab alio magistratu ad alium cum lictoribus transeunt, ferre ad aliquem qui, paria facturus, vult quicquid dixeris [1] audire? Ego nec decipere volo, nec decipi possum; laudari me a vobis, nisi laudaretis etiam malos, vellem." Quid autem necesse est in hoc descendere ut te petere comminus possint? Longum inter vos intervallum sit.

14. Cum cupieris bene laudari, quare hoc ulli debeas? Ipse te lauda. Dic: " Liberalibus me studiis tradidi. Quamquam paupertas alia suaderet [2] et ingenium eo duceret [3] ubi praesens studii pretium est, ad gratuita carmina deflexi me et ad salutare philosophiae contuli studium. 15. Ostendi in omne pectus cadere virtutem et, eluctatus natalium angustias nec sorte me sed animo mensus, par maximis steti. Non mihi in amicitia [4] Gaetulici Gaius fidem eripuit. Non in aliorum persona infeliciter amatorum

---

[1] *dixeris* Gronovius, Alexander for *dixerit* HP Oltramare; *dixit* Z; *dixerim* Gercke.
[2] *alias vaderet* HPE.
[3] Muret, Oltramare; *obduceret* MSS.
[4] *inimicitia* EJ².

---

[1] The *lictores* were attendants who carried the *fasces* before certain magistrates; they were transferred at the end of a year of office to new magistrates. The meaning of this passage is doubtful.

13. Model yourself after this pattern. When any flatterer approaches you, say: "Those words of yours are the formal compliments which pass from one magistrate to another along with the lictors.[1] Will you be pleased to take them to someone who, ready to render like for like, is willing to listen to anything you say? As for me, I am neither willing to be deceived nor can I be deceived. I would be glad to be praised by you except that you praise the bad as well as the good." But why is it necessary to descend to this level so that they can attack you at close quarters? Keep a big distance between yourself and them.

14. When you want to be praised sincerely, why be indebted to someone else for it? Praise yourself. Say: "I devoted myself to the liberal arts. Although my poverty urged me to do otherwise and tempted my talents towards a field where there is an immediate profit from study, I turned aside to unremunerative poetry and dedicated myself to the wholesome study of philosophy. 15. I have shown that virtue applies to every heart and, overcoming the limitations of my birth and measuring myself not by my lot but by my soul, I stood equal to the most important men. The Emperor Gaius did not rob me of my loyalty in my friendship with Gaetulicus.[2] Messallina and Narcissus,[3] long enemies of

[2] Cn. Cornelius Lentulus Gaetulicus was sent to his death by Gaius on charges of conspiracy.

[3] Messallina, the famously unchaste wife of the Emperor Claudius, was responsible for sending Seneca into exile. At one time she and Claudius' powerful freedman Narcissus plotted together as allies, but they later became enemies. She was put to death apparently at the instigation of Narcissus.

Messallina[1] et Narcissus, diu publici hostes antequam sui, propositum meum potuerunt evertere.
Cervicem pro fide opposui. Nullum verbum mihi
quod non salva bona conscientia procederet excussum
est. Pro amicis omnia timui, pro me nihil, nisi ne
parum bonus amicus fuissem. 16. Non mihi muliebres fluxere lacrimae; non e manibus ullius supplex
pependi; nihil indecorum nec bono nec viro feci.
Periculis meis maior, paratus ire in ea quae minaban-
tur, egi gratias fortunae quod experiri voluisset
quanti aestimarem fidem; non debebat mihi parvo
res tanta constare. Ne examinavi[2] quidem diu,
neque enim paria pendebant, utrum satius esset me
perire pro fide an fidem pro me. 17. Non praecipiti
impetu in ultimum consilium, quo me eriperem
furori potentium, misi. Videbam apud Gaium
tormenta, videbam ignes, sciebam olim sub illo in
eum statum res humanas decidisse ut inter miseri-
cordiae exempla[3] haberentur occisi; non tamen ferro
incubui nec in mare aperto ore desilui, ne viderer pro
fide tantum mori posse."

18. Adice invictum muneribus animum et in tanto
avaritiae certamine numquam suppositam manum
lucro; adice victus parsimoniam, sermonis modestiam,
adversus minores humanitatem, adversus maiores
reverentiam. Post haec ipse te consule, verane an

---

[1] Fortunatus, Oltramare for *Messala* HPE; *Messalia* ZO.
[2] Gercke, Oltramare for *examinavit* HPZ.
[3] *exempla* Z Oltramare; *opera* most MSS.

the state before they became enemies of each other, were not able to overturn my resolve in my allegiance to other people also whom it was unlucky to like. I risked my neck for my loyalty. No word was wrung from me which did not come unreservedly from a clear conscience. I feared everything for my friends, nothing at all for myself, except the fear that I had not been a good friend. 16. No womanly tears flowed from me, nor did I cling as a suppliant to anybody's hand. I did nothing a good man, or merely a man, should not do. Rising above my own danger and ready to meet the dangers that threatened, I was grateful to fortune because she was willing to test how much value I placed on loyalty. Such a great test could not stand for something of insignificant value to me. I did not even weigh matters very long, for the values did not balance: whether it were better for me to perish for loyalty or for loyalty to perish for me. 17. I did not rush headlong into the final decision in order to rescue myself from the rage of rulers. In the time of Gaius I saw tortures, I saw burnings, and under him I knew that men who were merely killed were considered among examples of mercy. Yet I did not fall upon my sword or leap open-mouthed into the sea, lest I seem only able to die for loyalty."

18. Add that your soul has been unconquered by bribes and in the great competition of avarice your hand has never been stretched out for money. Add the thriftiness of your way of life, the modesty of your speech, your courtesy towards inferiors, your respect for superiors. After this, ask yourself whether the things you said about yourself are true or false. If

falsa memoraveris.[1] Si vera sunt, coram magno teste laudatus es; si falsa, sine teste derisus es.

19. Possum et ipse nunc videri te aut captare aut experiri; utrumlibet crede et omnes timere a me incipe. Vergilianum illud exaudi

nusquam tuta fides,

aut Ovidianum

in facinus iurasse putes,
qua terra patet, fera regnat Erinys,

aut illud Menandri (quis enim non in hoc magnitudinem ingenii sui concitavit, detestatus consensum humani generis tendentis ad vitia): omnes ait malos vivere et in scaenam velut rusticus poeta prosiluit; non senem excipit, non puerum, non feminam, non virum, et adicit non singulos peccare nec paucos, sed iam[2] scelus esse contextum.

20. Fugiendum ergo et in se recedendum est; immo etiam a se recedendum. Hoc tibi, etsi dividimur mari, praestare temptabo ut subinde te iniecta manu ad meliora perducam, et, ne solitudinem sentias, hinc tecum miscebo sermones. Erimus una, qua

---

[1] *memoraverim* HPEZ.
[2] Warmington suggests *vitam* or *vitam iam*.

---

[1] *Aen.* 4.373.
[2] *Met.* 1.241.
[3] Seneca has in mind Menander's play Ὑποβολιμαῖος or Ἄγροικος.

they are true, you are praised in front of a great witness, yourself. If they are false, no one is a witness to your being made a fool of.

19. I myself now could appear to be either trapping or testing you. Believe either way and fear everybody, beginning with me. Listen to this line of Virgil:

> Nowhere is loyalty safe.[1]

or of Ovid:

> As far as the earth extends
> The savage Erinys rules.
> You would think
> Men had sworn an oath
> To commit crime.[2]

or consider the sentiment of Menander (for every intellectual has aroused the full greatness of his talents against this evil, detesting the universal consensus of a human race that tends towards vice): the poet says that all men live evil lives. He then springs forward on to the stage in the role of a man from the country. He excepts neither old man nor boy, neither woman nor man, and he adds that it is not just one or a few individuals who sin, but by now crime is woven into the fabric of society.[3]

20. It is necessary to flee the world and to return to oneself; better still, even to escape from one's self. Even though we are separated by the sea, I will try to supply this help to you: taking your hand in mine I will at once lead you away to a better life, and from here I will mingle my talk with yours so that you may not feel alone. We will be together

parte optimi sumus. Dabimus invicem consilia
non ex vultu audientis pendentia.

21. Longe te ab ista provincia abducam, ne forte
magnam historiis esse fidem credas et placere tibi
incipias, quotiens cogitaveris: " Hanc ego habeo sub
meo iure provinciam quae maximarum urbium exercitus et sustinuit et fregit, cum inter Carthaginem et
Romam ingentis belli pretium iacuit; quae[1] quattuor
Romanorum principum, id est totius imperii, vires
contractas in unum locum vidit aluitque; quae[2]
Pompeii fortunam erexit, Caesaris fatigavit, Lepidi
transtulit, omnium cepit; 22. quae illi ingenti
spectaculo interfuit ex quo liquere mortalibus posset
quam velox foret ad imum lapsus e summo quamque
diversa via magnam potentiam fortuna destrueret;
uno enim tempore vidit Pompeium Lepidumque ex
maximo fastigio aliter ad extrema deiectos, cum
Pompeius alienum exercitum fugeret, Lepidus
suum."[3]

[1] Gertz, Gercke, Oltramare, Alexander for *cum* HPEZ.
[2] Oltramare, Alexander for *aliudque* HPEZ; *aliud quoque* λ;
Antonii atque Gercke; *animumque* P. For *fatigavit* Z has
fastigavit.
[3] *et suum* Alexander.

in the part of us where we are best. We will give advice to each other, advice that will not depend on the facial expression of the listener.

21. I will lead you far away from that province of yours lest you put too much confidence in history and begin to be pleased with yourself whenever you think: " I have under my control a province which both maintained and crushed armies of the largest states when it lay as the prize of the great war between Carthage and Rome.[1] It saw and supported the strength of four Roman generals,[2] that is, of the whole empire, massed in one place. It raised high the fortunes of Pompey, exhausted Caesar's, transferred the power of Lepidus to his rivals, held the destiny of all. 22. Sicily was present at that great spectacle which made clear to the world how rapid a fall could be from the highest to the lowest, and by how different a road fortune could destroy a great power. For at the same time it saw Pompey and Lepidus cast down from the highest summit to the lowest depths, in different ways: while Pompey fled his enemy's army, Lepidus fled from his own."

[1] Seneca is probably thinking of both the First Punic War (264–241 B.C.) when Sicily was an important battleground, and of the Second Punic War (218–202 B.C.) during which Syracuse was captured by the Roman general Marcellus, 212 B.C.

[2] The four Roman generals were Sextus Pompey, Octavian, Lepidus, and Antony. Seneca refers to the struggle of the triumvirs against Sextus Pompey in Sicily in 36 B.C. Antony was not present but he participated by sending a fleet to aid Octavian and Lepidus. After the defeat and flight of Pompey, Lepidus tried to claim Sicily as his province and was promptly deserted by his army. From then on he held no real power, although Octavian allowed him to live.

1 1. Itaque, ut totum inde te [1] abducam, quamvis multa habeat Sicilia in se circaque se mirabilia, omnes interim provinciae tuae quaestiones praeteribo et in diversum cogitationes tuas abstraham. Quaeram enim tecum, id quod libro superiore distuli, quid ita Nilus aestivis mensibus abundet.

Cui Danuvium similem habere naturam philosophi tradiderunt, quod et fontis ignoti et aestate quam 2 hieme maior sit. Utrumque apparuit falsum. Nam et caput eius in Germania esse comperimus, et aestate quidem incipit crescere sed, adhuc manente intra mensuram suam Nilo, primis caloribus, cum sol vehementior intra extrema veris nives mollit, quas ante consumit quam tumescere Nilus incipiat; reliquo vero aestatis minuitur et ad hibernam magnitudinem redit atque ex ea demittitur. At Nilus ante exortum Caniculae augetur mediis aestibus ultra aequinoctium.

1 2. Hunc nobilissimum amnium natura extulit ante humani generis oculos et ita disposuit ut eo tempore inundaret Aegyptum quo maxime usta fervoribus terra undas altius traheret, tantum usura [2] quantum siccitati annuae sufficere posset. Nam in ea parte qua in Aethiopiam vergit aut nulli imbres sunt aut rari et qui insuetam aquis caelestibus terram non adiuvent. 2 Unam, ut scis, Aegyptus in hoc spem [3] suam habet;

[1] *mente* K.   [2] *mensuram* P; *hausura* E[2].
[3] *speciem* Pλ.

---

[1] Perhaps a reference to Bk. 6.8.3–5. Book Six was published before the " Nile " book.

1. And so, in order that I may lead you away 1
entirely from there, even though Sicily has many
marvels in and around it, I will for the time being pass
over all questions concerning your province and draw
your thoughts off into a different area. With you I
will investigate why the Nile overflows the way it
does in summer months, a subject which I postponed
in a previous book.[1]

Philosophers have maintained that the Danube has
the same characteristics as the Nile because its source
is unknown and it is larger in the summer than in the
winter. Both statements are now obviously false. 2
For we have found out that the source of the Danube
is in Germany. It does begin to rise in the summer
but at a time when the Nile is still flowing within its
normal limits, when a strong sun between the beginning and the end of spring softens the snows, which
the sun melts entirely before the Nile begins to rise.
In the rest of the summer the Danube diminishes and
returns to its winter level, and even falls below it.
But the Nile increases from the middle of the summer,
before the rise of the Dog Star, to beyond the equinox.

2. Nature has raised up this noblest of rivers 1
before the eyes of man and has arranged it to flood
Egypt at the very time the earth, especially parched
by heat, may draw in the waters more deeply, en-
joying a sufficient quantity to replenish the year's
dryness. For in that part of Egypt that stretches
towards Ethiopia there are either no rains at all or
they are rare and no help to a land which is un-
accustomed to water from the sky.

As you know, Egypt places her single hope in the 2

proinde aut sterilis annus aut fertilis est, prout ille
magnus influxit aut parcior; " nemo aratorum respicit
caelum." Quare non cum [1] poeta meo iocor [2] et
illi Ovidium suum impingo, qui ait

> nec Pluvio supplicat herba Iovi?

3   Unde crescere incipiat si comprehendi posset,
causae quoque incrementi invenirentur.   Nunc vero
magnas solitudines pervagatus et in paludes diffusus
herbisque ingentibus [3] sparsus circa Philas primum
ex vago et errante colligitur.   Philae insula est aspera
et undique praerupta; duobus in unum coituris
amnibus cingitur, qui Nilo mutantur et eius nomen
4   ferunt; urbem totam [4] complectitur.   Ab hac Nilus
magnus magis quam violentus Aethopiam harenasque
per quas iter ad commercia Indici maris est praelabi-
tur.   Excipiunt eum [5] Cataractae, nobilis insigni

[1] *nunc cum* EK.
[2] *in eo loco* Z.
[3] *herbisque ingentibus* Oltramare; *gentibus* most MSS.; *et
gentibus* T; *ingentibus* KJ[1]; *et ingentibus* POL; *arenisque
ingentibus* Diels; *ingentibus orbibus sparsas* Alexander.
[4] *urbe tota* Gercke; *urbs totam* Fortunatus.
[5] *enim* P; *autem* E; *eum* omitted in Z.

---

[1] Seneca may be quoting or parodying a verse of Lucilius,
his " poet friend." It is unclear whether the joke pertains
to this line or to the one that follows.

[2] Tibullus 1.7.26. Either Seneca's memory failed him
when he thought the line came from Ovid or he deliberately
made a mistake connected with some private joke between
himself and Lucilius.

Nile; hence the year is either sterile or fertile according to whether the Nile overflows in abundance or scantily. " Not one of the farmers looks at the sky." [1] Why should I not joke with my poet friend ? I will throw at him a line from Ovid, his favourite author, who says:

Nor does vegetation pray to the rain-god Jupiter.[2]

If it could be understood where the Nile begins to **3** rise, the causes of its flooding might also be found out. As it is now the river wanders through great waste-lands, spreads out into swamps and has patches of very thick vegetation,[3] and after uncertain wander-ing is collected for the first time near Philae. Philae is a rocky island, steep on all sides. It is surrounded by two branches of the river which then come together into one and are changed to the Nile and bear its name. The Nile encircles the entire city of Philae.[4] From here the Nile, large and **4** not very swift, glides past Ethiopia and the sands through which trade routes pass to the Indian Sea. The Cataracts receive it, a region famous for its

---

[3] Or " has scattered patches of very tall plants." Perhaps the so-called " sudd."

[4] Seneca makes a strange error. He describes the region of Meroë and calls it Philae. Lucan (10.302–303; 312–313), Pliny (5.53), Ammianus (22.15.12), and, in fact, all ancient authors clearly distinguish between Meroë and Philae. It was from Meroë that Nero had the distance measured to Aswan (cf. below, Bk. 6.8.3–4). Lucan in the *Pharsalia* devotes many lines (10.190–331) to the source and the flooding of the Nile. Since he was Seneca's nephew and closely asso-ciated with him in the court of Nero there was very likely some exchange of ideas. It is to be noted that in the identi-fication of Meroë Lucan is right and Seneca is wrong.

5 spectaculo locus; ibi per arduas excisasque pluribus
locis rupes Nilus insurgit et vires suas concitat.
Frangitur enim occurrentibus saxis et per angusta
luctatus, ubicumque vincit aut vincitur, fluctuat et,
illic excitatis primum aquis quas sine tumultu leni
alveo duxerat, violentus et torrens per malignos
transitus prosilit dissimilis sibi (quippe ad id lutosus et
turbidus fluit); at, ubi scopulos et acuta cautium
verberavit, spumat et illi non ex natura sua sed ex
iniuria loci color est, tandemque eluctatus obstantia
in vastam altitudinem subito destitutus cadit cum
ingenti circumiacentium regionum strepitu. Quem
perferre gens ibi a Persis [1] collocata non potuit obtusis
assiduo fragore auribus et ob hoc sedibus ad quietiora
translatis.

6 Inter miracula fluminis incredibilem incolarum
audaciam accepi. Bini parvula navigia conscen-
dunt, quorum alter navem regit, alter exhaurit;
deinde multum inter rapidam insaniam Nili et
reciprocos fluctus volutati tandem tenuissimos canales
tenent, per quos angusta rupium effugiunt et, cum
toto flumine effusi, navigium ruens manu temperant

[1] *aspersis* PKJ[1].

---

[1] Egypt was part of the old Persian Empire. Oltramare
comments on the papyri which show the existence of an important military colony of Jews established by the Persian
kings at Elephantine.

wonderful spectacle. There the Nile surges through 5
steep rocks which are jagged in many places, and
unleashes its forces. It is broken by the rocks it
runs against and, struggling through narrow places,
everywhere conquers or is conquered. It swirls,
and there for the first time its waters are aroused,
which had been flowing along without disturbance
in a smooth channel. Violent and torrential, it
leaps through narrow passes, unlike itself since up to
this point it had been flowing muddy and heavy, but
when it lashes against the boulders and the sharp
points of jagged rocks it foams and its colour comes
not from its own properties but from its rough treat-
ment in that place. Finally it struggles past the
obstacles and, suddenly deprived of support, falls
down a vast height with a great roar that fills all the
regions lying around. The people established there
by the Persians [1] were unable to endure the noise.
Their ears were deafened by the constant crash, and
for this reason they were removed from that settle-
ment to a quieter place.[2]

Among other marvels of the river I have heard 6
about the incredible daring of the inhabitants. Two
of them board a small boat. One rows, the other bails.
Then they are violently buffeted among the raging
rapids of the Nile and the back-swirling waves of
water. At last they reach the narrowest channels,
and through them escape the rocky gorge. Then
they are swept along by the entire force of the river,
guiding the rushing boat by hand, plunging head

[2] Pliny (6.181), Cicero (*De Rep.* 6.19), and Ammianus
(22.15.9) also speak of the deafness caused by the noise of the
Cataracts.

magnoque spectantium metu in caput missi, cum
iam adploraveris mersosque atque obrutos tanta mole
credideris, longe ab eo in quem ceciderunt loco
navigant tormenti modo missi; nec mergit illos
cadens unda sed planis aquis tradit.

7 Primum incrementum Nili circa insulam quam
modo rettuli Philas visitur.[1] Exiguo ab hac spatio
petra dividitur (Abaton Graeci vocant, nec illam ulli
nisi antistites calcant); illa primum saxa auctum
fluminis sentiunt. Post magnum deinde spatium
duo eminent scopuli (Nili venas vocant incolae) ex
quibus magna vis funditur, non tamen quanta operire
possit Aegyptum. In haec ora stipem sacerdotes et
aurea dona praefecti, cum sollemne venit sacrum,
8 iaciunt. Hinc iam manifestus novarum virium Nilus
alto ac profundo alveo fertur, ne in latitudinem[2]
excedat, obiectu montium pressus. Circa Memphim
demum liber et per campestria vagus in plura scin-
ditur flumina manuque canalibus factis, ut sit
modus in derivantium potestate, per totam discurrit
Aegyptum. Initio diducitur, deinde continuatis
aquis in faciem lati ac turbidi maris stagnat; cursum
illi violentiamque eripit latitudo regionum in quas

[1] *visitur* H²ZFλ; *nascitur* H¹PEL.
[2] Fortunatus, Gercke, Oltramare for *altitudinem* HPEZ.

---

[1] Lucan says the same thing (10.323–326) and points out
that here the obvious signs of the Nile flood begin. For a long

down. The onlookers are filled with fright. You would lament and believe that they were already drowned and that they had been crushed by such a mass of water. They are shot out as from a catapult and float in their vessel far from the place where they had fallen. The wave which drops them does not submerge them but carries them to smooth waters.

The first rise of the Nile is seen near the island of 7 Philae, which I just mentioned. A short distance away from there the river is divided by a rock. The Greeks call it Abatos " Untrodden ", and no one sets foot on it except priests. These cliffs first feel the rise of the river. Next, after a considerable distance two crags stick out—the natives call them the Veins of the Nile [1]—from which a great quantity of water pours, but not enough to flood over any expanse of Egypt. Into the mouth of this part the priests throw a ritual offering and the magistrates throw gold gifts when the sacred festival comes. From here the Nile, now showing its new strength, 8 is carried along in a channel of profound depth but hemmed in by a barrier of mountains so that it does not spread out in width. Near Memphis it is finally released, and splitting into several channels wanders over the fields. Canals are constructed by hand so that there might be a control on the power of distributing the water, and the water runs over all Egypt. At first it is split up; then it settles down in a continuous expanse of water with the appearance of a wide, muddy sea. The width of the regions over

time this place was considered the source of the Nile (Herodotus 2.28).

extenditur dextra laevaque totam amplexus Aegyptum.

9 Quantum crevit Nilus, tantum spei in annum est. Nec computatio fallit agricolam, adeo ad mensuram fluminis terra[1] respondet, quam fertilem facit Nilus. Is harenoso ac sitienti solo et aquam inducit et terram. Nam, cum turbulentus fluat,[2] omnem in siccis atque hiantibus locis faecem relinquit et, quicquid pingue secum tulit, arentibus locis allinit iuvatque agros duabus ex causis, et quod inundat, et quod oblimat. Itaque, quicquid non adivit,[3] sterile ac squalidum iacet; si crevit super debitum, nocuit.

10 Mira itaque natura fluminis quod, cum ceteri amnes abluant terras et eviscerent, Nilus, tanto ceteris maior, adeo nihil exedit nec abradit ut contra adiciat vires, minimumque[4] in eo sit quod solum temperat; illato enim limo harenas saturat ac iungit, debetque illi Aegyptus non tantum fertilitatem terrarum, sed ipsas.

11 Illa facies pulcherrima est cum iam se in agros Nilus ingessit: latent campi opertaeque sunt valles, oppida insularum modo extant, nullum mediterraneis nisi per navigia commercium est maiorque est laetitia gentibus quo minus terrarum suarum vident.

12 Sic quoque, cum se ripis continet Nilus, per septena

---

[1] *terra* Z; most MSS. omit *terra*.
[2] *fluat* ZT Oltramare, Alexander; *fiat* HPE; *fuit* Gercke.
[3] Leo, Gercke, Oltramare; *adiuvit* HEZ.
[4] *minimum* HZFλ Oltramare; *nimium* EL Gercke; *viriumque indicium* Alexander.

which it extends on the right and the left embraces all Egypt and deprives the current of its force.

The higher the Nile rises the greater the hope for 9 the year.[1] The farmer's estimate never fails, so much does the land respond to the measure of the water's rise, land which the Nile makes fertile. It brings both water and soil to the sandy and thirsty ground. For, when it flows down muddy it deposits all its sediment in the dry, gaping cracks, and smears over parched areas all the rich mud it carried down with it. It aids the fields for two reasons: it both inundates them and coats them with mud. And so, any area it does not reach lies barren and ugly. If it rises beyond what is needed it does damage.

Therefore the remarkable characteristic of the 10 river is that while other rivers wash away the land and exhaust it, the Nile, much larger than the others, is so far from eating away or rubbing away the soil that on the contrary it adds to the soil's vigour. The least good in it is that it conditions the soil; for when the mud is carried in it saturates and binds the sand. Egypt owes to the Nile not only the fertility of the land but the land itself.

It is a beautiful sight when the Nile has spread 11 itself over the fields: the plains lie hidden, the valleys are covered over, towns stand out like islands. In the interior of the country there is no communication except by boat. The less people see of their land the happier they are.

So also, when the Nile keeps within its normal 12

[1] Seneca contradicts himself at the end of this paragraph. Pliny (5.58; 18.168) and Ammianus (22.15.13) acknowledge the disaster of too much flooding.

ostia in mare emittitur; quodcumque ex his elegeris,
mare est. Multos nihilominus ignobiles ramos in
aliud atque aliud litus porrigit. Ceterum beluas
marinis vel magnitudine vel noxa pares educat, et ex
eo quantus sit aestimari potest quod ingentia animalia
et pabulo sufficienti et ad vagandum loco continet.

13 Balbillus, virorum optimus perfectusque in omni
litterarum genere rarissime, auctor est, cum ipse
praefectus obtineret Aegyptum, Heracleotico ostio
Nili, quod est maximum, spectaculo sibi fuisse
delphinorum a mari occurrentium et crocodillorum a
flumine adversum agmen agentium velut pro partibus
proelium; crocodillos ab animalibus placidis morsuque
innoxiis victos.

14 His superior pars corporis dura et impenetrabilis
est etiam maiorum animalium dentibus, at inferior
mollis ac tenera. Hanc delphini spinis quas dorso
eminentes gerunt submersi vulnerabant et in adversum enisi dividebant; rescissis hoc modo pluribus
ceteri velut acie versa refugerunt: fugax animal
audaci, audacissimum timido!

15 Nec illos Tentyritae generis aut sanguinis pro-
prietate superant, sed contemptu et temeritate.
Ultro enim insequuntur fugientesque iniecto trahunt

---

[1] The largest animal in the Nile is the hippopotamus, but
Seneca mentions the crocodile only.

[2] T. Claudius Balbillus was made prefect of Egypt in A.D.
55 (cf. Pliny 19.3).   [3] In fact a single fin.

channel it is discharged into the sea through seven mouths, and any one you choose is a sea in itself. In addition to this, it projects many unnamed branches to other places here and there along the coast. Moreover, it produces monsters equal in size to monsters of the sea and as capable of doing harm. How large it is can be judged from the huge animals [1] it maintains with food in abundance and room for ranging about. Balbillus,[2] a very distinguished man, **13** exceptionally accomplished in every type of literature, is my authority. When he himself governed Egypt as a prefect, he saw with his own eyes in the Heracleotic—which is the largest mouth of the Nile—what amounted to a pitched battle between dolphins rushing in from the sea, and crocodiles from the river organizing a battle-line against the dolphins. The crocodiles were defeated by the gentle animals with the harmless bite.

The upper part of a crocodile's body is hard and **14** impervious even for the teeth of larger animals, but the lower part is soft and tender. The dolphins swam under water and wounded this soft part with the spines[3] which they wear projecting from their backs. Pushing against the crocodiles in frontal attack they proceeded to cut them to pieces. After several crocodiles had been cut up this way the others wheeled their battle-line, so to speak, and fled. An animal that is very brave against the timid was ready to flee from the bold!

The natives of Tentyra overcome crocodiles not **15** because of any peculiar virtue of race or blood but merely through boldness and contempt for crocodiles. Taking the offensive against them they put

laqueo; plerique pereunt, quibus minus praesens animus ad persequendum fuit.

16 Nilum aliquando marinam aquam detulisse Theophrastus est auctor. Biennio continuo regnante Cleopatra non ascendisse, decimo regni anno et undecimo, constat. Significatam aiunt duobus rerum potientibus defectionem; Antonii enim Cleopatraeque defecit imperium. Per novem annos non ascendisse Nilum superioribus saeculis Callimachus est auctor.

17 Sed nunc ad inspiciendas causas propter quas aestate Nilus crescat accedam et ab antiquissimis incipiam. Anaxagoras ait ex Aethiopiae iugis solutas nives ad Nilum usque decurrere. In eadem opinione omnis vetustas fuit; hoc Aeschylus, Sophocles, Euripides tradunt. Sed falsum esse argumentis pluribus patet.

18 Primum Aethiopiam ferventissimam esse indicat hominum adustus color et Trogodytae, quibus subterraneae domus sunt. Saxa velut igni fervescunt non tantum medio sed inclinato quoque die; ardens pulvis nec humani vestigii patiens; argentum replumbatur; signorum coagmenta solvuntur; nullum

---

¹ Theophrastus was a pupil of Aristotle and like him probably wrote a book on the Nile (both books are now lost).

² 42–41 B.C. Antony and Cleopatra were defeated at Actium, 31 B.C.

³ Callimachus, born c. 310 B.C. at Cyrene, is the famous poet, literary critic, and bibliographer connected with the Alexandrian library.

⁴ See Diodorus Siculus (1.38) for the theory of Anaxagoras. Herodotus considers the theory false (2.22). Ammianus (22.15.5) reports it without much comment. Lucan (10.221–

them to flight, throw a noose around them, and drag them in. Many natives die, the ones who lose their nerve in the hunt.

Theophrastus [1] is my authority that the Nile 16 has sometimes carried down sea-water. It is well established that in the reign of Cleopatra the Nile did not flood for two successive years, the tenth and eleventh of her reign.[2] They say that this was a sign of the loss of power for the two rulers of the world, for the empire of Antony and Cleopatra did fall. Callimachus [3] is my authority that in earlier times the Nile did not flood for nine years.

But now I will come to a study of the explanations 17 of why the Nile rises in the summer, and I will start with the most ancient of them. Anaxagoras says that melted snows from the peaks of Ethiopia run down as far as the Nile.[4] All antiquity was of this same opinion; Aeschylus, Sophocles, and Euripides report it.[5] But it is patently wrong on the basis of many arguments.

First of all, the burnt colour of the people indi- 18 cates that Ethiopia is very hot, and so does the need of the Trogodytae [6] to have their homes underground. Rocks become as hot as though they had been heated over fire, not only at midday but even in the evening. Human feet cannot endure the hot dust. Silverwork is unsoldered, the joints of statues are melted; and

223) argues against it, using much the same reasoning as Seneca. Lucretius (6.735-737) seems to favour it.

[5] Aeschylus, fr. 300 N (*Aethiopis*) and *Suppliants* 497, 561; Sophocles, fr. 797; Euripides, *Helen*, 1 sqq.

[6] Usually called Troglodytes. Greek papyri found in Egypt and some Greek and Latin manuscripts of authors confirm the spelling Trogodytae, as here.

materiae superadornatae manet operimentum.
Auster quoque, qui ex illo tractu venit, ventorum
calidissimus est. Nullum ex his animalibus, quae
latent bruma, umquam reconditur; etiam per hiemes
in summo et aperto serpens est. Alexandriae
quoque, quae longe ab immodicis caloribus posita est,
19 nives non cadunt; superiora pluvia carent. Quemadmodum ergo regio tantis subiecta fervoribus
duraturas per totam aestatem nives recipit? Quas
sane aliqui montes illic quoque excipiant; numquid
magis quam Alpes, quam Thraciae iuga aut Caucasus?
Atqui horum montium flumina vere et prima aestate
intumescunt, deinde hibernis minora sunt. Quippe
vernis temporibus imbres nivem diluunt; reliquias
20 eius primus calor dissipat. Nec Rhenus, nec Rho-
danus, nec Hister, nec Hebrus [1] subiacens Haemo [2]
aestate proveniunt; et illis altissimae, ut in septem-
trionibus, iugiter sunt nives. Phasis quoque per
idem [3] tempus et Borysthenes crescerent, ut nives
flumina possent contra aestatem magna producere.
21 Praeterea, si haec causa attolleret Nilum, aestate
prima plenissimus flueret; tunc enim maxime in-
tegrae adhuc nives ex mollissimoque tabes est.
Nilus autem per menses quattuor liquitur et illi
aequalis [4] accessio est.
22   Si Thaleti credis, etesiae descendenti Nilo resistunt

[1] Oltramare for *caystrus* Z; *caistrus* P; *ei ystrus* E.
[2] Oltramare for *subiacent molo* (or *thmolo*) PEZ.
[3] *perinde* E; *perinde ad* Gercke.
[4] *qualis* EP.

no coating of plated material stays on. Also, the south wind, which comes from that region, is the hottest of winds. None of the animals that lie hidden in winter ever hibernates there. Snakes are on the surface and in the open even during winters. Also, snow never falls at Alexandria, which is located far from the excessive heat, and the southern regions do not even have rain. How, then, does a region 19 subjected to such heat get snow that will last through an entire summer? No doubt some mountains receive snow, even there—but more snow than the Alps, or the peaks of Thrace, or the Caucasus? The rivers of these mountains swell in the spring and early summer; subsequently in winter they diminish. In the springtime, of course, the rains wash down the snow. The first heat dissipates the snow that is left. Neither the Rhine, the Rhône, the Danube, 20 nor the Hebrus[1] (which lies below the Haemus) overflows in the summer; yet their snows are perpetually very deep, as is natural in northern regions. The Phasis, too, and the Borysthenes would rise in that same season if snows were able to make rivers swell in spite of summer heat. Besides, if this were 21 the cause of the Nile rising, its stream would be fullest in early summer since at that time the snows are still mostly intact and the melting comes from their excessive softness. The Nile, however, floods for four months and the additions to its water are constant.

If you believe Thales, the Etesian winds obstruct 22 the descent of the Nile and detain its current by

[1] The Maritza, the chief river in ancient Thrace. In its upper course it travels along the Haemus (Great Balkan). On the MSS readings see note on p. 70. The Phasis is the Rion; the Borysthenes, the Dnieper.

et cursum eius acto contra ostia mari sustinent. Ita
reverberatus in se recurrit, nec crescit, sed exitu
prohibitus resistit et quacumque mox potuit in se
congestus [1] erumpit. Euthymenes Massiliensis testimonium dicit: " Navigavi," inquit, " Atlanticum
mare. Inde Nilus fluit, maior, quamdiu etesiae tempus
observant; tunc enim eicitur mare instantibus ventis. Cum resederunt, et pelagus conquiescit minor-
que [2] descendenti inde vis Nilo est. Ceterum dulcis
mari sapor est et similes Niloticis beluae."

23 Quare ergo, si Nilum etesiae provocant, et ante
illos incipit incrementum eius et post eos durat?
Praeterea non fit maior quo illi flavere [3] vehementius,
nec remittitur incitaturque, prout illis impetus fuit;
quod fieret, si illorum viribus cresceret. Quid quod
etesiae litus Aegyptium verberant et contra illos
Nilus descendit,[4] inde venturus unde illi, si origo ab
illis esset? Praeterea ex mari purus et caeruleus
efflueret, non, et nunc, turbidus veniret.

---

[1] Oltramare for *in se concestus* Z; *inconcessus* E; *inconcestus*
P; *inconcessa* Diels; *vi congestus* Gercke.
[2] *maiorque* T.
[3] Fortunatus, Oltramare; *favere* PEZ.
[4] *ascendit* Z.

---

[1] Lucretius (6.712–720), Pliny (5.55), Lucan (10.239–247),
Mela (1.9), and Herodotus (2.28) mention this theory.
[2] Euthymenes (about 500 B.C.), about whom our information is vague, wrote an account of a voyage that probably took
him south along the Atlantic coast of Africa to the mouths of

driving the sea against its mouths.[1] Beaten back
in this way, it runs back on itself and does not actually
increase; but when a way out is blocked it stops and,
accumulating upon itself, next breaks out wherever
it can. Euthymenes [2] of Massilia tells an eyewitness
account: " I have," he says, " been on a voyage in
the Atlantic. The Nile flows from there, and in
greater volume as long as the Etesian winds are blowing in season, for at that time the sea is hurled out of
itself inland by the pressure of the winds. When the
winds subside, the sea is quiet and the descent of the
Nile has correspondingly less force. Moreover, the
taste of the sea is fresh and its monsters are like the
ones in the Nile."

But then if the Nile flood is provoked by the 23
Etesian winds why does it begin before them and last
after them? Besides, the Nile does not become
higher the more violently the winds blow, nor does it
fall back or rush forward in accordance with their
blast, which it would do if it flooded because of their
exertions. Also, there is the obvious fact that the
Etesian winds whip the Egyptian coast and the Nile
flows against them, whereas if the Nile flood origi-
nated from the Etesian winds it would come from the
same direction as the winds.[3] Besides, if it came from
the sea it would flow clear and blue, not muddy as it
does now.

certain rivers (not the Niger) where he would have seen crocodiles. Herodotus (2.21) believes that any account of the Nile
flowing from the Ocean is mere legend.

[3] Here Seneca seems to misunderstand the theory, which he
states correctly in the preceding paragraph, that the Etesian
winds cause the flood by blowing *against* the flow of the river
and making the water back up.

24 Adice quod testimonium eius testium turba coarguitur. Tunc erat mendacio locus; cum ignota essent externa, licebat illis fabulas mittere. Nunc vero tota exteri maris ora mercatorum navibus stringitur, quorum nemo narrat initium Nili aut mare saporis alterius: quod[1] natura credi vetat, quia dulcissimum quodque et levissimum sol trahit.

25 Praeterea quare hieme non crescit? Et tunc potest ventis concitari mare, aliquanto quidem maioribus; nam etesiae temperati sunt. Quod si e mari ferretur Atlantico, semel[2] oppleret Aegyptum. At nunc per gradus crescit.

26 Oenopides Chius ait hieme calorem sub terris contineri; ideo et specus calidos[3] esse et tepidiorem puteis aquam;[4] itaque venas interno calore siccari. Sed in aliis terris augeri imbribus flumina; Nilum, quia nullo imbre adiuvetur, tenuari; deinde crescere per aestatem, quo tempore frigent interiora terrarum et redit rigor fontibus.

27 Quod si verum esset, aestate flumina crescerent

---

[1] *quod* Z; *quae* PO Gercke; *que et* TKJ; *quam* E.
[2] *semper* E. [3] *calidos* ZT; *cavosos* PE.
[4] *aquam* ZT; *quam* PE.

---

[1] King Juba of Mauretania, a contemporary of Julius Caesar and Octavian, was a natural historian. He is given credit by Pliny (5.51) and by Ammianus (22.15.8) for identifying the source of the Nile in a mountain of lower Mauretania not far from the Ocean, and he brought back a crocodile from that area to prove his theory. According to Ammianus he obtained the information from Punic books. Lucan (10.255–257) simply reports the rumour that the Nile comes from the Ocean, and makes no mention of Juba as an authority. It is

Add that the testimony of Euthymenes is refuted 24
by a whole crowd of witnesses. At that time there was
opportunity for falsehood. Since foreign countries
were unknown it was easy for them to send out fabu-
lous stories. But now all the shores of the outer sea
are touched by the ships of merchants. No one of
them reports that the Nile begins there, or that the
sea is of a different taste there. Nature forbids this
last point from being believed because the sun draws
off from the sea all the fresh water, since it is also
the lightest. Besides, why does the Nile not rise 25
in the winter? At that time especially the sea can
be stirred up by the winds, and actually by winds
considerably stronger than the Etesian, for the Etesians are moderate. If the Nile came from the
Atlantic Ocean it would flood Egypt all at once.[1]
But in fact the Nile flooding is gradual.

Oenopides of Chios [2] says that in the winter heat is 26
contained under the ground and that is why caves are
warm and water from wells is fairly tepid. Therefore veins of water are dried up by the internal heat.
But in other countries, he says, rivers are swollen by
rains and the Nile diminishes because it is not supported by rainfall. Then it increases during the
summer, at which time the interiors of the earth become cold and frost returns to springs.

If what Oenopides says were true, all rivers would 27

curious that in what remains of Seneca's " Nile " book and the
résumé of Seneca's sources given by Lydus there is no reference
to Juba. Vitruvius (8.2.7) argues that the presence of crocodiles and other Nile creatures in springs flowing to the Western
Ocean proves that the source of the Nile is in Mauretania.

[2] Oenopides of Chios was a contemporary of Anaxagoras.
See Diodorus Siculus (1.41) for his theory on the Nile flood.

omnia,[1] putei aestate abundarent. Deinde falsum
est calorem [2] hieme sub terris esse maiorem. At
quare [3] specus et putei tepent? Quia aera rigentem [4]
extrinsecus non recipiunt; ita non calorem habent,
sed frigus excludunt. Ex eadem causa aestate [5]
frigidi [6] sunt, quia ad illos remotos seductosque [7]
calefactus aer non pervenit.

28 Diogenes Apolloniates ait: "Sol umorem ad se
rapit; hunc adsiccata tellus ex mari ducit; ipsum [8]
ex ceteris aquis. Fieri autem non potest, ut alia
sicca sit tellus, alia abundet; sunt enim perforata
omnia et invicem pervia, et sicca ab umidis sumunt.
Alioquin,[9] nisi aliquid terra acciperet, exaruisset.
Ergo undique sol trahit, sed ex his quae premit
29 maxime; haec meridiana sunt. Terra cum exaruit,
plus ad se umoris adducit; ut in lucernis oleum illo
fluit ubi exuritur, sic aqua illo incumbit quo vis caloris
et terrae aestuantis arcessit. Unde ergo trahit?
Ex illis scilicet partibus semper hibernis: septem-
trionales exundant (ob hoc Pontus in infernum mare

[1] Gercke, Oltramare for *omnes* PEZ.
[2] *falsum est calorem* Z Oltramare; most MSS. omit *falsum est.*
[3] *aquare* P; *ait. Quare* Gercke.
[4] *rigentem* ZT Oltramare; *et rigentem* PE; *frigentem* Leo,
Gercke.
[5] *est. at* P; *est ac* JK; *est aer* E.
[6] *frigidi sunt* Diels, Gercke, Oltramare for *frigidunt* Z;
refrigidunt JP²; *refrigidiunt* K; *frigidus* E; *frigidum* L.
[7] *sed ductos* PZ.
[8] Gercke, Oltramare for *cum* PE; *tum* Z.
[9] *alioquin* Z Oltramare; *aliquando* PE; *aliquid liquidi* Gertz.

---

[1] Diogenes of Apollonia was a contemporary of Anaxagoras.
[2] Lucan (10.248–254) presents the theory of these subterranean passages. Aristotle 2.7.365b 1–5: Democritus of

rise in the summer and all wells would have abundant water in the summer. Finally, it is not true that in winter there is greater heat underground. But why are caves and wells warm? Because they do not receive the freezing air from outside. Thus they do not have heat; they exclude cold. They are cold in the summer from the same cause; for, since they are remote and secluded, the heated air does not penetrate to them.

Diogenes of Apollonia [1] says: " The sun draws 28 moisture to itself; the land, dried out, takes moisture from the sea; the sea itself draws moisture from other waters. But it cannot happen that some land is dry, other land flooded, for all lands are perforated with communicating passages [2] and the dry sections draw from the moist. Otherwise, unless the land received some moisture it would have completely dried out. Accordingly, the sun draws up moisture, but only from those regions which the sun especially oppresses; that is, the southern regions. When the 29 land is parched it draws in more moisture. Just as in a lamp the oil flows to where it is burned, so water inclines to where the force of the heat and of the burning land draws it. But where does the land draw it from? Surely from areas of eternal winter. The northern regions abound in water. (For this reason the swift current of the Pontus [3] runs constantly towards the lower sea and does not ebb and flow in

Abdera says when the earth gets dried up water is drawn from the empty places to the fuller and causes earthquakes by the impact of its passage.

[3] The Pontus is the Black Sea and the " lower sea " is the Mediterranean.

assidue fluit rapidus, non, ut cetera maria, alternatis
ultro citro aestibus, in unam partem semper pronus
et torrens); quod nisi faceret his itineribus [1] ut [2]
quod cuique deest redderetur, quod cuique supérest
emitteretur, iam aut sicca essent omnia aut inundata."

30   Interrogare Diogenem libet quare, quoniam [3]
pertusa sunt cuncta et invicem commeant, non omnibus locis aestate maiora sint flumina. "Aegyptum
sol magis percoquit; itaque Nilus magis crescit;
sed [4] in ceteris quoque terris aliqua fluminibus fiat
adiectio." Deinde quare ulla pars terrae sine umore
est, cum omnis ad se ex aliis regionibus trahat, eo
quidem magis quo calidior est? Deinde quare
Nilus dulcis est, si haec illi e mari unda est? nec enim
ulli flumini dulcior gustus . . .

Joannes Laurentius Lydus (6th century of the Christian
era) in Book Four, Chapter 48, of his Greek work *On Months*
presents a résumé of Seneca's sources on theories that explain
the Nile flood in the lost portion of the *Natural Questions*:

Herodotus: When the sun traverses the (southern) zone near
the earth, it draws up liquid from all the rivers; but towards the
summer the sun turns to the north and calls the Nile from its
bed. That is why the river overflows in summer.

Egyptian theory: The Etesian winds drive all the clouds
from the upper regions towards the south, and the subsequent
heavy rains cause the Nile to rise.

Ephorus of Cyme [a pupil of Isocrates, mentioned by
Seneca 7.16.1]: In Book One of his *Histories* Ephorus says
Egypt is by nature porous, but mud carried down by the Nile

[1] *factis itineribus* Diels, Gercke.

[2] *ut* supplied by Oltramare.

[3] Gercke, Garrod, Oltramare for *quare cum* T; *quasi percussa sint* L; *quasi compertus animus cuncta et invicem commeant* PE.

[4] Gercke adds *quomodo fieri potest, ut absumptis aquis non
solum hic abundat sed* between *sed* and *in ceteris*.

alternating tides the way other seas do, but always
has a torrent descending in one direction). Unless
this happened—that is, unless these passage-ways
restored water to any land that lacked it and drained
away surplus water—everything would already have
been dried up or flooded."

I should like to ask Diogenes, since all lands are 30
perforated and have passages to each other, why rivers
do not everywhere become swollen in the summer.
"The sun bakes Egypt more, and so the Nile increases more; but in other countries too rivers may
develop some increase." Then why is any part of
the earth without water since every land attracts
moisture from other regions and the hotter the land
the more water it attracts? Next, why is the Nile
water fresh if its water comes from the sea? For no
river has fresher taste . . .[1]

fills up the soil so that it is no longer able to absorb water.
Then in the season of burning heat the Nile overflows to find
more porous ground.

Thrasyalces of Thasos ["one of the ancient physicians,"
Strabo 17.79]: The Etesian winds cause the Nile to overflow
because the high mountains in Ethiopia collect the rainclouds
that are pushed there by the Etesian winds.

Callisthenes the Peripatetic [nephew and pupil of Aristotle;
Seneca refers to him 6.23.2 sqq.; 7.5.3]: In Book Four of his
Greek Affairs Callisthenes says that he made an expedition
with Alexander the Macedonian into Ethiopia and discovered
that the endless rains there cause the Nile to rise.

Dicaearchus [a pupil of Aristotle]: In his *Tour of the Earth*
Dicaearchus assumes that the Nile flows from the Atlantic Ocean.

[1] In Bk. 6.8.3–5 Seneca discusses the Nile briefly in connection with the theory that the inundation of the Nile is
caused by waters from the earth's interior; and, whether a
source of the Nile or merely an addition to it, the water ascends
from a great underground lake.

BOOK IVB
HAIL AND SNOW

LIBER QUARTUS B[1]

DE GRANDINE ET NIVE[2]

1   3. Grandinem hoc modo fieri si tibi affirmavero
quo apud nos glacies fit, gelata nube tota, nimis
audacem rem fecero. Itaque ex his me testibus
numero secundae notae qui vidisse[3] quidem se negant.
Aut, quod historici faciunt, et ipse faciam; illi, cum
multa mentiti sunt ad arbitrium suum, unam aliquam rem nolunt spondere sed adiciunt: " Penes
2   auctores fides erit." Ergo si mihi parum credis,
Posidonius tibi auctoritatem promittit tam in illo
quod praeteriit[4] quam in hoc quod secuturum est;
grandinem enim fieri ex nube aquosa iam et in
umorem versa sic affirmabit tamquam interfuerit.

3   Quare autem rotunda sit grando, etiam sine
magistro scire possis, cum adnotaveris stillicidium
omne glomerari. Quod et in speculis apparet quae
umorem halitu[5] colligunt, et in poculis sparsis

---

[1] *l. primus* ST; *l. secundus* PKU; *l. tertius* HZ[2]; *l. quartus*
E; *libro qui fertur tertio adiunctus* ABV; [*Libri Quarti Qui
Fertur Pars Posterior*] *Liber Primus* Oltramare.

[2] *de grandine et nive* P; *de nubibus* H Oltramare; *de grandine
et nubibus* E; *de grandine* S; *de nivibus* Z.

[3] *vidisse* ZV Oltramare; *audisse* HPG; *qui audisse quidem
se vidisse negant* E.

[4] *praeiit* Garrod.

[5] *habitu* Z; *alicubi* ABV.

BOOK IVB

HAIL AND SNOW [1]

3. I would make too rash a statement if I assured 1
you that hail occurs in the same way as ice does on
earth, except that a whole cloud is frozen. And so I
consider myself one of those witnesses with a
secondhand brand of information, who say that they
themselves did not actually see it. Or I may do as
historians do. After they have lied to their own
satisfaction about a lot of things, they are unwilling
to guarantee some one point and toss out: "The
verification will be found among my sources." [2] So, 2
if you have too little confidence in me, Posidonius
guarantees you his authority both on the point he
omitted [3] and on what follows: for he will assure you,
just as though he had been present at the process,
that hail is formed in a cloud that is not only full of
water but has already changed into water.

Moreover, you can learn even without a teacher 3
why hail is round when you observe that every kind
of drop becomes globular. This appears on a mirror
which collects moisture from the breath, or is
obvious from drops scattered on cups or any other

---

[1] On the title of this book, see Introduction, p. XX.
[2] Sallust *B. Jug.* 17.
[3] A reference to some lost section of the book.

47

aliaque omni levitate. Non minus foliis si quae guttae
adhaeserunt in rotundum iacent.

4   Quid magis est saxo durum ?   Quid mollius unda ?
Dura tamen molli saxa cavantur aqua ;

aut, ut alius poeta ait :

Stillicidi casus lapidem cavat ;

haec ipsa excavatio rotunda fit. Ex quo apparet
illud quoque huic esse simile quod cavat ; locum enim
5 sibi ad formam et habitum sui exculpit. Praeterea
potest, etiamsi non fuit grando talis, dum defertur,
corrotundari et, totiens per spatium aeris densi
devoluta, aequabiliter atque in orbem teri. Quod
nix pati non potest, quia non est tam solida, immo
quia fusa est, et non per magnam altitudinem cadit,
sed circa terras initium eius est ; ita non longus
illi per aera sed ex proximo lapsus est.

6   Quare non et ego mihi idem permittam quod
Anaxagoras ?   Inter nullos magis quam inter philoso-
phos esse debet aequa libertas.   Grando nihil aliud
est quam suspensa glacies, nix pruina pendens.   Illud
enim iam diximus, quod inter rorem et aquam interest,

---

[1] Ovid *Ars Amatoria* 1.475–476.

[2] Lucretius 1.314. Nowhere in the *Naturales Quaestiones*
does Seneca name Lucretius ; here he identifies him only as
" another poet."

[3] Aristotle (1.12.348a 34–37) makes much the same statement ; however, he considers that hail formed near the earth
is correspondingly not round.

smooth surface. Also, any drops clinging to leaves
lie in a round shape.

> What is harder than rock   4
> Or softer than water?
> Yet hard rocks are made hollow
> By soft water.[1]

or, as another poet says:

> Drops falling
> Make stones hollow.[2]

This hollow is itself round. From which it is obvious
that the shape in the rock is similar to that which
hollowed it out, for the drops sculpture a spot according to their own shape and character. Besides, even if   5
hail did not have such a shape, it could be rounded
when it fell. Rolling over and over again through a
space of thick air it is worn down equally on all sides
into a globe.[3] But snow cannot be affected this
way because it is not as solid and because, moreover,
it is loosely made and falls from no great height.
Its origin is near the earth. Its descent through the
air is thus not prolonged since it falls from near by.

Why should I not permit myself the same liberties   6
Anaxagoras takes?[4] Equal freedom ought to exist
among no group more than among philosophers.
Hail is nothing more than ice in suspension, snow is
suspended frost. I have already said[5] that the same
distinction between frost and ice exists as between

---

[4] In a lost section Seneca has evidently objected to the
theories of Anaxagoras, perhaps following Aristotle (1.12.348b
12–16).

[5] In a part of the book now lost.

hoc inter pruinam et glaciem nec non inter nivem
et grandinem [1] interesse.

1   4. Poteram me peracta quaestione dimittere, sed
bene mensum dabo et, quoniam coepi tibi molestus
esse, quicquid in hoc loco quaeritur dicam (quaeritur
autem quare hieme ningat, non grandinet, vere iam
frigore infracto grando cadat); nam, ut fallar [2] tibi,
verum mihi quidem persuadetur, qui me usque ad
mendacia haec leviora in quibus os percidi, non
oculi erui solent, credulum praesto.

2   Hieme aer riget et ideo nondum in aquam vertitur
sed in nivem, cui aer propior est; cum ver coepit,
maior inclinatio [3] temporis [4] sequitur et calidiore
caelo maiora fiunt stillicidia.   Ideo, ut ait Vergilius
noster,

cum ruit imbriferum ver,

vehementior mutatio est aeris undique patefacti et
solventis se ipso tempore [5] adiuvante; ob hoc nimbi
graves magis vastique quam pertinaces deferuntur.

3   Bruma lentas pluvias habet et tenues, quales saepe
solent intervenire, cum pluvia rara et minuta nivem
quoque admixtam habet; dicimus nivalem diem,

[1] *glaciem* HEGλAV.
[2] *ni fallar* B; *ut fatear* Gercke.
[3] *indignatio* H[1]F.
[4] *aeris* PZ; *temporis vel aeris* λ.
[5] *tepore* Gronovius, Haase, Alexander.

---

[1] The Latin is extremely puzzling here.   I follow William
Hardy Alexander, who makes the best sense of it in English

dew and water. There is the same distinction between snow and hail.

4. I could stop now, since the investigation is complete, but I will give you your money's worth; and since I have already started to be a nuisance to you I will discuss everything asked about this subject. For example, a common question is why does it snow in winter but does not hail, yet hail falls in spring after the cold is broken. I may be wrong, in your opinion, but *I* am convinced of its truth, and I am a man who shows himself credulous up to the limit of those trivial falsehoods for which the face is usually slapped but the eyes are not put out.[1]

In winter the atmosphere becomes stiff and so is not yet converted into water but into snow, which the atmosphere more nearly resembles. When spring begins there follows a greater variation of climate and larger drops form in the warmer sky. So, as our Virgil says:

> When rain-bearing spring
> Marches in,[2]

there is a more violent change in the atmosphere, and everywhere it opens up and relaxes with the help of the season itself. For this reason heavy and abundant showers rather than long lasting rains are discharged. Winter has sluggish and thin rains, the sort that often fall when a scattered and fine rain is mixed with snow. We call it a snowy day when the

which, as he says, has at least the "virtue of being recognizably connected with the Latin original." [Seneca may mean "falsehoods which hit one in the face but no worse."—E.H.W.]

[2] Virgil *Georgics* 1.313.

cum altum frigus et triste caelum est. Praeterea,
aquilone flante aut suum caelum habente, minutae
pluviae sunt; austro imber improbior est et guttae
pleniores.

1   5. Rem a nostris positam nec dicere audeo, quia
infirma videtur, nec praeterire. Quid enim mali est
aliquid et faciliori iudici scribere? Immo, si omnia
argumenta ad obrussam coeperimus exigere, silen-
tium indicetur. Pauca enim admodum sunt sine
adversario; cetera, etsi vincunt, litigant.

2   Aiunt vere, quicquid circa Scythiam et Pontum et
septemtrionalem plagam glaciatum et astrictum est,
relaxari; tunc flumina gelata discedere, tunc obrutos
montes nivem solvere. Credibile est ergo frigidos
3   spiritus inde fieri [1] et verno [2] caelo remisceri. Illud
quoque adiciunt, quod nec sum expertus nec experiri
cogito (tu quoque, censeo, si volueris verum ex-
quirere, nivem in Care [3] experiaris); minus algere
aiunt pedes eorum qui fixam et duram nivem calcant
quam eorum qui teneram et labefactam.

4   Ergo, si non mentiuntur, quicquid ex illis septem-
trionalibus locis iam disturbata nive et glacie fran-
gente se fertur, id meridianae partis tepentem iam

---

[1] *ferri* Gercke.
[2] *uno* AV; *imo* BC.
[3] Gronovius, Gercke, Oltramare for *cane* HPSABV; *carne* Z.

---

[1] Oltramare explains that Seneca is using a Greek proverb
which meant (in a roundabout way having to do with Caria

cold is intense and the sky gloomy. Besides, the rains are fine when the north wind blows or the sky has a typically north wind look. From the south wind the rain is more violent and the drops are larger.

5. I am afraid either to mention or to omit a 1 theory established by our Stoic friends, because it seems without basis. But what is wrong in writing about it to so indulgent a judge as you? Actually, if we started to subject every argument to a rigid test we would be compelled by command to silence. There are only a few theories without opposition; the others are pleading in court, even though they eventually win their case.

The Stoics say that all the ice-bound, frozen 2 district around Scythia and the Pontus and the northern regions is released in the spring. Then the frozen rivers start to move along again; then the snow that covered the mountains melts. It is accordingly conceivable that cold air rises from there and mixes with the spring climate. They add a proof which 3 I have never tested and do not plan to test (but you, I think, might test snow at your own risk [1] if you want to find out the truth); they say that feet feel less cold when they step on hard, solid snow than on soft, slushy snow.

If then the Stoics are not in error, all the cold air 4 which moves from those northern regions when the snow is dislodged, and the ice is breaking up, immobilizes and condenses the air of the southern

and Carian slaves) that you undertook something at your own risk, or with caution. In any case the *cane* and *carne* in the manuscripts are incomprehensible.

umidumque aera alligat et praestringit; itaque
pluvia futura erat, grando fit iniuria frigoris.

1 6. Non tempero mihi quominus omnes nostrorum
ineptias proferam. Quosdam peritos observandarum
nubium esse affirmant et praedicere cum grando
ventura sit. Hoc intellegere usu ipso potuerunt,
cum colorem nubium notassent, quem grando totiens
insequebatur.

2 Illud incredibile, Cleonis fuisse publice praepositos
chalazophylacas, speculatores venturae grandinis.
Hi cum signum dedissent adesse iam grandinem, quid
expectas? Ut homines ad paenulas discurrerent aut
ad scorteas? Immo pro se quisque alius agnum
immolabat, alius pullum. Protinus illae nubes alio
declinabant, cum aliquid gustassent sanguinis.

3 Hoc rides? Accipe quod magis rideas. Si quis
nec agnum nec pullum habebat, quod sine damno
fieri poterat, manus sibi afferebat et, ne tu avidas aut
crudeles existimes nubes, digitum suum bene acuto
graphio pungebat et hoc sanguine litabat; nec minus
ab huius agello grando se vertebat quam ab illo in
quo maioribus hostiis exorata erat.

1 7. Rationem huius rei quaerunt. Alteri, ut
homines sapientissimos decet, negant posse fieri ut
cum grandine aliquis paciscatur et tempestates

regions, which is warming and already moist. And so, what was going to be rain becomes hail because of the effect of this cold.

6. I cannot restrain myself from publishing all the silly theories of our Stoic friends. They assert that there are some experts in observing clouds and in predicting when hail will come. They are able to know this just from experience, since they have noted in the clouds a colour which is in every case followed by hail.

It is incredible that at Cleonae there were " hail-officers " appointed at public expense who watched for hail to come. When they gave a signal that hail was approaching, what do you think happened? Did people run for woolly overcoats or leather rain-coats? No. Everybody offered sacrifices according to his means, a lamb or a chicken. When those clouds had tasted some blood they immediately moved off in another direction.

Are you laughing at this? Here is something to make you laugh even more. If someone did not have a lamb or a chicken he laid hands on himself, which could be done without great expense. But do not think the clouds were greedy or cruel. He merely pricked his finger with a well-sharpened stylus and made a favourable offering with this blood, and the hail turned away from his little field no less than it did from the property of a man who had appeased it with sacrifices of larger victims.

7. People seek an explanation for this sort of thing. Some, as is fitting for thoroughly educated men, say it is impossible for anyone to make a bargain with hail or buy off a storm with little gifts, even though

munusculis redimat, quamvis munera et deos vincant. Alteri suspicari ipsos aiunt esse in ipso sanguine vim quandam potentem avertendae nubis ac
2 repellendae. Sed quomodo in tam exiguo sanguine potest esse vis tanta ut in altum penetret et illam sentiant nubes? Quanto expeditius erat dicere: mendacium et fabula est. At Cleonaei[1] iudicia reddebant in illos quibus delegata erat cura providendae tempestatis, quod neglegentia eorum vineae vapulassent aut segetes procidissent. Et apud nos in XII tabulis cavetur: "ne quis alienos fructus excantassit."

3 Rudis adhuc antiquitas credebat et attrahi cantibus imbres[2] et repelli, quorum nihil posse fieri tam palam est ut huius rei causa nullius philosophi schola intranda sit.

1 8. Unam rem ad hoc[3] adiciam et favere te ac plaudere iuvabit. Aiunt nivem in ea parte aeris fieri quae prope terras est. Hanc enim plus habere caloris ex quattuor[4] causis: una, quod omnis terrarum evaporatio, cum multum in se fervidi aridique habeat, hoc est calidior quo recentior; altera, quod radii solis a terra resiliunt et in se recurrunt (horum duplicatio proxima quaeque a terris calefacit, quae ideo plus habent teporis[5] quia solem bis sentiunt); tertia

1 Gercke, Oltramare for *Cleonae* ZHP; *decuriones* E[2]; *cleonis* ABV.
2 *nubes* ABV.
3 *adhuc* ABV.

presents do win over even the gods. Others say they suspect that there is in blood itself some powerful force for averting and repelling clouds. But how can the power in a little drop of blood be so great that it penetrates to the heights and influences clouds? It is much easier to say: it is an untrue fable. But the people of Cleonae passed harsh judgements on those who had been delegated the task of forecasting storms, because through their negligence vines were beaten down or crops flattened. And among ourselves, in the Twelve Tables there is the warning: " No one may make incantations against another's crop."[1]

Antiquity, still uneducated, used to believe that rains were attracted or repelled by incantations. It is so obvious none of these things can happen that it is unnecessary to enroll in the school of some philosopher to learn it.

8. I will add one thing to this and you will be glad to approve and applaud it. They say that snow is formed in that part of the atmosphere which is near the earth. This part has more heat, for four reasons: one, because all the evaporation from the earth, since it contains much heat and dryness, is hotter the more recently it has left the ground; two, because the rays of the sun bounce back from the earth and run back into themselves and their double trip heats up all the air closest to the earth (which then has more warmth because it feels the

---

[1] Cf. Pliny 28.18; E. H. Warmington, *Remains of Old Latin*, *LCL*, vol. 3, pp. 474–475; 478–479.

---

⁴ *tribus* BV.   ⁵ *temporis* H¹λZ.

SENECA

causa est quod magis superiora perflantur, at quaecumque depressa sunt minus ventis verberantur.

1   9. Accedit his ratio Democriti: " Omne corpus,
quo solidius est, hoc calorem citius concipit, diutius
servat. Itaque si in sole posueris aeneum vas et
vitreum,[1] aeneo citius calor accedet, diutius haere-
bit." Adicit deinde quare hoc existimet fieri.
" His," inquit, " corporibus quae duriora et pressiora
sunt necesse est minora foramina esse et tenuiorem
in singulis spiritum; sequitur ut, quemadmodum
minora balnearia et minora miliaria[2] citius calefiunt,
sic haec foramina occulta et oculos effugientia et
celerius fervorem sentiant et propter easdem angustias, quicquid receperunt, tardius reddant."
Haec longe praeparata ad id perducunt de quo nunc
quaeritur.

1   10. Omnis aer quo propior est terris, hoc crassior.
Quemadmodum in aqua et in omni umore faex ima
est, ita in aere spississima quaeque desidunt. Iam
autem probatum est omnia, quo crassioris solidiorisque
materiae sunt, hoc fidelius custodire calorem receptum. Editior aer, quo longius a terrarum colluvie
recessit, hoc sincerior puriorque est; itaque solem
non retinet, sed velut per inane transmittit; ideo
minus calefit.

[1] *vitreum et argenteum* MSS.; Gercke and Oltramare delete
et argenteum.
[2] *militaria* ABSTV.

58

sun's heat twice); third, because upper regions are blown around more, while all lower regions are less lashed by the winds.

9. The theory of Democritus [1] belongs to the above reasons. " The more solid an object is the more quickly it absorbs heat and the longer it retains it. And so, if you place a bronze vase and a glass vase in the sun, the heat will communicate itself more quickly to the bronze vase and cling to it longer." Next, he adds why he thinks this happens. " In objects which are harder and more compact," he says, " the openings are necessarily smaller and in each opening the air is thinner. It follows that just as smaller bathtubs and smaller containers become hot more quickly, so those openings which are concealed and too small for the eye to see feel the heat more quickly and, because of this same littleness, lose more slowly whatever they receive." This long preamble leads up to the point to be discussed next.

10. The closer all air is to the earth, the thicker it is. Just as in water and in all liquids the dregs are at the bottom, so in air all the thickest particles settle downward. But it has already been proven that all things which have thick and solid matter preserve more faithfully the heat they receive. The higher the air is, the farther it withdraws from the pollution of the earth, the less contaminated and purer it is. And so it does not retain the sun's heat but transmits it as through a vacuum. Accordingly, it becomes less warm.

[1] Democritus of Abdera lived in the second half of the fifth century. Seneca discusses his " atomic " theory in 5.2.1.

1 11. Contra quidam aiunt cacumina montium hoc
calidiora esse debere quo propiora soli sunt. Qui
mihi videntur errare quod Apenninum et Alpes et
alios notos ob eximiam altitudinem montes in tantum
putant crescere ut illorum magnitudo sentire solis
viciniam possit.

2 Excelsa sunt ista, quamdiu nobis comparantur;
at vero, ubi ad universum respexeris, manifesta est
omnium humilitas; inter se vincuntur et vincunt.
Ceterum in tantum nihil attollitur ut in collatione
totius ulla[1] sit vel maximis portio. Quod nisi esset,
non diceremus totum orbem terrarum pilam esse.

3 Pilae proprietas est cum aequalitate quadam rotun-
ditas; aequalitatem autem hunc accipe quam vides
in lusoria pila; non multum illi commissurae et rimae
earum nocent quo minus par sibi ab omni parte
dicatur. Quomodo in hac pila nihil illa intervalla
officiunt ad speciem rotundi, sic ne in universo quidem
orbe terrarum editi montes, quorum altitudo totius
mundi collatione consumitur.

4 Qui dicit altiorem montem, quia solem propius
excipiat, magis calere debere, idem dicere potest
longiorem hominem citius quam pusillum debere
calefieri et caput citius quam pedes. At quisquis
mundum mensura sua aestimaverit et terram cogi-
taverit tenere puncti locum, intelleget nihil in illa

---

[1] *nulla* AV.

11. Some say, on the contrary, that the peaks of 1
mountains ought to be warmer the nearer they are to
the sun. They seem to me to be wrong because they
believe that the Apennines and the Alps and other
mountains famed for their great heights reach such
an altitude that their elevation enables them to feel
the nearness of the sun.

Such mountains are high as long as they are 2
compared to ourselves; but surely when you look at
the whole earth, the lowness of all of them is obvious
to everybody. Mountains are excelled or excel in
size only in relation to each other. However,
nothing is elevated so high that even the greatest
parts have any proportion to the whole earth. If this
were not so we would not usually say that the whole
globe of the earth is a ball. A characteristic of a 3
ball is its roundness and a certain uniformity. However, take the uniformity which you see in balls used
in games. The seams and chinks do not keep them
from being spoken of as equal on all sides. In a ball
of this type those areas do not interfere with the
appearance of roundness; and in the same way the
height of mountains projecting from the sphere as a
whole even of the earth is brought to nothing by
comparison with the whole world.

Anyone who says that a higher mountain ought to 4
be warmer because it receives the sun's heat closer,
could also say that a tall man ought to become hot
sooner than a short man, and his head sooner than
his feet. But anyone who judges the universe by its
own measure and reflects that the earth occupies
only the position of a pinpoint, will realize that
nothing on earth can be so high that it can feel more

posse ita eminere ut caelestia magis sentiat, velut in propinquum illis accesserit.

5 Montes isti quos suspicimus et vertices aeterna nive obsessi nihilominus in imo sunt; et propius quidem est a sole mons quam campus aut vallis, sed sic quomodo est pilus pilo crassior. Isto enim modo et arbor alia magis quam alia dicetur vicina caelo. Quod est falsum, quia inter pusilla[1] non potest magnum esse discrimen, nisi dum inter se comparantur. Ubi ad collationem immensi corporis ventum est, nihil interest quanto sit alterum altero maius, quia, etiamsi magno discrimine, tamen minima vincuntur.

1 12. Sed ut ad propositum revertar, propter has quas rettuli causas plerisque placuit in ea parte aeris nivem concipi quae vicina terris est, et ideo minus alligari quia minore rigore coit. Nam vicinus aer et plus habet frigoris quam ut in aquam imbremque transeat, et minus quam ut duretur in grandinem; hoc medio frigore non nimis intento[2] nives fiunt coactis aquis.

1 13. "Quid istas," inquis, "ineptias, quibus litteratior est quisque, non melior, tam operose persequeris? Quomodo fiant nives dicis, cum multo magis ad nos dici a te pertineat quare emendae non sint nives." Iubes me tu[3] cum luxuria litigare?

---

[1] *illa* ABV.   [2] *in alto* Z.

strongly the influences from the sky as though it had approached close to them.

Those mountains we look up to, whose tops are 5 covered with eternal snow, are really quite low. A mountain is closer to the sun than a plain or a valley is, but in the way that one hair is thicker than another. In the same way one tree will be said to be closer than another tree is to the sky. This is false, because between little things there cannot be a great difference, except when they are compared with each other. When it comes to a comparison with an immense object it does not matter how much larger one little thing is than another because both are still dwarfed even if the difference between them is great.

12. But to return to the subject. For reasons 1 which I have given, most authorities are of the opinion that snow is formed in that part of the atmosphere which is near the earth and so is less compact than hail because it is congealed by less cold. For the nearby atmosphere has too much cold to be transformed into rainwater, and too little cold to be hardened into hail. In this moderate and not too intense cold, snow is formed from congealed water.

13. " Why," you say, " do you so laboriously 1 pursue these trivialities by which any person is made more cultured, not more virtuous? You describe how snow is formed when it matters much more to us to be told by you why snow should not be bought." *You* want me to quarrel with luxury? This quarrel

---

³ *iubes me tu* ES Oltramare; *iubes mentem* HPZAB; *iubes autem* V; *iubes me litem* Gercke; *iubes medentem* Alexander.

Cotidianum istud et sine effectu iurgium est. Litigemus tamen, etiamsi superior futura est; pugnantes ac reluctantes vincat.

2 Quid porro? Hanc ipsam inspectionem naturae nihil iudicas ad id quod vis conferre? Cum quaerimus quomodo nix fiat et dicimus illam pruinae [1] similem habere naturam, plus illi spiritus quam aquae inesse, non putas exprobrari illis, cum emere aquam turpe sit, si ne [2] aquam quidem emunt?

3 Nos vero quaeramus potius quomodo fiant nives quam quomodo serventur, quoniam, non contenti vina diffundere, veteraria per sapores aetatesque disponere, invenimus quomodo stiparemus [3] nivem, ut ea aestatem evinceret et contra anni fervorem defenderetur loci frigore. Quid hac diligentia consecuti sumus? Nempe ut gratuitam mercemur aquam. Nobis dolet quod spiritum, quod solem emere non possumus, quod hic aer etiam delicatis divitibusque ex facili nec emptus venit. O quam nobis male est quod quicquam a rerum natura in

4 medio relictum est! Hoc quod illa fluere et patere omnibus voluit, cuius haustum vitae publicum fecit, hoc quod tam homini quam feris avibusque et inertissimis animalibus in usum large ac beate profudit, contra se ingeniosa luxuria redegit ad pretium, adeo nihil illi potest placere nisi carum. Unum hoc erat quod divites in aequum turbae deduceret, quo non

---

[1] *pluvie* ABV.
[2] *sine* PZ; *si nec* AV.
[3] *isti paremus* HPZ; *istis paremus* ES.

goes on daily without effect. Nevertheless, let us argue against luxury. Even if luxury wins, it should defeat us while we are fighting and resisting.

What then? Do you judge that this examination 2 of nature contributes nothing to the objective you want? When we investigate how snow is formed and we say that it has properties similar to frost, that there is more air than water in it, do you not think that this is a reproach to people who, while it is a disgrace to buy water, do not even get water for their money but mostly air?

But let us investigate how snow is formed rather 3 than how it is preserved. Since we are not content with racking off wines and arranging vaults for older vintages by taste and age, we have found out how we may compress snow so that it prevails over summer and is protected in a cold place against the season's heat. What have we accomplished by this diligence? Only that we trade in free water. We are sad because we cannot pay for air and sunlight, and because this air comes easily and without cost to the fastidious also and the rich. How unfortunate it is for us that nature has left anything as common property. This water, which nature has allowed to 4 flow for everyone and be available to all, the drinking of which she has made common to life; this water which she has poured forth abundantly and generously for the use of men as well as wild animals, birds, and the laziest creatures; on this water luxury, ingenious against itself, has put a price. So, nothing can please luxury unless it is expensive. Water was the one thing which reduced the wealthy to the level of the mob. In this, the wealthy could not be

possent antecedere pauperrimum; illi cui divitiae
molestae sunt excogitatum est quemadmodum etiam
caperet aqua luxuriam.

5   Unde hoc perventum sit ut nulla nobis aqua satis
frigida videretur quae flueret dicam. Quamdiu
sanus et salubris cibi capax stomachus est impletur-
que, non premitur, naturalibus fomentis contentus
est; ubi, cotidianis cruditatibus perustus,[1] non temporis aestus, sed suos sentit, ubi ebrietas continua
visceribus insedit et praecordia bile in quam vertitur
torret, aliquid necessario quaeritur quo aestus ille
frangatur qui ipsis aquis incalescit. Remediis
incitatur [2] vitium; itaque non aestate tantum, sed
6   et media hieme nivem causa pari [3] bibunt. Quae
huius rei causa est nisi intestinum malum et luxu
corrupta praecordia? Quibus nullum intervallum umquam quo interquiescerent datum est, sed prandia
cenis usque in lucem perductis ingesta sunt, et dis-
tentos copia ferculorum ac varietate comessatio
altius mersit; deinde numquam intermissa intem-
perantia quicquid alimenti [4] decoxerat efferavit et in
desiderium semper novi rigoris accendit.

7   Itaque quamvis cenationem velis ac specularibus
muniant et igne multo doment [5] hiemem, nihilo-

[1] *perustus* Z Oltramare; omitted in the other MSS.
[2] Leo, Oltramare for *incitat* MSS.; *incitat se* Garrod.
[3] Oltramare for *causa pati* Z; *hac causa* in most of the
MSS.; *hac de causa* B.
[4] Oltramare for *animi* HPFABV; *anima* Z; *avide* ES;
nivis Leo; *alui* Garrod.
[5] *amoveant* B.

superior to the poorest man. Someone burdened by riches has thought out how even water might become a luxury.

I will explain how it happens that no water which 5 is flowing seems cold enough to us. As long as the stomach is healthy and receptive to wholesome food, and is filled up, not overloaded, it is satisfied with natural stimulants. When it is burned up by daily indigestion and feels the heat, not of the season but of itself, when continuous drunkenness takes possession of the viscera and the bile into which it is turned burns the internal organs, out of necessity something is searched for to quench that burning which is inflamed by mere water. The malady is aggravated by remedies. So, for one and the same reason people drink snow not only in the summer but also in the middle of winter. What reason is there for drinking 6 snow except an intestinal illness and internal organs ruined by debauchery? The organs are never given any interval in which to rest. Breakfasts are heaped on banquets lasting till dawn. When people are distended by the abundance and variety of the dishes, drunkenness submerges them deeper. Then the uninterrupted excesses aggravate the food already half-digested and inflame a continuous craving for a new cold stimulant.[1]

And so, although people protect the dining hall 7 with draperies and window-panes, and they control the winter temperature with a huge fire, none the less

[1] In Seneca's time *decoquere* usually meant " to boil down." But Seneca here probably hits at Nero's drinking hot water suddenly cooled by thrusting the drinking glass in snow (cf. Pliny 31.40).

minus stomachus ille solutus et aestu suo languidus
quaerit aliquid quo erigatur. Nam sicut animo
relictos stupentesque frigida[1] spargimus, ut ad sen-
sum[2] sui redeant, ita viscera istorum vitiis tor-
pentia nihil sentiunt, nisi frigore illa vehementiore
8 perusseris.[3]   Inde est, inquam, quod ne nive quidem
contenti sunt, sed glaciem, velut certior illi ex solido
rigor sit, exquirunt ac saepe repetitis aquis diluunt.
Quae non e summo tollitur sed, ut vim maiorem habeat
et pertinacius frigus, ex abdito effoditur.   Itaque ne
unum quidem eius est pretium, sed habet institores
aqua et annonam, pro pudor! variam.

9   Unguentarios Lacedaemonii urbe expulerunt et
propere cedere finibus suis iusserunt, quia oleum
disperderent.   Quid illi fecissent, si vidissent repo-
nendae nivis officinas et tot iumenta portandae aquae
deservientia, cuius colorem saporemque paleis quibus
custodiunt inquinant?

10   At, dii boni, quam facile est extinguere sitim
sanam!   Sed quid sentire possunt emortuae fauces et
occallatae cibis ardentibus?   Quemadmodum nihil
illis satis frigidum, sic nihil satis calidum est, sed ardentes boletos et raptim in condimento[4] suo mer-
satos demittunt paene fumantes, quos deinde
restinguant nivatis[5] potionibus.   Videbis, inquam,

---

[1] *aqua frigida* EB.
[2] *animum* A[1]B.
[3] *perfuderis* ABV; *percusseris* P[2]S Alexander.

the stomach, debilitated and languid from its own burning, seeks something by which it may be revived. For just as we sprinkle cold water on people who have fainted and are dazed, so that they may return to consciousness, so the internal organs of these people, made numb by excesses, feel nothing unless you inflame them to feverish activity by a more extreme cold. This is why, I say, they are not satis- 8 fied even with snow but look for ice, as though it had a more reliable cold because of its solidarity; and they melt it by pouring water over it repeatedly. The ice is not taken from the surface but is dug out from a covered layer in order that it might have more strength and its cold last longer. And so water does not even have a uniform price but has hucksters and—for shame!—quotations for its value.

The Lacedaemonians expelled perfumers from the 9 city and ordered them to leave the country in a hurry because they were wasting oil. What would they have done if they had seen shops for storing snow and so many pack-animals devoted to carrying frozen water, its colour and taste spoiled by the straw with which they protect it?

But, good gods, how easy it is to quench a healthy 10 thirst! Yet what can gullets feel when they have been deadened and hardened by scalding food? Just as nothing is cold enough for them, so nothing is hot enough. They greedily swallow down hot mushrooms dipped in their own sauce and almost smoking, only to extinguish them with snowed drinks. You will see, I tell you, skinny youths wrapped in

---

4 *in condimento* Z Alexander for *indumento* most MSS.
5 *vinatis* λ.

quosdam graciles et palliolo focalique circumdatos, pallentes et aegros non sorbere solum nivem sed etiam esse et frusta eius in scyphos suos deicere, ne tepescant inter ipsam bibendi moram.

11 Sitim istam esse putas? Febris est, et quidem eo acrior quod non tactu venarum nec in cutem effuso calore deprehenditur, sed cor ipsum excoquit. Luxuria invictum malum et ex molli fluidoque durum atque patiens. Non intellegis omnia consuetudine vim suam perdere? Itaque nix ista, in qua iam etiam natatis, eo pervenit usu et cotidiana stomachi servitute ut aquae locum obtineat. Aliquid adhuc quaerite illa frigidius, quia pro nihilo est familiaris rigor.

[Additional note to pp. 34–35, Book IVA, 2.20. Prof. Corcoran accepts Oltramare's *Hebrus* . . . . *Haemo*. But if Seneca wrote this, why did any scribe alter it to the geographically less happy *Caystrus* (Kara Su river in Lydia) . . . . *Tmolo* (Tmolus =Musa Dagh mountain) from which the Caystrus rises? I would conclude that it was Seneca himself, none too good a geographer, who wrote *Caystrus* . . . . *Tmolo*.—E.H.W.]

cloaks and mufflers, pale and sickly, not only sipping
the snow but actually eating it and tossing bits of
it into their glasses lest they become warm merely
through the time taken in drinking.

Do you consider this thirst? It is a fever, and all 11
the more severe because it is not detected by the
pulse or by heat suffused through the skin; indeed it
burns the heart itself. Luxury is an incurable malady
and from being soft and weak it hardens to endure
anything. Do you not realize that all things lose
their force because of familiarity? And so, that
snow, in which you are even now swimming,[1] has
come to such a pitch, by constant use, and daily
slavery of the stomach, that it takes the place of water.
Search now for something still colder than snow,
because cold that is familiar is nothing.

---

[1] During noon to midnight revels Nero restored his en-
durance by frequent plunges in a pool chilled with ice (Suetonius *Nero* 27.2).

BOOK V
WINDS

LIBER QUINTUS[1]

DE VENTIS[2]

1   1. VENTUS est fluens aer. Quidam ita definierunt: ventus est aer fluens[3] in unam partem. Haec definitio videtur diligentior, quia numquam aer tam immobilis est ut non in aliqua sit agitatione. Sic tranquillum mare dicitur, cum[4] leviter commovetur nec in unam partem inclinatur; itaque si legeris

> cum placidum ventis staret mare,

scito illud non stare, sed succuti[5] leviter, et dici tranquillum, quia nec hoc nec illo impetum capiat.[6]

2 Idem et de aere iudicandum est, non esse umquam immobilem, etiamsi quietus sit. Quod ex hoc intellegas licet: cum sol in aliquem clausum locum infusus est,[7] videmus corpuscula minima in adversum[8]

---

[1] *liber secundus* PK; *quartus* HZMV; *quintus* E; [*Liber Quintus*] *Liber Secundus* Oltramare.

[2] *de ventis* HPEZ; *de vento* S.

[3] *agitatus* ABV.

[4] *non cum* HPZ; *cum non* L.

[5] *concuti* ABV.

[6] *faciat* EF.

[7] *inclusus est* A²V.

[8] *adversum* most MSS.; *diversum* Z.

74

BOOK V

WINDS

1. WIND is flowing air.[1] Some have defined it this 1
way: wind is air flowing in one direction.[2] This
definition seems more accurate because air is never
so immobile that it is not in some sort of motion.
Thus, the sea is called calm when it rolls gently and
does not veer in a single direction. And if you read:

> When the winds were silent
> And the sea stood still [3]

you know that the sea does not really stand still, but
rocks gently and is called calm because it receives
no impetus from one side or the other. The same 2
concept must also be used concerning the air: it is
never without motion even though it is quiet.
You may realize this from the following: when the
sun pours into any closed place we see very tiny
particles moving in opposing directions, some up, some

---

[1] Aristotle (1.13.349a 12) says that some authorities define
wind as air in motion; yet he remarks (2.4.360a 28–29) that it
is absurd to suppose air becomes wind by simply being in
motion. Pliny (2.114) describes wind as a *flatus* (" puff " or
" wave ") of air.

[2] This theory probably belongs to Posidonius. Oltramare
believes Posidonius was Seneca's principal source on winds.

[3] Virgil *Ec.* 2.26.

ferri, alia sursum, alia deorsum varie concursantia.

3 Ergo, ut parum diligenter comprehendet quod vult qui dixerit, "fluctus est maris agitatio," quia tranquillum quoque agitatur, at ille abunde sibi caverit cuius definitio haec fuerit: " fluctus est maris in unam partem agitatio," sic in hac quoque re quam cum maxime [1] quaerimus non circumscribetur qui ita se gesserit ut dicat: " ventus est fluens in unam partem aer," aut: " aer fluens impetu," aut: " vis aeris in unam partem euntis,"[2] aut: " cursus aeris aliquo concitatior."

4 Scio quid responderi pro altera definitione possit. Quid necesse est adicere te " in unam partem "? Utique enim quod fluit in unam partem fluit; nemo aquam fluere dicit, si tantum intra se movetur, sed si aliquo ferter; potest ergo aliquid moveri et non fluere et e contrario non potest fluere nisi in unam partem.

5 Sed sive haec brevitas satis a calumnia tuta est, hac utamur; sive aliquis circumspectior est, verbo non parcat cuius adiectio cavillationem omnem poterit excludere. Nunc ad ipsam rem accedamus, quoniam satis de formula disputatum est.

1 2. Democritus ait, cum in angusto inani multa sint corpuscula, quae ille atomos vocat, sequi ventum; at contra quietum et placidum aeris statum esse, cum

---

[1] *nunc maxime* ABV.　　　[2] *fluentis* ABV.

down, running into each other in random patterns.[1]
Therefore you do not express accurately what you **3**
mean when you say, " A wave is the motion of the
sea," because the sea has motion even when still.
But you sufficiently protect yourself if your definition
is thus: " A wave is the motion of the sea in one
direction." Such is the case especially in the subject
we are now examining. You will not be trapped if
you so express yourself that you say: " Wind is air
flowing in one direction," or " wind is air flowing from
a force pushing it," or " wind is the force of air
moving in one direction," or " a rush of fairly forcible
air in one direction."

I know the reply that can be given in favour of the **4**
first definition. Why is it necessary for you to add
" in one direction"? For surely anything that
flows, flows in one direction. No one says that water
flows if it moves simply within itself, but only if it is
carried in some direction. Accordingly, something
can move and yet not flow; on the other hand, nothing can flow except in one direction.

If this brief definition is secure enough from **5**
captious objection let us use it; yet if you are a more
precise person you should not avoid a word if its
addition can eliminate all carping. Now let us get
to the subject itself, since there has been sufficient
discussion of our method.

2. Democritus says that when there are many little **1**
particles, which he calls atoms, in a small empty
space, wind is the result; on the other hand, when
there are only a few little particles in a vast void the

---

[1] Lucretius (2.113–122) uses dust-motes seen in the sunshine to illustrate the random motion of atoms.

in multo inani pauca sint corpuscula. Nam quemadmodum in foro aut vico, quamdiu paucitas est, sine
tumultu ambulatur, ubi turba in angustum concurrit,
aliorum in alios incidentium rixa fit, sic in hoc quo
circumdati sumus spatio, cum exiguum locum multa
corpora impleverint, necesse est alia aliis incidant et
impellant[1] ac repellantur implicenturque et com-
primantur. Ex quibus nascitur ventus, cum illa quae
colluctabantur incubuere et diu fluctuata ac dubia
inclinavere se. At, ubi in magna laxitate corpora
pauca versantur, nec arietare possunt nec impelli.

1   3. Hoc falsum esse vel ex eo colligas licet quod tunc
minime ventus est cum aer nubilo gravis est; atqui
tunc plurima corpora se in angustum contulerunt et
2   inde est spissarum nubium gravitas. Adice nunc
quod circa flumina et lacus frequens nebula est artatis
congestisque corporibus, nec tamen ventus est.
Interdum vero tanta caligo effunditur ut conspectum
in vicino stantium eripiat, quod non eveniret, nisi in
parvum locum corpora se multa compellerent. Atqui
nullum tempus magis quam nebulosum caret vento.
3   Adice nunc quod e contrario evenit ut sol matutinum
aera spissum et umidum ortu suo tenuet; tunc
surgit aura, cum datum est laxamentum corporibus
et stipatio illorum ac turba resoluta est.

[1] *incitentur et impellantur* AV.

condition of the air is quiet and calm. For example, as long as only a few people are in a market-place or on a side-street they walk about without disturbance, but when a crowd comes running together into a narrow place people bump into each other and start quarrelling. The same thing happens in the space surrounding us. When many bodies fill a tiny space they unavoidably knock against each other and push, are shoved back, entwined, and squeezed. Winds are produced from these activities. The particles which are struggling with one another press hard and, after being tossed about and in confusion for a long time, start to move in one direction. Whereas, when only a few bodies are moving around in plenty of room they cannot ram each other or be pushed.

3. You can realize that Democritus' theory is 1 wrong from the fact that there is very little wind when the atmosphere is heavy with clouds; yet at that time many bodies have collected in a narrow space and as a result there is a heavy mass of thick clouds. Now 2 add the fact that around rivers and lakes there is frequent cloudiness from the particles that are closely packed together—and yet there is no wind. Sometimes, indeed, so much darkness surrounds everything that it cuts off the view of objects standing close by, which would not happen unless there were a great many particles packing themselves together into a tiny space. Yet there is never less wind than at a cloudy period. Now consider, on the contrary, 3 that the rising sun thins out the thick and humid morning air. When the particles have been given room, and their close-packed crowd has been dispersed, then a breeze rises.

1   4. " Quo modo ergo," inquis, " venti fiunt, quoniam hoc negas fieri ? " Non uno modo. Alias enim terra ipsa magnam vim aeris eicit et ex abdito spirat; alias, cum magna et continua ex imo evaporatio in altum egit quae emiserat, mutatio ipsa halitus mixti in ventum vertitur.

2   Illud enim nec ut credam mihi persuaderi potest nec ut taceam: quomodo in nostris corporibus cibo fit inflatio—quae non sine magna narium iniuria emittitur et ventrem interdum cum sono exonerat, interdum secretius—sic putant et hanc magnam rerum naturam alimenta mutantem emittere spiritum. Bene nobiscum agitur, cum quod edit semper concoquit;[1] alioquin immundius aliquid timeremus.

3   Numquid ergo hoc verius est dicere multa ex omni parte terrarum et assidua ferri [2] corpuscula ? Quae cum coacervata sunt, deinde extenuari sole coeperunt, quia omne quod in angusto dilatatur spatium maius desiderat, ventus existit.

1   5. Quid ergo ? Hanc solam esse causam venti existimo, aquarum terrarumque evaporationes; ex his gravitatem aeris fieri, deinde solvi impetum, cum

---

[1] *agitur, quod* BC; *edit* supplied by Oltramare, who suggests as an alternative *agitur quod semper concoquit* for *quod semper concoquit sic emittit* ES; *cum quod semper concoquit raro emittit* Gercke.

[2] *fieri* E.

---

[1] Lucan (10.247–248) refers to air-holes in the earth and exhalations from caves.

4. " But," you say, " since you argue that Demo- 1
critus' theory is not true, how are winds formed? "
Not in one way only. Sometimes the earth itself
ejects a great quantity of air, which she breathes
out from hidden recesses.[1] Sometimes when the
great and continuous evaporation from below drives
into the upper atmosphere particles which the
earth emits, the simple change of the earth's exhalations mixed with these particles becomes wind.[2]

Here is a theory which I cannot persuade myself 2
either to believe or to remain silent about. In our
bodies flatulence is caused by food. This flatulence
is not emitted without great offence to our sense of
smell—sometimes it unburdens the stomach noisily,
sometimes more discreetly. In the same way,
people think, this great nature of the world emits air
in digesting its nourishment. It is lucky for us that
nature always digests thoroughly what she consumes,
otherwise we might fear a more offensive atmosphere.[3]

It is truer, surely, to say that many little particles 3
are constantly being carried up from all parts of the
earth. When they are accumulated and then begin
to be thinned out by the sun a wind develops because anything expanding in a narrow space needs
more room.

5. What then? Do I think that evaporation from 1
water and land is the sole cause of wind? Do I
think that weight in the atmosphere is produced by
these evaporations and that next there is set free

[2] Aristotle (2.4.361a–361b) says that only the dry exhalations produce wind; the wet exhalations produce rain.
[3] Aristotle (2.8.366b 15–20) explains earthquakes as similar
to flatulence and other tremors in the human body.

quae densa steterant, ut est necesse, extenuata nitun-
tur in ampliorem locum? Ego vero et hanc iudico.
Ceterum illa est longe valentior veriorque, habere
aera naturalem vim movendi se, nec aliunde concipere, sed inesse illi, ut aliarum rerum, ita huius
2 potentiam. An hoc existimas nobis quidem datas
vires quibus nos moveremus, aera autem relictum
inertem et inagitabilem esse, cum aqua motum
suum habeat etiam ventis quiescentibus? Nec enim
aliter animalia ederet; muscum quoque innasci
aquis et herbosa quaedam videmus summo innatantia;
est ergo aliquid in aqua vitale.

1 6. De aqua dico; ignis, qui omnia consumit,
quaedam creat et, quod videri non potest simile veri,
tamen verum est animalia igne generari. Habet
ergo aliquam vim talem aer et ideo modo spissat se
modo expandit et purgat et alias contrahit diducit
ac differt. Hoc ergo interest inter aera et ventum
quod inter lacum et flumen.

Aliquando per se ipse sol causa venti est fundens
rigentem aera et ex denso coactoque explicans.

1 7. In universum de ventis diximus; nunc viritim
incipiamus illos excutere. Fortasse apparebit quemadmodum fiant, si apparuerit quando et unde
procedant.

---

¹ Seneca follows the belief that a life principle exists in
certain elements. Cf. Pliny 2.10; 11.119; Cicero *Nat. D.*
2.24.
² The meaning seems to be that both winds and rivers are
in motion whereas lakes and air are comparatively still.

a rush of air, when things which were dense and stationary are rarefied and so struggle, as they must, towards a roomier space? I do judge that this is sometimes the true explanation; however, there is a far stronger and more accurate theory: air has a natural force for moving itself. It does not take this force from elsewhere; but just as it has within itself other properties so it has this power of moving itself. Or do you suppose that we have been given 2 strength to move but air has been left inert and immobile? Water, also, has its own motion even when the winds are quiet; otherwise it would not produce animal life.[1] Yet, we see moss produced in water, and various forms of vegetation floating on the surface. Therefore, some principle of life exists within water.

6. Why am I talking about water! Fire, too, which 1 consumes everything, creates certain things. It seems unbelievable that animals are generated by fire, and yet it is true. Air has some sort of similar power; and that is why air sometimes makes itself thick, sometimes expands and eliminates impurities, and at other times contracts, separates, and disperses itself. Accordingly, there is the same relationship between air and wind as there is between a lake and a river.[2]

Sometimes the sun by itself is the cause of wind, when it makes the stiff air flow and expand from its dense and compressed state.

7. We have talked about winds in general. Now let 1 us undertake to discuss them individually. Perhaps it will be clear how they are formed if it is clear where they come from, and when.

Primum ergo antelucanos flatus [1] inspiciamus, qui aut ex fluminibus aut ex convallibus aut ex aliquo
2 sinu feruntur. Nullus ex his pertinax est, sed cadit fortiore iam sole nec fert ultra terrarum conspectum. Hoc ventorum genus incipit vere; non ultra aestatem durat et inde maxime venit ubi aquarum plurimum et montium est. Plana, licet abundent aquis, carent aura; hac, dico, quae pro vento valet.

1 8. Quomodo ergo talis flatus concipitur quem Graeci ἐγκολπίαν vocant? Quicquid ex se paludes et flumina remittunt—id autem et multum est et assiduum—per diem solis alimentum est, nocte non exhauritur et montibus inclusum in unam regionem colligitur. Cum illam implevit et iam se non capit, exprimitur aliquo et in unam partem procedit; hic ventus est. Itaque eo incumbit quo liberior exitus invitat et loci laxitas, in quam coacervata decurrant.
2 Huius rei argumentum est quod prima noctis parte non spirat; incipit enim fieri illa collectio, quae circa lucem iam plena est; onerata quaerit quo defluat et eo potissimum exit ubi plurimum vacui est et magna ac patens area. Adicit autem ei [2] stimulos ortus solis feriens gelidum aera. Nam, etiam antequam ap-

---

[1] *flatus* ZSABV; *fluctus* HPE.
[2] *eis* HPEλS; *illis* Z.

First, then, let us look at the pre-dawn breezes, which are carried from rivers, valleys, or some bay. None of these breezes lasts long but falls when the 2 sun becomes stronger. They do not pass beyond sight of the earth. This type of wind begins in the spring, does not last beyond summer, and comes mostly from places where there are mountains and an abundance of water. Plains, although they abound in water, lack these breezes. I mean breezes which are strong enough to be considered winds.

8. Next, how is that breeze formed which the 1 Greeks call *Encolpias* [" gulf breeze "]? All the exhalations of the swamps and rivers (which are, by the way, considerable and continuous) provide nourishment for the sun during the day. At night they are not drained off and since they are hemmed in by mountains they accumulate in one region. When they have filled this region and no longer have room they are squeezed towards some point and move in one direction. This becomes wind. Of course, it inclines towards any place where it is attracted by a fairly free exit with open space. The accumulated exhalations rush into that open space. A proof of this is that a gulf breeze does not blow in 2 the early part of the night, for the accumulation I recently mentioned has just begun to form. Towards daylight it is at the full stage. When it is overfull it searches for a direction in which to flow out and by preference leaves wherever there is the largest empty space and a big open area. Moreover, the rising sun strikes the cold air and applies a stimulus to the accumulation. For even before the sun appears even its light has power. It does not, it is

85

pareat, lumine ipso valet et nondum quidem radiis
aera impellit, iam tamen lacessit et irritat [1] luce
3 praemissa; nam, cum ipse processit, alia superius
rapiuntur, alia diffunduntur tepore.[2] Ideo non ultra
matutinum illis datur fluere; omnis illorum vis conspectu solis extinguitur. Etiamsi violentiores [3] flavere, circa medium tamen diem relanguescunt nec
unquam usque in meridiem aura producitur; alia
autem alia [4] imbecillior ac brevior est, prout valen-
tioribus minoribusve collecta causis est.

1   9. Quare tamen tales venti vere et aestate validiores
sunt?—levissimi enim cetera parte anni nec qui
vela impleant surgunt. Quia ver [5] aquosum est ex
pluvialibus [6] aquis locisque [7] ob umidam caeli
naturam saturis et redundantibus maior evaporatio
est.

2   At quare aestate aeque profunditur? Quia post
occasum solis remanet diurnus calor et magna noctis
parte perdurat. Qui evocat exeuntia ac vehementius
trahit quicquid ex his sponte reddi solet, deinde non
tantum habet virium ut quod evocavit absumat; ob
hoc diutius corpuscula emanare solita et efflari terra
ex se atque umor emittit.[8]

---

[1] *invitat* AV; *inmutat* BC.
[2] *tempore* Z; *terre* ABV.
[3] *insolentiores* BA².
[4] *alia* supplied by Haase, Gercke, Oltramare.
[5] *aer* HP²S; *aer vere* ABV.
[6] Gercke, Oltramare for *pluribus* MSS.
[7] *lacis* S.

true, as yet push the air with its rays; none the less the sun already harasses and stimulates the air with the light that precedes its rays. For when the sun **3** itself comes out some of the exhalations are carried off to a higher altitude, others are dissipated by the heat. For this reason the gulf breezes are not given the power to blow beyond morning. All their strength is extinguished at the appearance of the sun. Even if they do blow more strongly, they none the less subside around midday; and in fact the breeze never lasts till noon. However, some breezes are weaker and briefer according to whether they are derived from stronger or weaker sources.

9. Yet why are winds of this sort stronger in spring **1** and summer? They are very light the rest of the year and do not rise enough to fill sails. The explanation is that spring is full of moisture from rainwater, and there is greater evaporation from places saturated and oversaturated by the humid conditions of the sky.

But why does the wind blow equally strong in the **2** summer? The reason is that the day's heat remains after sunset and lasts most of the night. This heat draws out exhalations and more forcefully attracts anything ordinarily given off by the ground in any case. Soon the heat does not have enough strength to absorb what it draws out. For this reason the soil and its moisture emit for a longer time the particles that are ordinarily exhaled by the earth or made to ooze out.

---

[8] Oltramare for *humorem mittit* HPZABV; *aqua humorem mittit* ES.

3   Facit autem ventum ortus [1] non calore tantum sed
etiam ictu; lux enim, ut dixi, quae solem antecedit,
nondum aera calefacit sed percutit tantum; percus-
sus autem in latus cedit.   Quamquam ego ne illud
quidem concesserim lucem ipsam sine calore esse, cum
4   ex calore sit.   Non habet forsitan tantum teporis [2]
quantum tactu appareat, opus tamen suum facit et
densa diducit ac tenuat; propterea [3] loca quae aliqua
iniquitate naturae ita clausa sunt ut solem accipere
non possint illa quoque nubila et tristi luce calefiunt et per diem minus quam noctibus rigent.
5   Etiamnunc natura calor [4] omnis abigit nebulas
et a se repellit; ergo sol quoque idem facit.   Et ideo,
ut quibusdam videtur, inde flatus est unde [5] sol.
1   10. Hoc falsum esse ex eo apparet quod aura [6] in
omnem partem vehit et contra ortum plenis velis [7]
navigatur; quod non eveniret, si semper ventus
ferretur a sole.
Etesiae quoque, qui in argumentum a quibusdam
2   advocantur, non nimis [8] propositum adiuvant.   Dicam
primum quid illis placeat, deinde cur displiceat mihi.
Etesiae, inquiunt, hieme non sunt, quia brevissimis
diebus sol desinit, priusquam frigus evincatur; itaque

[1] *sol ortus* E; *ortus sol* S.   [2] *temporis* KLABVH[1]Z[1].
[3] Gertz, Oltramare for *praeterea* MSS.
[4] *caloris* ABV.   [5] *esse* ABV.
[6] *natura* HES.   [7] *ventis* HE.
[8] *minus* HC; *minus his* A[2].

---

[1] Seneca is arguing against the theory that morning breezes,
such as the pre-dawn and gulf-breezes, are caused by the

Moreover, the sunrise creates wind not only by its **3** heat but also by its pressure. For the light which precedes the sun, as I said, does not yet make the atmosphere warm but only strikes it. When the atmosphere is struck it gives way to one side. And yet I certainly would not concede that light is without heat, since light is derived from heat. Per- **4** haps light does not have as much heat as appears from contact. None the less it accomplishes its task and separates and rarefies dense things. This is why places which are so shut in by some imbalance of nature that they are not able to receive sunshine become warmed even in cloudy and bleak light and are less frozen in the day than at night.

Also, heat by its very nature dispels all clouds and **5** drives them away; therefore the sun, too, does the same thing. And so, as some think, the wind blows only from the direction of the sun.

10. That this is wrong is obvious from the fact that **1** the breeze blows vessels in every direction and a ship can be navigated with full sails against the sunrise. This would not happen if the wind were always coming from the direction of the sun.

Also, the Etesian winds, which are brought into the discussion by some authorities, do not help the theory too much.[1] First, I will tell you what their opinion **2** is, then why I disagree. The Etesian winds do not exist in the winter, they say, because in a season of very short days the sunshine ends before the cold

pressure of sunlight and so can come only from the direction of the sunrise. The Etesian winds of the Mediterranean blow from the north in summer, as Seneca knows, and from the south in winter—a fact which he seems not to know.

nives et ponuntur et durant. Aestate incipiunt
flare, cum et longius extenditur dies et recti in nos
3 radii diriguntur. Veri ergo simile est concussas
calore magno nives plus umidi efflare, item terras
exoneratas nive retectasque spirare liberius; ita
plura ex septemtrionali parte caeli corpora exire et
in haec loca quae sunt summissiora ac tepidiora de-
4 ferri; sic impetum etesias sumere. Et ob hoc a solstitio illis initium est—ultraque ortum Caniculae
non valent—quia iam multum e frigida caeli parte in
hanc egestum est ac sol mutato cursu in nostram
rectior tendit et alteram partem aeris attrahit,
alteram vero impellit. Sic ille etesiarum flatus aestatem frangit et a mensium ferventissimorum
gravitate defendit.

1   11. Nunc, quod promisi, dicendum est quare
etesiae nos [1] non adiuvent nec quicquam huic conferant causae. Dicimus ante lucem auram incitari;
eandem [2] subsidere, cum illam sol attigit. Atqui
etesiae ob hoc somniculosi a nautis et delicati vocan-
tur quod, ut ait Gallio, " mane nesciunt surgere."
Eo tempore fere incipiunt prodire quo ne pertinax
quidem aura est. Quod non accideret, si ut auram

----

[1] *vos* E.   [2] *tandem* E.

----

[1] Seneca's brother, whom he praises in Book Four A, Pr. 10.

is overcome. As a result, snow piles up and freezes hard. In the summer the Etesians begin to blow when the day is extended longer and the sun's rays are directed straight down upon us. Therefore, it is 3 probable that the snows struck by great heat exhale more moisture. Likewise when the earth is unburdened by snow and uncovered it breathes more freely. Thus more particles move out from the northern region of the sky and are carried down to our regions which are lower and warmer. In this way, they say, the Etesian winds get their start. And 4 for this reason the Etesians have their beginning at the summer solstice. They do not blow strong after the rise of the Dog Star, because by then much of the cold section of the sky has been carried down to this region; and the sun, after changing direction, moves towards our region more directly and attracts one part of the atmosphere while repelling another part. Accordingly, the blowing of the Etesians breaks the summer heat and protects us from the severity of the hottest months.

11. Now, as I promised, I must tell why the Etesian 1 winds do not help us explain morning breezes and do not contribute anything to the present subject of discussion. We say that a pre-dawn breeze is stirred before daylight and that it subsides when the sun's rays touch it. And yet the Etesians, on the contrary, are called " sleepy " and " lazy " by sailors because, as Gallio [1] says, " They do not know how to get up in the morning." The Etesians begin to come out at about the same time the most persistent pre-dawn breeze has stopped. This would not happen if the sun broke up the Etesians as it does

91

2 ita illos comminueret sol. Adice nunc quod, si
causa illis flatus esset spatium diei ac longitudo, et
ante solstitium flarent, cum longissimi dies sunt et
cum maxime nives [1] tabescunt. Iulio enim mense
iam despoliata sunt omnia aut certe admodum pauca
iacent adhuc sub nive.

1   12. Sunt quaedam genera ventorum quae ruptae
nubes et in pronum solutae emittunt; hos Graeci
ventos ἐκνεφίας vocant. Qui hoc, ut puto, modo
fiunt. Cum magna inaequalitas ac dissimilitudo
corporum quae vapor terrenus emittit in sublime eat
et alia ex his corporibus sicca sint, alia umida, ex
tanta discordia corporum inter se pugnantium, cum
in unum conglobata sunt, verisimile est quasdam
cavas effici nubes et intervalla inter illas relinqui
2 fistulosa et in modum tibiae angusta. His intervallis tenuis includitur spiritus, qui maius desiderat
spatium, cum everberatus cursu parum libero in-
caluit et ob hoc amplior fit, scinditque cingentia [2] et
erumpit in ventum, qui fere procellosus est, quia
superne demittitur, et in nos cadit vehemens et acer,
quia non fusus nec per [3] apertum venit sed laborat et
iter sibi vi ac [4] pugna parat. Hic fere brevis flatus
est, quia receptacula nubium per quae ferebatur ac
munimenta perrumpit; ideo tumultuosus venit,
aliquando non sine igne ac sono caeli.

[1] *dies* ABV.
[2] *scindentia* ABV.
[3] *et per* Z.
[4] *in hac* E¹OABV (instead of *vi ac*).

the pre-dawn breeze. Add now the fact that if the 2
cause of their blowing were the lengthened space of
the day, they would also blow before the solstice
when days are longest and when snows are mostly
melted. For in the month of July everything is clear
of snow, or at least very few places still lie under snow.

12. There are certain types of wind which clouds 1
emit when they are burst and rent from top to bottom.
The Greeks call these winds *ecnephiae* [" cloudbursts "].[1] They develop, I suppose, in this way:
there is a great inequality and dissimilarity among
the particles which are emitted by earthly vapor
and travel to the upper atmosphere. Some of these
particles are dry, others wet. When they have
massed together in one body there is a great discord
of particles struggling internally; from which it is
probable that some clouds are formed hollow like a
flute, and narrow tubular spaces are left inside them.
Thin air is confined in these spaces. When it is 2
buffeted about on a restricted track it becomes hot,
and for this reason expands and needs more room.
It splits its envelope and bursts forth in wind which,
generally, is a squall because it hurtles down from
above; and it falls on us with severe force, since it is
not diffused and does not come come through an
opening but struggles and makes a path for itself
by force and fighting. Usually this is a brief gust,
because it breaks through confining barriers and ram-
parts of the clouds through which it was travelling;
so it arrives violently, sometimes with fire and thunder
in the sky.

[1] Pliny (2.131) gives a description of these cloudbursts.

3 Hi venti multo maiores diuturnioresque sunt, si alios quoque flatus ex eadem causa ruentes [1] in se abstulerunt et in unum confluxere plures. Sicut torrentes modicae magnitudinis sunt,[2] quamdiu separatis suus cursus est; cum vero plures in se aquas converterunt, fluminum iustorum [3] ac peren-

4 nium magnitudinem excedunt, idem credibile est fieri et in procellis ut breves sint, quamdiu singulae sunt; ubi vero sociavere vires et ex pluribus caeli partibus elisus spiritus eodem se contulit, et impetus illis accedit et mora.

5 Facit ergo ventum resoluta nubes, quae pluribus modis solvitur: nonnumquam conglobationem [4] illam spiritus rumpit, nonnumquam inclusi et in exitum nitentis luctatio, nonnumquam calor, quem modo sol facit, modo ipsa arietatio magnorumque [5] inter se corporum attritus.

1 13. Hoc loco, si tibi videtur, quaeri potest cur turbo fiat. Evenire in fluminibus solet ut, quamdiu sine impedimento feruntur, simplex et rectum illis iter sit; ubi incurrerunt in aliquod saxum ad latus ripae prominens, retorqueantur et in orbem aquas sine exitu flectant, ita ut circumlata in se sorbeantur et

2 verticem [6] efficiant. Sic ventus, quamdiu nihil obstitit, vires suas effundit; ubi aliquo promontorio

---

[1] *fluentes* E.
[2] Gercke, Oltramare for *eunt* MSS.
[3] *istorum* HZλAV.
[4] *conglobatio* Axelson, supported by Alexander.

These winds are much greater and longer lasting **3** if several of them have flowed together into one and have also absorbed within themselves other gusts rushing along for the same reason. In the same way, rivers are of moderate size as long as they are separate with their own streams, but when many have combined their currents they exceed the size of regular and constant rivers. It is believable that **4** the same thing also happens in storms: they are of brief duration as long as they are single, but when they have combined their forces, and the air, driven from many sections of the sky, has massed itself into one place, the storms acquire both force and duration.

Therefore, the breaking up of a cloud makes wind. **5** The cloud is broken up in several ways: sometimes by a current of air scattering the cloud's mass, sometimes by the struggle of air that is enclosed and striving for an exit, sometimes by heat produced either by the sun or by the simple ramming together and friction of large bodies.

13. At this point, if you like, we may ask why a **1** whirlwind occurs. In the case of rivers it usually happens that as long as the rivers move along without obstruction their channels are uniform and straight. When they run into some boulder projecting on the side of the bank they are forced back and their waters twist in a circle with no way out. Thus they are swirled around, sucked into themselves, and form a whirlpool. In the same way the wind blows in **2** full force as long as nothing obstructs it. When it is

---

[5] *vagorum* Leo, Gercke, Alexander.   [6] *vorticem* V.

repercussus est aut locorum [1] coeuntium in canalem
devexum tenuemque collectus, saepius in se volutatur similemque illis quas diximus converti aquis [2]
3 facit verticem.[3] Hic ventus circumactus et eundem
ambiens locum ac se ipsa vertigine concitans turbo
est. Qui si pugnacior est ac diutius volutatus, in-
flammatur et efficit quem πρηστῆρα Graeci vocant;
hic est igneus turbo. Sic [4] fere omnia pericula
venti erupti de nubibus produnt, quibus armamenta
rapiantur et totae naves in sublime tollantur.

4   Etiamnunc quidam [5] venti diversos ex se generant
et impulsum aera in alias quoque partes quam in
quas ipsi inclinavere dispergunt. Illud quoque dicam
quod mihi occurrit. Quemadmodum stillicidia,
quamvis iam inclinent se et labantur, nondum tamen
effecere lapsum, sed ubi plura coiere et turba vires
dedit, tunc fluere et ire dicuntur, sic, quamdiu leves
sunt aeris motus agitati pluribus locis,[6] nondum
ventus est; tunc esse incipit, cum omnes illos miscuit
et in unum impetum contulit. Spiritum a vento
modus separat; vehementior enim spiritus ventus est,
invicem spiritus leniter fluens aer.

1   14. Repetam nunc quod in primo dixeram edi e

----

[1] *iugorum* Alexander.
[2] *aquas* ES.
[3] *vorticem* V.
[4] Gercke, Oltramare for *haec* HPEZV; *hic* AB[2]. Alexander
suggests *ad haec, fere omnia pericula.*
[5] *et nunc quia* ABV.
[6] *ventis* ABV.

beaten back by some projecting height or is collected in the thin downward channel of a canyon, the wind often revolves upon itself and makes an eddy similar to those waters which we said are altered into whirlpools. This wind, revolving and passing round the 3 same spot and gathering momentum by its very rotation, is a whirlwind. If it is fairly violent and has been revolving a fairly long time, it ignites and makes what the Greeks call *Prester*; that is, a fiery whirlwind.[1] Winds that have burst their way from the clouds generally produce all the disasters whereby tackle is carried away and entire ships are lifted into the air.

Also, some winds generate from themselves different 4 winds by scattering the air and driving it in other directions also than the one in which the winds themselves were moving. I will say something which also occurs to me : drops of moisture do not yet manage to fall even though they have already started downwards and are slipping; but when many drops have come together and mass has given them strength, then they are said to flow and move. In the same way, as long as there are only slight movements of an atmosphere which is agitated at several points there is not yet wind. Wind begins to develop at the same time that it combines all those movements and concentrates them in a single effort. The degree of movement separates air from wind; for the more violently moving air is wind. On the other hand, gently flowing atmosphere is air.

14. Let me repeat now what I said in the first 1

---

[1] Lucretius (6.422–540) and Pliny (2.133) refer to this fiery whirlwind.

specu ventos recessuque interiore terrarum. Non
tota solido contextu terra in imum usque fundatur,
sed multis partibus cava et

caecis suspensa [1] latebris,

aliubi aquis plena,[2] aliubi habet inania sine umore.[3]

2 Ibi etiamsi nulla lux discrimen aeris monstrat, dicam
tamen nubes nebulasque in obscuro consistere.
Nam ne haec quidem supra terras, quia videntur,
sunt, sed, quia sunt, videntur; illic quoque nihilo
minus ob id sunt quod non videntur flumina. Illic
scias licet nostris paria sublabi, alia leniter ducta,
alia in confragosis locis praecipitando sonantia.
Quid ergo? Non illud aeque dabis esse aliquos et
sub terra lacus et quasdam aquas sine exitu stagnare?

3 Quae si ita sunt, necesse est et illud: aera onerari
oneratumque incumbere et ventum propulsu suo
concitare. Et ex illis ergo subterraneis nubibus
sciemus nutriri inter obscura flatus,[4] cum tantum
virium fecerint [5] quanto aut terrae obstantiam
auferant aut aliquod apertum ad hos efflatus iter

[1] Ovid has *obscura*.
[2] Haase, Gercke, Oltramare for *aliubi habet* HP[1]Z; *alicubi habet* Eλ; *alia* ABV.
[3] *lumine* V.
[4] *flatus qui cum* Garrod.
[5] *dum tantum virium ceperint* Alexander.

---

[1] Above, Chapter Four.
[2] Ovid *Met.* 1.388. The words are incorrectly quoted by

part of this book, that winds issue from caves and recesses in the interior of the earth.[1] The whole earth is not constructed of solid texture all the way to the bottom, but is hollow in many places and

> suspended
> over dark recesses.[2]

In some places it has voids filled with water, in other places voids without moisture. Even though no light is there to show differences in atmosphere, I will say that, none the less, clouds and mist exist in the gloom. For even these do not exist above ground merely because they are seen, but they are seen because they exist. Also, by the same reasoning, rivers are no less existent under the earth merely because they are not seen. You must understand that down there rivers as large as our own glide along, some flowing gently, others resounding in their tumbling over the broken ground. What then? Will you not equally allow that there are some lakes underground and some waters stagnating there without an exit? If true, this also necessarily follows: air is laden with moisture and when laden it exerts pressure and the pressure itself stirs up wind. Therefore, we will understand that blasts of wind from these subterranean clouds are nurtured in darkness when they have made sufficient strength to overcome the resistance of the earth or seize some

2

3

Seneca. The misquotation has given rise to speculation about the relationships among Lucretius, Ovid, the *Aetna*, and Seneca (see Oltramare, p. 214). However, Seneca so frequently misquotes, or adapts, that a discrepancy here should be no cause for excitement.

occupent et [1] per hanc cavernam in nostras sedes efferantur.

4 Illud vero manifestum est magnam esse sub terris vim sulphuris et aliorum non minus ignem alentium. Per haec loca cum se exitum quaerens spiritus torsit, accendat flammam ipso affrictu [2] necesse est, deinde, flammis latius fusis, etiam si quid ignavi aeris erat, extenuatum moveri et viam cum fremitu vasto atque impetu quaerere. Sed haec diligentius persequar, cum quaeram de motibus terrae.

1 15. Nunc mihi permitte narrare fabulam. Asclepiodotus auctor est demissos quam plurimos [3] a Philippo in metallum antiquum olim destitutum, ut explorarent quae ubertas [4] eius esset, quis status, an aliquid futuris reliquisset vetus avaritia; descendisse illos cum multo lumine et multos duraturo dies, deinde longa via fatigatos vidisse flumina ingentia et conceptus aquarum inertium vastos, pares nostris nec compressos quidem terra supereminente sed liberae laxitatis, non sine horrore visos.

2 Cum magna hoc legi voluptate. Intellexi enim saeculum nostrum non novis vitiis sed iam inde anti-

---

[1] *et* eliminated by Garrod.
[2] *affrictu* A; *astrictu* HPV; *adflictu* Z; *attritu* B.
[3] *complures* Z.
[4] *utilitas* AV.

---

[1] Seneca apparently promises to treat fully the subject of volcanoes along with earthquakes. He never does so, al-

open path for this puffing out and pass through this cave towards our world.

It is surely obvious that under the earth there is a 4 great supply of sulphur and other substances which feed fire. When the air, searching for a way out, twists itself through these places, it necessarily kindles fire by its very friction. Then, as the flames spread more extensively, even any sluggish air that is present is rarefied and set in motion and seeks an outlet with great noise and violence. But I will take this matter up in more detail when I investigate earthquakes.[1]

15. Now permit me to tell a story. Asclepio- 1 dotus is my authority that many men were sent down by Philip [2] into an old mine, long since abandoned, to find out what riches it might have, what its condition was, whether ancient avarice had left anything for future generations. They descended with a large supply of torches, enough to last many days. After a while, when they were exhausted by the long journey, they saw a sight that made them shudder: huge rivers and vast reservoirs of motionless water, equal to ours above ground and yet not pressed down by the earth stretching above, but with a vast free space overhead.

I read this story with great enjoyment. For I 2 realized that our age suffers not from new vices but from vices that have been handed down all the way

though in *Epistulae 79* he indicates that he plans to study Aetna and other volcanoes.

[2] As in paragraph three below, Seneca means Philip II of Macedon (382–336 B.C.), the father of Alexander the Great. Philip opened new mines (Diodorus, 16.8).

SENECA

quitus traditis laborare, nec nostra aetate primum
avaritiam venas terrarum lapidumque rimatam in
tenebris male abstrusa quaesisse: illi maiores nostri,
quos celebramus laudibus, quibus dissimiles esse nos
querimur, spe ducti montes ceciderunt et supra
lucrum sub ruina steterunt.

3   Ante Philippum Macedonum regem [1] fuere qui
pecuniam in altissimis usque latebris sequerentur et
recto spiritu liberoque in illos se demitterent specus
in quos nullum perveniret noctium dierumque discrimen.   A tergo lucem relinquere quae tanta spes
fuit? quae tanta necessitas hominem ad sidera
erectum incurvavit et defodit et in fundum telluris
intimae mersit, ut erueret aurum non minore peri-
4   culo quaerendum quam possidendum?   Propter hoc
cuniculos egit et circa praedam lutulentam incer-
tamque reptavit oblitus dierum, oblitus rerum
naturae melioris, a qua se avertit.   Ulli ergo mortuo
terra tam gravis est quam istis supra quos avaritia
ingens [2] terrarum pondus iniecit, quibus abstulit
caelum, quos in imo, ubi illud malum virus latitat,
infodit?   Illo descendere ausi sunt ubi novam rerum
positionem, terrarum pendentium habitus ventosque

---

[1] Gercke, Oltramare for *reges* MSS.;   Leo omits *reges*.
[2] *urgens* E.

from antiquity, and it is not in our age that avarice
first pried into the veins of earth and rock searching
for treasure poorly hidden in the darkness. Those
famous ancestors of ours, whom we are always heaping
with praises, whom we complain that we do not
resemble, cut down mountains, lured as they were by
hope, and stood there over their profit—but under
a mass of rubble.

Even before King Philip of Macedon there were 3
men who followed after money down into the deepest
hiding-places and, of upright and freeborn spirit[1] as
they were, let themselves down into those caverns
where no difference between night and day reaches.
What did they hope to find that was great enough to
leave daylight behind? What powerful necessity
bent man down, man ordinary erect to the stars,
and buried him and plunged him to the bottom of the
innermost earth so that he might dig out gold, no
less dangerous to search for than it is to possess?
On account of this he dug shafts and crawled around 4
the mud-smeared, uncertain booty, forgetful of day,
forgetful of the better nature of things from which
he turned himself away. Is the earth so heavy on
any dead man as it is on those upon whom great
avarice has cast the weight of the earth, from whom
avarice has taken away the sky, whom it has buried
in the depths where that evil poison lurks? They
dared to descend to a place where they found a strange
order of things, layers of earth hanging overhead,

---

[1] [Seneca seems to have a sarcastic moral tone here. But
Oltramare takes it that Seneca means physically breathing up-
right and freely, in contrast with the buried dead. Perhaps
Seneca presents both meanings here.—E.H.W.]

per caecum inanes experirentur et aquarum nulli
fluentium horridos fontes et alteram [1] perpetuamque
noctem; deinde, cum ista fecerunt, inferos metuunt!
1   16. Sed ut ad id de quo agitur revertar, venti
quattuor sunt, in ortum, occasum, meridiem septem-
trionemque divisi; ceteri, quos variis nominibus
appellamus, his applicantur.

Eurus ad Auroram Nabataeaque regna recessit
Persidaque et radiis iuga subdita matutinis.
Vesper et occiduo quae litora sole tepescunt
Proxima sunt zephyris.   Scythiam septemque triones
Horrifer invasit boreas.   Contraria tellus
Nubibus assiduis pluvioque madescit ab austro.

2   Vel, si brevius illos complecti mavis, in unam
tempestatem, quod fieri nullo modo potest, congre-
gentur:

[1] *altam* HV.

---

[1] Pliny (2.119) says that the ancients recognized four winds
only, but it was a poor system of reasoning; later eight more
winds were added, making twelve winds which, however,
seemed too cumbersome. A compromise was reached with
only four of the eight winds added to the four original ones.
The result: two winds from each of the four quarters of the
sky.

[2] Nabataea was a country in Arabia Petraea. Naba-
taean came to mean Arabian, Eastern, Oriental.

[3] The Septemtriones were the seven stars of the North Pole,
i.e. the Wain and the Great or the Little Bear. The word
was used for the northern regions, or simply the north.
Among the Greeks βορέας was properly the north-north-east
wind; but the name was used for the north wind also, properly
ἀπαρκτίας. See further p. 311 and the folder on this.

dead winds in the darkness, dreadful springs of water
flowing for no man, and a night other than our own,
and perpetual. Then, after doing these things, they
fear the Underworld!

16. But to return to the subject which is being 1
discussed: there are four winds,[1] divided amongst the
East, the West, the South, and the North. To these
the other winds, which we called by various names,
are attached:

> Eurus has gone toward the Dawn
> And the Nabataean [2] realms
> And to Persia
> And the ridges lying under
> The morning rays.
> Evening and the coasts
> Which are warmed by the setting sun
> Are close to Zephyrus.
> The gusty Boreas has possessed
> Scythia and the Septemtriones.[3]
> The land facing these
> Drips
> With continuous clouds
> From the rainy Auster.[4]

Or if you prefer them to be compressed more 2
briefly, they may be bunched together in one storm
(which cannot occur under any circumstances):[5]

[4] Ovid *Met.* 1.61–66.
[5] Aristotle 2.6.363a 21: opposing winds cannot blow simultaneously. Pliny (2.128) says all the winds take turns
blowing. Homer (*Od.* 5.295–296) puts Eurus, Notus, Zephy-
rus, and Boreas together in the storm that harassed Odysseus
on his way from Calypso's island to the land of the Phaeacians.

Una eurusque notusque ruunt creberque procellis
Africus

et, qui locum in illa rixa non habuit, aquilo.

3 Quidam illos duodecim faciunt. Quattuor enim
caeli partes in ternas dividunt et singulis ventis
binos subpraefectos dant. Hac arte Varro, vi diligens, illos ordinat, nec sine causa. Non enim eodem
semper loco sol oritur aut occidit, sed alius est ortus
occasusque aequinoctialis—bis autem aequinoctium
4 est—alius solstitialis, alius hibernus. Qui surgit ab
oriente aequinoctiali, subsolanus apud nos dicitur,
Graeci illum ἀφηλιώτην vocant. Ab oriente hiberno
eurus exit, quem nostri vocavere vulturnum—T.
Livius [1] hoc illum nomine appellat in illa pugna
Romanis parum prospera in qua Hannibal et contra
solem orientem exercitum nostrum et contra ventum
constitutum [2] venti adiutorio ac fulgoris praestrin-

---

[1] Gertz, Oltramare for *et L.* in the MSS.
[2] Gercke, Oltramare for *constituit tum* H²PZAB; *constituit
cum* Pλ; *instituit tum* V.

---

[1] Virgil *Aen.* 1.85–86.
[2] A little later on Virgil adds Aquilo to this same storm
(*Aen.* 1.102).
[3] Varro wrote a work on the winds and navigation, titled
De Ora Maritima, now lost. Pliny (2.119–121) gives sub-
stantially the same names of winds as Seneca does reaching,
however, a total of fourteen winds. He also gives (2.122–125)
the seasons when particular winds blow. Cf. Aristotle
2.6.363b–365a; Gellius 2. 22.
[4] All that is enclosed in [] in Sections 3–6 explains Seneca's

> Both Eurus and Notus
> Rush together,
> And Africus
> Packed with squalls [1]

and Aquilo, which has had no part in this famous squabble.[2]

Some make them twelve winds. For they divide **3** the four sections of the sky into three parts each and assign two subsidiary winds to each of the other winds. Varro, a diligent man, classifies them according to this system, and with good reason.[3] For the sun does not always rise or set in the same place. One rising and setting is the equinoctial [i.e., rising due E., setting due W.][4]—moreover, the equinox occurs twice a year—another is the summer-solstitial [i.e., rising in the N.E., setting in the N.W.], and still another the winter-solstitial [i.e. rising in the S.E., setting in the S.W.]. The wind which **4** rises from the equinoctial sunrise [E.] is called by us Subsolanus; the Greeks call it the *Apheliotes*. Eurus comes from the winter sunrise [S.E.], a wind which our people call Vulturnus. T. Livy calls it by this name in connection with that famous battle which was disastrous for the Romans when Hannibal defeated our army which was drawn up facing the rising sun and wind.[5] He had the help of the wind and the glare that dazzled the eyes of his enemy.

---

meaning. For a diagram showing the Graeco-Roman system of winds see folder and pp. 311–312.

[5] Livy 22.43.10. It is the famous Battle of Cannae, 216 B.C. The wind blows from the south-east or east-south-east and is now called the scirocco by the Italians and produces very oppressive climatic conditions.

gentis oculos hostium vicit; Varro quoque hoc nomen
usurpat—sed et eurus iam civitate donatus est et
nostro sermoni non tamquam alienus intervenit.
Ab oriente solstitiali excitatum κaικίαν Graeci
appellant; apud nos sine nomine est.

5   Aequinoctialis occidens favonium mittit, quem
zephyrum esse dicent tibi etiam qui graece nesciunt
loqui. A solstitiali occidente corus venit, qui apud
quosdam argestes[1] dicitur—mihi non videtur, quia
cori violenta vis est et in unam partem rapax,
argestes fere mollis est et tam euntibus communis
quam redeuntibus—ab occidente hiberno africus
furibundus et ruens; apud Graecos λίψ dicitur.

6   A septemtrionali latere summus est aquilo, medius
septemtrio, imus θρασκίας;[2] huic deest apud nos
vocabulum. A meridiano axe εὐρόνοτος est; deinde
νότος, latine auster; deinde λευκόνοτος, apud nos
sine nomine est.

1   17. Placet autem duodecim ventos esse, non quia
ubique tot sunt—quosdam enim inclinatio terrarum
excludit—sed quia plures nusquam sunt. Sic casus
sex dicimus, non quia omne nomen sex recipit, sed

---

[1] Erasmus, Gercke, Oltramare for *ergastes* HPEZ; *ergates*
ABV.

[2] *thrascias* Fortunatus; *thrachias* H; *trachias* PZST; *tracias*
AB; θρᾳκίας Gercke.

---

[1] Pliny (2.119) explains that Corus is the Latin name,
Argestes the Greek name for the same wind. To show that
some winds are called by different names in different places,
Pliny says (2.121) that Argestes is called Sciron at Athens and
Olympias in the rest of Greece. Aristotle (2.6.363b 23–24)

Varro also uses the name Vulturnus. But Eurus
is already Latinized and does not come into our speech
as though it were a foreign word. The wind which
is aroused from the summer-solstitial sunrise [N.E.,
though in fact *Caecias* is the E.N.E. wind] the Greeks
call *Caecias*; it has no name in our language.

The equinoctial sunset [W.] sends Favonius, which 5
even those who do not know how to speak Greek will
tell you is Zephyr. From the summer-solstitial
setting [N.W.] comes Corus, which is called Argestes
by some.[1] This does not seem right to me, because
the force of Corus is violent, gusting in one direction,
while Argestes is ordinarily gentle and hits travellers
the same coming and going. From the winter
sunset [S.W.] comes the furious rushing Africus; it
is called *Lips* among the Greeks. In the northern 6
section the highest is Aquilo [N.N.E.], the middle
Septemtrio [N.], the lowest [2] is *Thrascias* [N.N.W.],
for which there is lacking a word in our language.
At the southern axis there is the *Euronotus* [S.S.E.];
then the *Notus* [S.], or in Latin the Auster; then the
Leuconotus [S.S.W.],[3] which has no Latin name.

17. We like to say there are twelve winds, not 1
because there are that many winds everywhere—
for the curve of the lands blocks some—but because
nowhere are there more than twelve. In the same
way we say there are six cases, not because every

gives the same explanation: Sciron and Olympias are called
Argestes. See further pp. 311–312 and folder on Argestes.

[2] Seneca is apparently thinking of the arrangement of a
triclinium (set of three *lecti*-couches) at table during a dinner-
party, having however especially in mind the three places on
one of the couches.

[3] Pliny (2.120) calls this wind *Libonotus*.

2 quia nullum plures quam sex. Qui duodecim ventos
esse dixerunt, hoc secuti sunt totidem ventorum esse
quot caeli discrimina. Caelum autem dividitur in
circulos quinque, qui per mundi cardines eunt: est
septemtrionalis, est solstitialis, est aequinoctialis,
est brumalis, est contrarius septemtrionali. His
sextus accedit, qui superiorem partem mundi ab
inferiore secernit;[1] ut scis enim, dimidia pars mundi
3 semper supra, dimidia infra est. Hanc lineam, quae
inter aperta et occulta est (id est hunc circulum),
Graeci ὁρίζοντα vocant, nostri finitorem esse dixerunt,
alii finientem. Adiciendus est adhuc meridianus
circulus, qui ὁρίζοντα rectis angulis secat.[2] Ex his
quidam circuli in transversa currunt et alios inter-
ventu suo scindunt.

Necesse est autem tot aeris discrimina esse quot
4 partes. Ergo ὁρίζων, sive finiens circulus, quinque
illos orbes quos modo dixi fieri scindit et efficit decem
partes, quinque ab ortu, quinque ab occasu. Meridianus circulus, qui in ὁρίζόντα incurrit, regiones duas
adicit.[3] Sic duodecim aer discrimina accipit et
totidem facit ventos.

5 Quidam sunt quorundam locorum proprii, qui
non transmittunt, sed in proximum ferunt; non est

---

[1] *secrevit* L¹A¹B; *discernit* V.
[2] *segregat* BV; *segregavit* A¹.
[3] *efficit* AV.

noun has six but because no noun has more than six. Those who say there are twelve winds follow **2** this reasoning: there are the same number of winds as there are sectors of the sky. The sky is divided into five circles which pass through the cardinal points of the universe. In these five circles are the northern circle, the summer solstitial circle, the equinoctial circle, the wintry circle, and the one that is opposite to the northern.[1] To these is added a sixth circle, the one which separates the upper part of the universe from the lower (for as you know, half of the universe is always above us, half below us). The line (that is, this circle) which exists between the **3** visible and the invisible sector is what the Greeks call the horizon line; some of us call it the limiter line,[2] others call it the limiting line. We still have to add the meridian circle, which cuts the horizon at right angles. Out of these some circles run transversely and split the other circles by intersecting them.

Moreover, there must be as many divisions of the lower sky as there are parts. Accordingly, the **4** horizon, or limiting circle, splits those five belts, whose location I just described, into ten sectors, five in the east and five in the west. The meridian circle, which meets the horizon, adds two more sectors. In this way the lower sky gets twelve sectors and produces the same number of winds.

Some winds are associated only with certain **5** localities. They do not convey ships to another region but bring them only into their own neighbourhood.

---

[1] That is, the circles we now call arctic circle, tropic of Cancer, equator, tropic of Capricorn, antarctic circle. See folder.

[2] *Finitor* is the word used by Lucan (9.496).

illis a latere universi mundi impetus. Atabulus
Apuliam infestat, Calabriam iapyx, Athenas sciron,
Pamphyliam crageus,[1] Galliam circius, cui aedificia
quassanti tamen incolae gratias agunt, tamquam
salubritatem caeli sui debeant ei—divus certe
Augustus templum illi, cum in Gallia moraretur, et
vovit et fecit. Infinitum est, si singulos velim
persequi; nulla enim propemodum regio est quae
non habeat aliquem flatum ex se nascentem et circa
se cadentem.

1 18. Inter cetera itaque providentiae opera hoc
quoque aliquis ut dignum admiratione suspexerit.
Non enim ex una causa ventos aut invenit aut per
diversa disposuit, sed primum ut aera non sinerent
pigrescere, sed assidua vexatione utilem redderent
2 vitalemque tracturis;[2] deinde ut imbres terris sub-
ministrarent idemque nimios[3] compescerent. Nam
modo adducunt nubes, modo deducunt, ut per totum
orbem pluviae dividi possint. In Italiam auster
impellit; aquilo in Africam reicit; etesiae non
patiuntur apud nos nubes consistere; idem totam
Indiam et Aethiopiam continuis per id tempus aquis

[1] Müller, Gercke, Oltramare for *chagreus* HPZ; *cragreus*
Eλ; *chagreis* ABV.
[2] *terris* ABV.
[3] *nubes* A¹B.

---

[1] Horace (*Sat.* 1.5.78) says the Atabulus parches Apulia.
[2] Horace (*Odes* 1.3) invokes Iapyx to convey Virgil safely
from Calabria to Attica.

They are not propelled from any part of the world as a whole. Atabulus [1] infests Apulia; Iapyx,[2] Calabria; Sciron, Athens; Crageus,[3] Pamphylia; Circius, Gaul. Even though the last one shakes their buildings, the inhabitants give thanks to it in the belief that they owe the healthfulness of their climate to it. At any rate, the deified Augustus built a temple and dedicated it to Circius, when he was staying in Gaul. I would have an infinite chore if I wanted to discuss each and every wind. Practically every place has some wind that rises from it and falls only there.

18. And so, among the other works of Providence, 1 this, too, should be respected as worthy of admiration. Providence devised winds and scattered them about for several reasons. But first, so that the winds might prevent the atmosphere from becoming stagnant and by continual agitation make it wholesome and life-supporting for all that will breathe it. Second, to 2 supply rain for the earth while checking excessive moisture, for the winds collect clouds in one place, scatter them in another, in order that precipitation may be distributed all over the world. The Auster drives rainfall to Italy; the Aquilo sends it back to Africa.[4] The Etesian winds do not permit rain clouds to stay in our part of the world, yet during their season they irrigate all India and Ethiopia

[3] The Crageus is not mentioned anywhere else. A Mt. Cragus forms part of the Taurus chain in Lycia. Pamphylia is between Lycia and Cilicia. According to Oltramare's reasoning, the Crageus is perhaps a local name for a wind associated with Mt. Cragus. Circius is the mistral.

[4] Lucan (9.422–423) says the Aquilo occasionally carries rain from Italy to refresh the fields in Africa.

3 irrigant. Quid quod fruges percipi [1] non possent, nisi
flatu supervacua et mixta servandis ventilarentur,
nisi esset quod segetem excitaret et latentem frugem
ruptis velamentis suis—folliculos agricolae vocant—
adaperiret ?

4 Quid quod omnibus inter se populis commercium
dedit et gentes dissipatas locis miscuit ? Ingens
naturae beneficium, si illud in iniuriam suam non
vertat hominum furor ! Nunc, quod de Caesare [2]
maiore [3] vulgo dictatum est et a Tito Livio positum
in incerto esse utrum illum magis nasci an non nasci
reipublicae profuerit, dici etiam de ventis potest;
adeo quicquid ex illis utile et necessarium est non
potest his repensari quae in perniciem suam generis
5 humani dementia excogitat. Sed non ideo non
sunt ista natura bona, si vitio male utentium nocent.
Non in hoc providentia ac dispositor ille mundi deus
aera ventis exercendum dedit et illos ab omni parte
ne quid esset situ squalidum effudit, ut nos classes
partem freti occupaturas compleremus milite ar-
mato et hostem in mari aut post mare quaereremus.

6 Quae nos dementia exagitat et in mutuum com-
ponit exitium ? Vela ventis damus bellum petituri

[1] *percoqui* Gercke.
[2] *de C.* Z; *decens* HPAV.
[3] *marior* Z; *maiori* in most of the MSS.

---

[1] One MS. (Z) gives *de C. marior*, which suggests changing
Caesar to Marius. Oltramare presents three good arguments

with continuous rain. Moreover, crops could not **3**
be gathered if the useless parts, which are mixed in
with the parts worth saving, were not winnowed out
by the wind; or if the wind did not stimulate the
growing crop and uncover the hidden fruit by
breaking open its wrappings (called " follicles " by
farmers).

And, too, the wind has made communication **4**
possible between all peoples and has joined nations
which are separated geographically. A great benefit of nature, if the madness of man did not turn it to
his own destruction! As things are, however, it
could be said of winds what was commonly said of
Julius Caesar,[1] as reported by Titus Livy; it is
uncertain whether it was better for the state that
Caesar had been born or not. Indeed, whatever
is useful and necessary from the winds cannot be
balanced by the things which the madness of mankind
devises for its own destruction. Even if they do **5**
cause harm by the wrongdoing of men who use them
evilly, not on this account are the winds evil by
nature. Actually, Providence and that god who is
the organizer of the universe did not arrange to move
the atmosphere by winds and to distribute winds
from all directions (lest anything become barren
because of inactivity) only so that we might fill up
our fleets with armed soldiers to seize part of the
deep waters and only so that we might seek out an
enemy on the sea or even beyond the sea!

What madness drives us and makes us ready to **6**
destroy one another? We spread sails to the winds

for making such a change but admits that the weight of MSS.
evidence is against it.

et periclitamur periculi causa; incertam fortunam experimur, vim tempestatum nulla ope humana
7 superabilem et mortem sine spe sepulturae. Non erat tanti, si ad pacem per ista veheremur; nunc, cum evaserimus tot scopulos latentes et insidias vadosi maris, cum effugerimus procellosos desuper montes, per quos praeceps in navigantes ventus impingitur, cum involutos nubilo dies et nimbis ac tonitribus horridas noctes, cum turbinibus divulsa navigia, quis erit huius laboris ac metus fructus, quis nos fessos tot malis portus excipiet? Bellum scilicet et obvius in litore hostis et trucidandae gentes tracturaeque magna ex parte victorem et antiquarum urbium flamma.

8   Quid in arma cogimus populos? Quid exercitus scribimus directuros aciem in mediis fluctibus? Quid maria inquietamus? Parum videlicet ad mortes nostras terra late patet; nimis delicate fortuna nos tractat; nimis dura dedit nobis corpora, felicem valetudinem; non depopulatur nos casus incurrens; emetiri cuique annos suos ex commodo licet et ad senectutem decurrere! Itaque eamus in pelagus et
9 vocemus in nos fata cessantia. Miseri, quid quaeritis mortem, quae ubique superest? Petet illa vos et ex lectulo. Sed innocentes petat! Occupabit vos

intending to seek war; we endanger ourselves for the sake of danger. We risk an uncertain future, storms so violent that they cannot be overcome by any human endeavour, a death without hope of burial. It would not be worthwhile even if we were sailing to 7 peace through these risks. As things are, when we have escaped so many hidden rocks and the dangers of a sea full of shallows, when we have fled stormy mountains above us, through which the wind is driven headlong against sailors; after days enveloped in cloud and nights horrid with rain and thunderstorms, when the ship has been torn apart by whirlwinds—what reward will there be for this suffering and fear, what port will welcome us exhausted by so many evils? Surely war will meet us, an enemy on the shore, ancient cities burning, and nations destined to be slaughtered but also likely to drag most of the conquerors with them.

Why do we drive peoples to armament? Why do 8 we enlist armies that will marshal their battle-line in the midst of waves? Why do we disturb the seas' rest? Supposedly the land does not open wide enough for our deaths; chance deals with us too tenderly; supposedly fortune has given us bodies too tough, a health too sound; perhaps onrushing disasters do not thin our population; or maybe each man is allowed to measure out his life-span at his own convenience and trot along to old age! Well, then, let us go down to the sea and summon dallying death against us. Miserable mankind, why do you search 9 for death, which is plentiful everywhere? Death will look for you, even in bed. Only let it look for you innocent! It will catch up with you in your own

in vestra domo. Sed occupet nullum molientes malum!

Hoc vero quid aliud quis dixerit quam insaniam, circumferre pericula et ruere in ignotos, iratum sine iniuria occurrentia devastantem, ac ferarum more occidere quem non oderis? Illis tamen in ultionem aut ex fame morsus est; nos sine ulla parsimonia nostri alienique sanguinis movemus manum et navigia deducimus, salutem committimus fluctibus, secundos optamus ventos, quorum felicitas est ad bella perferri.

10 Quousque nos mala nostra rapuerunt? Parum est intra orbem suum furere. Sic Persarum rex stolidissimus in Graeciam traiciet,[1] quam exercitus non vincet, cum impleverit. Sic Alexander ulterior[2] Bactris et Indis volet quaeretque quid sit ultra magnum mare et indignabitur esse aliquid ultimum sibi. Sic Crassum avaritia Parthis dabit; non horrebit revocantis diras[3] tribuni, non tempestates longissimi maris, non circa Euphratem praesaga

---

[1] *traiciet* Haase, Gercke, Oltramare for *traiecit* most MSS.
[2] *ulteriora* Gercke.
[3] *minas* Z.

---

[1] Xerxes led the second Persian attack on Greece and was defeated by sea at Salamis in 480 B.C. and then on land at Plataea in 479 B.C.
[2] Alexander the Great did not travel beyond India, in fact he knew only north-west India; Seneca is vaguely referring to what was known of the Indian Ocean in his time.

home. But hope that it does catch you not plotting evil.

What else could you call it except a form of insanity to carry destruction with you, to attack men you do not even know, to be enraged without having been wronged, to destroy everything you come across, and like wild beasts to kill whom you do not hate? Yet beasts bite in revenge or hunger; we, without sparing any bloodshed, our own or another's, put our hands to work and launch ships, entrust our safety to the waves and hope for favourable winds, happy to be sailing to war.

How far have our evils swept us along? It is 10 not enough to be insane in our own part of the world. In the same way a mad Persian king [1] will cross over into Greece and practically fill it with an army that cannot conquer it. An Alexander will travel fast far beyond Bactria and India and will seek what lies past the great sea,[2] and will complain that there is some limit beyond which even he cannot go. And greed will consign a Crassus to the Parthians; he will not fear the foreboding threats of a tribune calling him back,[3] nor the storms of a long sea voyage, nor the ominous lightning around the Euphrates, nor even the opposition of the gods. He

[3] When Crassus, the " triumvir," was setting out to make war on the Parthians and to meet his death at their hands, C. Ateius Capito, a tribune of the people for 55 B.C., made every effort to stop the expedition. He even ordered an officer to seize Crassus, which, however, was not permitted by the other tribunes. Finally, Ateius ran ahead to the gate where he burned incense and cursed Crassus " with dreadful imprecations, naming several strange and horrible deities " (Plutarch *Crassus* 6.4–6 553).

fulmina et deos resistentes: per hominum et deorum
iras [1] ad aurum ibitur.

11 Ero non immerito quis dixerit rerum naturam
melius acturam fuisse nobiscum, si ventos flare vetuis-
set et inhibito discursu furentium in sua quemque
terra stare iussisset. Si nihil aliud, certe suo quisque
tantum ac suorum malo nasceretur. Nunc parum
mihi domestica, externis [2] quoque laborandum est.

12 Nulla terra tam longe remota est quae non emittere
aliquod suum malum possit. Unde scio an nunc
aliquis magnae gentis in abdito dominus, fortunae
indulgentia tumens, non contineat intra terminos
arma, an paret classes ignota moliens? [3] Unde scio
hic mihi an ille ventus bellum invehat? Magna pars
erat pacis humanae maria praecludi.

13 Non [4] tamen, ut paulo ante dicebam, queri possumus de auctore [5] nostri deo, si beneficia eius
corrupimus et ut essent contraria effecimus. Dedit
ille ventos ad custodiendam caeli terrarumque tem-
periem, ad evocandas supprimendasque aquas, ad
alendos satorum [6] atque arborum fructus, quos ad
maturitatem, cum aliis causis, adducit ipsa iactatio
attrahens cibum in summa et ne torpeant permovens.

14 Dedit ventos ad ulteriora noscenda. Fuisset enim
imperitum animal et sine magna experientia rerum
homo, si circumscriberetur natalis soli fine. Dedit

[1] minas Z.   [2] exterius EAB.
[3] cupiens Z.   [4] num ABV.
[5] actore Z.   [6] segetum ABV.

will make a journey for gold in spite of the anger of gods and men.

Accordingly, someone sensibly said that nature 11 would have done better for us if she had forbidden the winds to blow and, by restraining the varied extent of their raging, had arranged that each man stay in his own land. If nothing else, a man would then be born to do evil only to himself or to his countrymen. As it is now, domestic evils are not enough for me; I have to suffer also ills from abroad. No country is so distantly remote that it cannot ex- 12 port some of its own ills. For all I know even now some ruler of a great nation (hitherto unknown to me), puffed up by the indulgence of fortune, is not restricting his armies within his own country but is outfitting fleets and moving against people who never even heard of him. How do I know but that this wind or that is bringing war to me? A great measure of peace would be granted to humans if the seas were closed.

None the less, as I said before, we cannot com- 13 plain against god, our author, if we have corrupted his benefits and cause them to be evil. He gave winds to maintain the temperature of sky and earth, to produce and to check moisture, to nurture the crops of the fields and the trees, crops which the very agitation of the winds ripens (for this movement, along with other causes, draws the nutriment to the top so that the crops do not wilt). He gave us 14 winds so that we might get to know distant lands. For man would have been an untaught animal and without experience of affairs if he had been circumscribed by the limits of the land where he was born.

ventos, ut commoda cuiusque regionis fierent communia, non ut legiones equitemque gestarent nec ut
perniciosa gentium [1] arma transveherent.

15   Si beneficia naturae utentium pravitate perpen-
dimus, nihil non nostro malo accepimus.   Cui videre
expedit? Cui loqui? Cui non vita tormentum
est?   Nihil invenies tam manifestae utilitatis quod
non in contrarium transeat [2] culpa. Sic ventos
quoque natura bono futuros invenerat; ipsi illos
contrarios fecimus.

16   Omnes in aliquod nos malum ducunt.   Non eadem
est his et illis causa solvendi, sed iusta nulli.   Diversis
enim irritamentis ad temptandum mare [3] impellimur;
utique alicui vitio navigatur. Egregie Plato dicit,
qui nobis circa exitum iam testium loco dandus est,
minima esse quae homines emant vita. Immo,
Lucili carissime, si bene illorum furorem aestimaveris
—id est nostrum, in eadem enim turba volutamur—
magis ridebis, cum cogitaveris vitae parari in quae
vita consumitur.

[1] *civium* ABV.
[2] *transferat* ABV.
[3] Pincianus, Oltramare for *ire* MSS.

He gave us winds in order that the advantages of each region might become known to all; but not in order to carry legions and cavalry or to transport weapons to destroy mankind.

If we evaluate the benefits of nature by the 15 depravity of those who misuse them, there is nothing we have received that has not hurt us. Who has been helped by being able to see? Or by being able to speak? In fact, who has not found life a torment? You will find nothing, even of obvious usefulness, such that it does not change over to its opposite through man's fault. So, nature created winds also to exist for a good purpose. We ourselves have made them otherwise.

All the winds lead us towards some sort of evil. 16 Men do not give the same reason for launching a ship, but none gives a good reason. We are impelled by different motivations to try the sea; yet surely each man sets sail to harm someone else. Plato made a famous remark (*he* must be produced in the role of witness now that I am about to close) that it is trifles men buy with their lives.[1] Yes, my friend Lucilius, if you judge rightly the madness of these people—that is, ours, for we wallow in the same herd —you will laugh all the more when you consider that things are acquired for living which are the very things for which life is destroyed.

---

[1] This passage of Plato is otherwise unknown.

BOOK VI
EARTHQUAKES

LIBER SEXTUS[1]

DE TERRAE MOTU [2]

1   1. Pompeios, celebrem Campaniae urbem, in
quam ab altera parte Surrentinum Stabianumque
litus, ab altera Herculanense conveniunt et mare ex
aperto reductum amoeno sinu cingunt, consedisse
terrae motu, vexatis quaecumque adiacebant regionibus, Lucili, virorum optime, audivimus, et quidem
hibernis diebus, quos vacare a tali periculo maiores
2   nostri solebant promittere. Nonis Februariis hic
fuit motus Regulo et Verginio consulibus, qui Campaniam, numquam securam huius mali, indemnem
tamen et totiens defunctam metu, magna strage
vastavit. Nam et Herculanensis oppidi pars ruit
dubieque stant etiam quae relicta sunt, et Nuceri-
norum colonia, ut sine clade, ita non sine querela

[1] *liber sextus* E; *liber tertius* PKTU; *liber quintus* HZGLMV;
[*Liber Sextus*] *Liber Tertius* Oltramare.
[2] *de terrae motu* HPEZMT.

---

[1] Aristotle 2.8.366b 2–5: earthquakes occur most often in
spring and autumn.   Pliny (2.195) says the same thing.
[2] Of course this is not the famous disaster of A.D. 79 when
an eruption of Vesuvius buried Pompeii and Herculaneum.
C. Memmius Regulus and L. Verginius Rufus were consuls in

BOOK VI

EARTHQUAKES

1. LUCILIUS, my good friend, I have just heard 1
that Pompeii, the famous city in Campania, has been
laid low by an earthquake which also disturbed all
the adjacent districts. The city is in a pleasant bay,
back a ways from the open sea, and bounded by the
shores of Surrentum and Stabiae on one side and the
shores of Herculaneum on the other; the shores
meet there. In fact, it occurred in days of winter,
a season which our ancestors used to claim was free
from such disaster.[1] This earthquake was on the 2
Nones of February, in the consulship of Regulus and
Verginius.[2] It caused great destruction in Campania, which had never been safe from this danger
but had never been damaged and time and again
had got off with a fright. Also, part of the town
of Herculaneum is in ruins and even the structures
which are left standing are shaky. The colony of
Nuceria escaped destruction but still has much to

A.D. 63. However, Tacitus seems to place the earthquake in
A.D. 62, a little before their consulship (*Ann.* 15.22–23).
Below, in 13, Seneca indicates an earthquake struck Achaia
and Macedonia the "year before" the one at Pompeii;
it was the effect of a comet (7.28.2) that appeared in the
consulship of Paterculus and Vopiscus (in A.D. 60). The Campanian earthquake probably occurred in A.D. 62 (February 5).

est. Neapolis quoque privatim multa, publice
nihil amisit leviter ingenti malo perstricta; villae
3 vero prorutae, passim sine iniuria tremuere. Adi-
ciuntur his illa: sexcentarum ovium gregem exanimatum et divisas statuas, motae post hoc mentis
aliquos atque impotentes sui errasse. Quorum ut
causas excutiamus, et propositi operis contextus
exigit et ipse in hoc tempus congruens casus.

4 Quaerenda sunt trepidis solacia[1] et demendus
ingens timor. Quid enim cuiquam satis tutum videri
potest, si mundus ipse concutitur et partes eius
solidissimae labant? Si quod unum immobile est in
illo fixumque, ut cuncta in se intenta sustineat,
fluctuatur;[2] si quod proprium habet terra perdidit,
stare, ubi tandem resident metus nostri? Quod
corpora receptaculum invenient, quo sollicita con-
fugient, si ab imo metus nascitur et funditus trahitur?

5 Consternatio omnium est, ubi tecta crepuerunt et
ruina signum dedit. Tunc praeceps quisque se
proripit et penates suos deserit ac se publico credit.[3]
Quam latebram prospicimus, quod auxilium, si
orbis ipse ruinas agitat, si hoc quod nos tuetur ac
sustinet, supra quod urbes sitae sunt, quod funda-
mentum quidam mundi[4] esse dixerunt, discedit ac

6 titubat? Quid tibi esse—non dico auxilii—sed solacii
potest, ubi timor fugam perdidit? Quid est,

[1] *remedia* ABV.
[2] *fluctuat* ESTABV.
[3] *condit* ABV.
[4] *mundi* Z Oltramare; the other MSS. have *orbis*.

complain about. Naples also lost many private dwellings but no public buildings and was only mildly grazed by the great disaster; but some villas collapsed, others here and there shook without damage. To these calamities others were added: they say that 3 a flock of hundreds of sheep was killed, statues were cracked, and some people were deranged and afterwards wandered about unable to help themselves. The thread of my proposed work, and the concurrence of the disaster at this time, requires that we discuss the causes of these earthquakes.

It is necessary to find solace for distressed people 4 and to remove their great fear. Yet can anything seem adequately safe to anyone if the world itself is shaken and its most solid parts collapse? Where will our fears finally be at rest if the one thing which is immovable in the universe and fixed, so as to support everything that leans on it, starts to waver; if the earth loses the characteristic it has, stability? What hiding-place will creatures find, where will they flee in their anxiety, if fear arises from below and is drawn from the depths of the earth? There is 5 panic on the part of all when buildings creak and give signs of falling. Then everybody hurls himself headlong outside, abandons his household possessions, and trusts to his luck in the outdoors. What hiding-place do we look to, what help, if the earth itself is causing the ruin, if what protects us, upholds us, on which cities are built, which some speak of as a kind of foundation of the universe, separates and reels? What solace—I do not say what help—can 6 there be for you when fear has lost a way of escape? What, I say, is adequately defended?

inquam, satis munitum, quid ad tutelam alterius ac
sui firmum? Hostem muro repellam, et praeruptae
altitudinis castella vel magnos exercitus difficultate
aditus morabuntur; a tempestate nos vindicat
portus; nimborum [1] vim effusam et sine fine cadentes
aquas tecta propellunt; fugientes non sequitur
incendium; adversus tonitruum et minas caeli
subterraneae domus et defossi in altum specus remedia
sunt. Ignis ille caelestis non transverberat terram,
sed exiguo eius obiectu retunditur. In pestilentia
mutare sedes licet. Nullum malum sine effugio est.

7 Numquam fulmina populos perusserunt; pestilens
caelum exhausit urbes, non abstulit. Hoc malum
latissime patet inevitabile, avidum, publice noxium.
Non enim domos solum aut familias aut urbes sin-
gulas haurit; gentes totas regionesque submergit,
et modo ruinis operit, modo in altam voraginem
condit, ac ne id quidem relinquit ex quo appareat
quod non est saltem fuisse, sed supra nobilissimas
urbes sine ullo vestigio prioris habitus solum extenditur.

8 Nec desunt qui hoc genus mortis magis timeant
quo in abruptum cum sedibus suis eunt et e vivorum
numero vivi auferuntur, tamquam non omne fatum
ad eundem terminum veniat. Hoc habet inter cetera
iustitiae suae natura praecipuum quod, cum ad exi-
9 tum ventum est, omnes in aequo sumus. Nihil
itaque interest utrum me lapis unus elidat, an monte

---

[1] *imbrium* ABV.

What is firm for the protection of the persons of others and of oneself? I will repel the enemy from the wall, and fortifications on a sheer height will stop even great armies with the difficulties of approach. The harbour shelters us from a storm. Roofs ward off the force poured down from the clouds, waters falling without end. A fire does not pursue the ones who flee from it. Against the threats of thunderstorms and of heaven houses underground and caves dug in deep are a remedy. That great fire from the sky does not penetrate the earth; it is beaten back by the slightest obstruction of the ground. In time of plague we can change our place of residence. No disaster is without means of escape. Lightning 7 bolts have never burned up entire nations. A pestilential season has emptied cities, not carried them away. But the disaster of an earthquake extends far and wide, is inevitable, insatiable, deadly for the entire state. It gulps down not only homes or families or individual cities; it inters entire nations and regions. Sometimes it covers them with ruins, sometimes buries them in a deep abyss, and does not even leave anything to indicate that what does not exist, at least once was. Soil extends over the noblest cities, without any trace of the way they used to look.

Many people fear this kind of death most of all, 8 in which they go down into a pit with their own houses, and while still alive are carried off from the number of the living; as though every death did not come to the same end. Nature has, among other aspects of its fairness, this as a principal point: when we come to death we are all on the same level. It does not 9 matter, therefore, whether I am struck dead by one

toto premar; utrum supra me domus unius onus
veniat et sub exiguo eius cumulo ac pulvere expirem,
an totus caput meum terrarum orbis abscondat; in
luce hunc et in aperto spiritum reddam an in vasto
terrarum dehiscentium sinu; solus in illud profundum
an cum magno comitatu populorum concadentium
ferar. Nihil interest mea quantus circa mortem
meam tumultus sit. Ipsa ubique tantundem est.

10   Proinde magnum sumamus animum adversus
istam cladem quae nec evitari nec provideri potest,
desinamusque audire istos qui Campaniae reuntia-
verunt quique post hunc casum emigraverunt negant-
que ipsos umquam in illam regionem accessuros.
Quis enim illis promittit melioribus fundamentis hoc
11 aut illud solum stare? Omnia eiusdem sortis sunt
et, si nondum mota, tamen mobilia. Hunc fortasse
in quo securius consistitis locum haec nox aut hic
ante noctem dies scindet. Unde scis an melior
eorum locorum condicio sit in quibus iam vires suas
fortuna consumpsit et quae in futurum ruina sua
12 fulta sunt? Erramus enim, si ullam terrarum partem
exceptam immunemque ab hoc periculo credimus.
Omnes sub eadem iacent lege; nihil ita ut immobile
esset natura concepit; alia temporibus aliis cadunt
et, quemadmodum in urbibus magnis nunc haec
domus nunc illa suspenditur, ita in hoc orbe terrarum
nunc haec pars facit vitium nunc illa.

rock or I am crushed by an entire mountain; whether the weight of a single house covers me over and I expire beneath its little dust heap or the whole earth covers my head. It does not matter whether I give up this ghost in broad daylight or in the vast bosom of the gaping earth, whether I am carried alone to the depths or with a great crowd of peoples perishing along with me. It makes no difference to me how great a tumult accompanies my death. Death amounts to the same thing everywhere.

Accordingly, let us have great courage in the face 10 of that disaster, which can neither be averted nor foreseen. Let us stop listening to those who have renounced Campania and who have emigrated after this catastrophe and say they will never visit that district again. For who promises them better foundations for this or that soil to stand on? All 11 places have the same conditions and if they have not yet had an earthquake, they none the less can have quakes. Perhaps this night or, before tonight, this day will split open the spot where you stand securely. How do you know whether conditions are better in those places against which fortune has already exhausted her strength or in those places which are supported on their own ruins henceforth? We are 12 mistaken if we believe any part of the world is exempt and safe from the danger of an earthquake. All regions lie under the same laws: nature has not created anything in such a way that it is immobile. Some things fall at one time, others at another, and just as in large cities one home here another home there is propped up, so on the globe of earth now this part now that has a flaw.

13 Tyros aliquando infamis ruinis fuit; Asia duodecim urbes simul perdidit; anno priore Achaiam et Macedoniam,[1] quaecumque est ista vis mali quae incurrit nunc Campaniam, laesit. Circumit fatum et, si quid diu praeterit, repetit. Quaedam rarius sollicitat, saepius quaedam; nihil immune esse et
14 innoxium sinit. Non homines tantum, qui brevis et caduca res nascimur, urbes oraeque terrarum et litora et ipsum mare in servitutem fati venit. Nos tamen nobis permansura promittimus bona fortunae, et felicitatem, cuius ex omnibus rebus humanis velocissima est levitas, habituram in aliquo pondus ac
15 moram credimus. Et perpetua sibi omnia promittentibus in mentem non venit id ipsum supra quod stamus stabile non esse. Neque enim Campaniae istud aut Achaiae sed omnis soli vitium est, male cohaerere et ex causis pluribus solvi et summa manere, partibus ruere.

1 2. Quid ago?[2] Solacium adversus pericula rara promiseram. Ecce undique timenda denuntio. Nego quicquam esse quietis aeternae, quod perire possit et perdere. Ego vero hoc ipsum solacii loco pono, et quidem valentissimi, quando quidem sine remedio timor stultis est: ratio terrorem prudentibus excutit; imperitis magna fit ex desperatione securi-

---

[1] Fortunatus for *in Achaia et Macedonia* HPEZS.
[2] *ergo* ABV.

Tyre was once notorious for its ruinations. Asia 13
lost twelve cities at one time.[1] Last year the same
disastrous force, whatever it is, that now has fallen
upon Campania, struck Achaia and Macedonia.
Fate travels in a circuit and returns to a place it has
long passed by. Some regions it rarely troubles,
others it disturbs frequently. But it permits nothing
to be immune and unharmed. Not only we men, who 14
are born short-lived and frail things, but cities also,
and regions and coasts of earth, and even the sea,
are slaves of fate. None the less we promise ourselves that benefits from fortune will be permanent,
and we believe that happiness, whose fickleness is the
most fleeting of all human affairs, will in some person
have stability and duration. And since men prom- 15
ise themselves that all things are perpetual it does
not enter the mind that the very land on which we
stand is unstable. The flaw in Campania or Achaia
exists not only there but in every ground. The earth
stays together poorly and is disintegrated by many
causes; it is permanent as a whole but its parts collapse.

2. What am I up to? I had promised solace 1
against dangers that are rare. Instead I am now
reporting dangers to be feared on all sides. I say
that there is no lasting peace for anything that can
perish and cause to perish. But I place this fact in
the category of solace, actually a very powerful
solace, since fear without remedy is what foolish
men have. Reason frees wise men from terror, and
for the uneducated great confidence comes from

[1] Tacitus (*Ann.* 2.47) describes the collapse of these twelve
cities in Asia and names them. The date was A.D. 17.

2 tas. Hoc itaque generi humano dictum puta quod
illis subita captivitate inter ignes et hostem stupen-
tibus dictum est:

Una salus victis nullam sperare salutem.

3 Si vultis nihil timere, cogitate omnia esse metuenda.
Circumspicite quam levibus causis discutiamur.
Non cibus nobis, non umor, non vigilia, non somnus
sine mensura quadam salubria sunt. Iam intelle-
getis nugatoria esse nos et imbecilla corpuscula,[1]
fluida, non magna molitione perdenda. Sine dubio
id unum periculi nobis est quod tremunt terrae,
quod subito dissipantur ac superposita deducunt!

4 Magni se aestimat qui fulmina et motus terrarum
hiatusque formidat. Vult ille imbecillitatis sibi suae
conscius timere pituitam? Ita videlicet nati sumus,
tam felicia sortiti membra, in hanc magnitudinem
crevimus! Et ob hoc, nisi mundi partibus motis, nisi
caelum intonuerit, nisi terra subsederit, perire non
5 possumus! Unguiculi nos et ne totius quidem dolor
sed aliqua ab latere eius scissura conficit! Et ego
timeam terras trementes, quem crassior saliva
suffocat? Ego extimescam emotum sedibus suis
mare et ne aestus maiore quam solet cursu plus

---

[1] *corpora* EB.

---

[1] Virgil *Aen.* 2.354.
[2] Catarrh was a persistent ailment of Seneca (cf. *Ep.* 78.1).

despair. So, consider that this statement was made 2
to the human race, which was addressed to men dazed
by sudden entrapment between fire and enemy:

> The one safety
> For the conquered
> Is to hope
> For no safety.[1]

If you wish to fear nothing, consider that every- 3
thing is to be feared. See how we are shattered by
only trivial causes. Neither food, drink, waking, or
sleeping is healthful for us without certain limitations. You will soon realize that we are insignificant, weak little bodies, unstable, to be destroyed
by a slight effort. Undoubtedly, the only danger to
us is the lands trembling, suddenly breaking up and
dragging down all that is situated on their surface.

The man who fears lightning bolts, earthquakes, 4
and gaping cracks in the ground esteems himself
highly. But is he willing to be aware of his own
frailty and to fear a cold in the head? *That*, to be
sure, is how we were born, have been allotted such
goodly limbs, have grown to this stature! And for
this reason we are not able to die unless sections of
the world are moved, unless the sky thunders, unless
the earth settles! The pain of a fingernail, and not 5
even of the whole nail but just a split on one side of it,
finishes us off! Also, should *I* fear an earth tremor
because a thick catarrh chokes me?[2] Am *I* to fear
the sea moved from its place and the tide with a
greater rush than usual, pulling more water and

Today it would probably be diagnosed as a chronic upper
respiratory infection.

aquarum trahens superveniat, cum quosdam stran-
gulaverit potio male lapsa per fauces? Quam stultum
est mare horrere, cum scias stillicidio perire te posse!

6   Nullum maius solacium est mortis quam ipsa
mortalitas; nullum autem omnium istorum quae
extrinsecus terrent quam quod innumerabilia pericula [1] in ipso sinu sunt. Quid enim dementius quam
ad tonitrua succidere et sub terram correpere [2]
fulminum metu? Quid stultius quam timere nuta-
tionem [3] terrae aut subitos montium lapsus et irrup-
tiones maris extra litus eiecti, cum mors ubique
praesto sit et undique occurrat nihilque sit tam
exiguum quod non in perniciem generis humani satis
7   valeat? Adeo non debent nos ista confundere,
tamquam plus in se mali habeant quam vulgaris
mors, ut contra, cum sit necessarium e vita exire et
aliquando emittere animam, maiore perire ratione
iuvet. Necesse est mori ubicumque, quandoque;
stet licet ista humus et se teneat suis finibus nec ulla
iactetur iniuria, supra me quandoque erit. Quid [4]
interest, ego illam mihi an ipsa se mihi imponat?

8   Diducitur et ingenti potentia nescio cuius mali
rumpitur et me in immensam altitudinem abducit.
Quid porro? Mors levior in plano est? Quid habeo
quod querar, si rerum natura me non vult iacere

---

[1] *exempla* ABV.
[2] *correpere* Erasmus for *corripere* HPE; *se corripere* ABV;
corruere ZS.
[3] *mutationem* λ.
[4] *Quid* supplied by Gercke, Oltramare.

drowning me when a drink has strangled some people as it slipped down the throat the wrong way? How foolish to fear the sea when you know you can die from a drop of water!

There is no greater solace in dying than mortality 6 itself. Moreover, of all those dangers which terrify us from without there is no solace greater than the realization that there are innumerable dangers in our own bosoms. For what is more insane than to collapse at the noise of thunder and to creep underground from fear of lightning bolts? What is more foolish than to fear the earth's swaying or the sudden collapse of mountains or the eruptions of a sea cast beyond the shore, when death is present everywhere and meets us on all sides, and nothing is so lacking in strength that it is not strong enough to destroy the human race? These dangers ought not to throw us 7 into confusion, as though they contained more evil than a common death. So true is this that, on the contrary, when it is necessary to leave this life and some time give up the ghost, it should be a joy to die in a grander manner. It is necessary to die somewhere, some time. Although the ground is stable and keeps itself within its own limits and is not tossed about by any violence, it will some day be above me. What difference does it make whether I place the ground on me or the ground places itself on me?

The earth is split and burst by the great power 8 of I know not what calamity and carries me off into the immense depths. So what? Is death easier on a level surface? What do I have to complain about if nature does not want me to lie in an ordinary

9 ignobili leto,[1] si mihi inicit sui partem? Egregie Vagellius [2] meus in illo inclito carmine:

                                    Si cadendum est,
  inquit,[3]
E caelo cecidisse velim.

Idem mihi [4] licet dicere: si cadendum est, cadam orbe concusso, non quia fas est optare publicam cladem, sed quia ingens mortis solacium est terram quoque videre mortalem.

1   3. Illud quoque proderit praesumere animo nihil horum deos facere nec ira numinum aut caelum converti [5] aut terram; suas ista causas habent nec ex imperio saeviunt sed quibusdam vitiis, ut corpora nostra turbantur, et tunc, cum facere videntur,

2 iniuriam accipiunt. Nobis autem ignorantibus verum [6] omnia terribiliora sunt, utique quorum metum raritas auget; levius accidunt familiaria; ex insolito formido maior est. Quare autem quicquam nobis insolitum est? Quia naturam oculis, non ratione, comprehendimus, nec cogitamus quid illa facere possit, sed tantum quid fecerit. Damus

----

[1] *lecto* λ; *loco* ABV.
[2] *Vagellius* S; *vero agellius* ABV.
[3] *inquit mihi* HPESA; *mihi* deleted by Gercke, Oltramare.
[4] *mihi* supplied by Gercke, Oltramare.
[5] *concuti* AV; Alexander proposes *nec iram numinum aut caelum conqueri aut terram.*
[6] *unde veniant* ABV (instead of *verum*).

----

[1] We do not know of any Latin poet named Vagellius. Attempts to emend the manuscripts to read Valgius (Valgius Rufus, a poet friend of Horace), Gallio (Seneca's brother), or a hypothetical A. Gellius are all mere guesses.

death, if she places upon me a part of herself? My 9
friend Vagellius [1] expresses it well in that famous
poem of his:

If I must fall,

he says,
  I would prefer to fall
  From heaven.

I might say the same thing: if I must fall, let me fall
with the world shattered, not because it is right to
hope for a public disaster but because it is a great
solace in dying to see that the earth, too, is mortal.

3. It will help also to keep in mind that gods cause 1
none of these things and that neither heaven nor
earth is overturned by the wrath of divinities. [2] These
phenomena have causes of their own; [3] they do not
rage on command but are disturbed by certain de-
fects, just as our bodies are. At the time they seem
to inflict damage they actually receive damage. All 2
these phenomena are terrible to us since we do not
know the truth, and all the more terrible since
the rarity of their occurrence increases our fear.
Familiar things affect us lightly. The fear from
unusual occurrences is greater. But why is anything unusual to us? Because we comprehend
nature with our eyes, not our reason. We do not reflect upon what nature can do but only on what she has
done. Accordingly, we pay the penalty for this negli-

[2] Pliny (2.200) says every earthquake at Rome was a warning
of something about to happen.
[3] Seneca (*Dial.* 1.1.3) says that phenomena which seem
irregular and without fixed purpose, such as earthquakes, do
not happen without reason, but have their own cause.

itaque huius neglegentiae poenas tamquam novis
3 territi, cum illa non sint nova sed insolita. Quid
ergo? Non religionem incutit mentibus, et
quidem publice, sive deficere sol visus est, sive luna
(cuius obscuratio frequentior) aut parte sui aut tota
delituit? Longeque magis illa, actae in transversum
faces et caeli magna pars ardens et crinita sidera et
plures solis orbes et stellae per diem visae subitique
transcursus ignium multam post se lucem trahentium?
4 Nihil horum sine timore miramur. Et cum
timendi sit causa nescire, non est tanti scire, ne
timeas? Quanto satius est causas inquirere, et
quidem toto in hoc intentum animo. Neque enim
illo quicquam inveniri dignius potest cui se non
tantum commodet, sed impendat.

1 4. Quaeramus ergo quid sit quod terram ab infimo
moveat, quod tanti molem ponderis pellat; quid
sit illa valentius quod tantum onus vi sua labefactet;
cur modo tremat, modo laxata subsidat, nunc in
partes divisa discedat et alias intervallum ruinae
suae diu servet, alias cito comprimat; nunc amnes
magnitudinis notae convertat introrsum, nunc novos
exprimat; aperiat aliquando aquarum calentium
venas, aliquando refrigeret, ignesque nonnumquam
per aliquod ignotum antea montis aut rupis foramen

gence in being terrified by things as new when they are not new but merely unusual. What, therefore? 3 Does it not inspire religion in men's minds, and even on a nationwide scale, if the sun is seen in eclipse, or the moon (whose eclipses are more frequent) is obscured in part or entirely? And this is far more so in the case of torches driven across the scene, much of the sky burning, comets, several suns, stars appearing in the daytime, and the sudden passage of fires dragging a long trail of light after them.

We marvel at none of these phenomena without 4 fear. And since the cause of fear is ignorance, is it not worth a great deal to have knowledge in order not to fear? It is much better to investigate the causes and, in fact, to be intent on this study with the entire mind. For nothing can be found worthier than a subject to which the mind not only lends itself but spends itself.

4. Let us ask, then, what it is that moves the earth 1 from the depths, what pushes such a great mass of weight; what is stronger than the earth that by its force it can shake so great a load. Let us investigate why the earth sometimes trembles, sometimes collapses and sinks, now is divided into sections and gapes open; why in one place it preserves for a long time the gap caused by its destruction, in other places it quickly compresses it again. Why at one time does it channel within itself rivers of noteworthy size, and at another time causes new rivers to appear. Why does it sometimes open veins of hot water, sometimes makes the water cold, and sometimes emits fire through a previously unknown opening of a mountain or a rock, but at other times

emittat, aliquando notos et per saecula nobiles
supprimat.[1] Mille miracula movet faciemque mutat
locis et defert montes, subrigit plana, valles extuberat,
novas in profundo insulas erigit. Haec ex quibus
causis accidant, digna res excuti.

2 Quod, inquis, erit pretium operae? Quo nullum
maius est, nosse naturam. Neque enim quicquam
habet in se huius materiae tractatio pulchrius, cum
multa habeat futura usui, quam quod hominem [2]
magnificentia sui detinet nec mercede sed miraculo
colitur. Inspiciamus ergo quid sit propter quod haec
accidant. Quorum adeo est mihi dulcis inspectio
ut, quamvis aliquando de motu terrarum volumen
iuvenis ediderim, tamen temptare me voluerim et
experiri aetas aliquid nobis aut ad scientiam aut
certe ad diligentiam adiecerit.

1 5. Causam qua terra concutitur alii in aqua esse,
alii in ignibus, alii in ipsa terra, alii in spiritu puta-
verunt, alii in pluribus, alii in omnibus his; quidam
liquere ipsis [3] aliquam ex istis causam esse dixerunt,
sed non liquere quae esset.

2 Nunc singula persequar. Illud ante omnia mihi
dicendum est opiniones veteres parum exactas esse
et rudes. Circa verum adhuc errabatur; nova omnia
erant primo temptantibus; postea eadem illa limata
sunt. Et, si quid inventum est, illis nihilominus

---

[1] *supprimat* Z Oltramare; *comprimat* most MSS.
[2] *omnes* ABV.
[3] *sibi* ABV.

suppresses fires that have been known and famous for ages? An earthquake produces a thousand strange things and changes the appearance of places and carries away mountains, elevates plains, pushes valleys up, raises new islands in the sea. What causes these things to happen is a subject worth investigating.

What, you ask, will make it all worth while? To 2 know nature—no reward is greater than this. Although the subject has many features which will be useful, the study of this material has nothing more beautiful in itself than that it involves men in its magnificence and is cultivated not for profit but for its marvellousness. Let us examine, then, why these phenomena occur. The investigation of them is so appealing to me that, even though at one time as a young man I published a volume on earthquakes, none the less I would wish to test myself and find out whether age has added anything to me in the way of knowledge or at any rate in the way of diligence.

5. Some think the cause of earthquakes exists in 1 water, others in fire, or in the earth itself, or even in the air, or in several of these elements, or in all of them. Certain writers have said that it was clear to them that some cause of earthquakes came from those elements; but it was not clear what the cause was.

I will now pursue each theory. Before anything 2 else, I must say that the old theories are crude and inexact. Men were still in error about the truth. Everything was new for men who were making the first attempts. Later these same theories were refined. Yet, if anything has been discovered, it

referri debet acceptum; magni animi res fuit rerum
naturae latebras dimovere nec contentum exteriore
eius aspectu introspicere et in deorum secreta
descendere. Plurimum ad inveniendum contulit
3 qui speravit posse reperiri. Cum excusatione itaque
veteres audiendi sunt. Nulla res consummata est,
dum incipit; nec in hac tantum re omnium maxima
atque involutissima, in qua, etiam cum multum actum
erit,[1] omnis tamen aetas quod agat inveniet, sed et
in omni alio negotio longe semper a perfecto fuere
principia.

1   6. In aqua causam esse nec ab uno dictum est nec
uno modo. Thales Milesius totam terram subiecto
iudicat umore portari et innare,[2] sive illud oceanum
vocas, sive magnum mare, sive alterius naturae
simplicem adhuc aquam et umidum elementum.
Hac, inquit, unda [3] sustinetur orbis velut aliquod
grande navigium et grave his aquis quas premit.

2   Supervacuum est reddere causas propter quas
existimat gravissimam partem mundi non posse
spiritu tam tenui fugacique gestari; non enim nunc
de situ terrarum sed de motu agitur. Illud argu-

[1] *actum erit* λ; *acti erit* most MSS.; *erit quesitum* AV.
[2] *in mare* Z[1]λ; *mare* OS; *in mari* ABV.
[3] *aqua* P.

---

[1] Seneca presents Thales' theory and objects to it in Book
3. 14.1. Apparently Thales envisaged no globe but only a

none the less ought to be acknowledged as having been received from them. It was the achievement of a great spirit to move aside the veil from hidden places and, not content with the exterior appearance of nature, to look within and to descend into the secrets of the gods. The man who had the hope that the truth could be found made the greatest contribution to its discovery. And so the ancients must be 3 listened to, indulgently. Nothing is completed while it is beginning. This is true not only in this subject (which is the greatest and most complex of all), but in every other business as well. Even though much will have been done on this subject every age will none the less find something to do. As in every other subject, the first beginnings have always been far away from the completed knowledge.

6. The cause of earthquakes is said to be in water 1 by more than one authority but not in the same way. Thales [1] of Miletus judges that the whole earth is buoyed up and floats upon liquid that lies underneath, whether you call it the ocean, the great sea, or consider it the as yet elementary water of a different character and call it merely a humid element. The disc is supported by this water, he says, just as some big heavy ship is supported by the water which it presses down upon.

It is pointless for me to give the reasons for his 2 belief that the heaviest part of the universe cannot be carried by air, which is so tenuous and mobile; for the point now does not deal with the location of the earth but with earthquakes. By way of proof that

flat disc of lands floating on water. To Seneca the whole earth is a globe of land and water.

menti loco ponit aquas esse in causa quibus hic orbis
agitetur, quod in omni maiore motu erumpunt
fere novi fontes, sicut in navigiis quoque evenit ut,
si inclinata sunt et abierunt in latus, aquam sorbeant,
quae in omni† [1] eorum onerum† [2] quae vehit, si [3]
immodice depressa sunt, aut superfunditur aut certe
dextra sinistraque solito magis surgit.

3 Hanc opinionem falsam esse non est diu colligen-
dum. Nam, si terra aqua sustineretur et ea aliquando concuteretur, semper moveretur, nec agitari
illam miraremur sed manere; deinde tota concuteretur, non ex parte; numquam enim navis
dimidia iactatur. Nunc vero terrarum non univer-
sarum sed ex parte motus est. Quomodo ergo fieri
potest ut, quod totum vehitur, totum non agitetur,
4 si eo quo vehitur agitatum est? " At quare aquae
erumpunt? " Primum omnium saepe tremuit terra
et nihil umoris novi fluxit. Deinde, si ex hac causa
unda prorumperet, a lateribus terrae circumfun-
deretur, sicut in fluminibus ac mari videmus in-
cidere ut incrementum aquarum, quotiens navigia
desidunt, in lateribus maxime appareat. Ad ultimum non tam exigua fieret quam tu [4] dicis eruptio
nec velut per rimam sentina subreperet, sed fieret
ingens inundatio ut ex infinito liquore et ferente
universa.

---

[1] *vi omni* Gercke (instead of *in omni*).
[2] *onerum* most MSS.; *onere* Koeler, Oltramare; *oneri* ABV.
[3] *vehit situ, si* Alexander.
[4] *quantum* HPZ (instead of *quam tu*).

waters exist as the cause of earthquakes and that the earth is agitated by these waters, he proposes this: in every great earthquake new springs usually break out, just as it also happens that if ships tilt and lean to one side they take in water. In the case of all heavy objects which water carries, if they are submerged considerably, the water either flows over them or at least the water rises on the right or left more than usual.[1]

It need not take long to deduce that Thales' theory **3** is false. For, if the earth were supported by water and sometimes shaken by it, there would always be earthquakes and we would not be amazed that the earth is shaken but that it remains at rest. Finally, the whole earth would be shaken, not just a part; for never is half a ship tossed about. As things are, a quake is not over the entire earth but on a part of it. Therefore, how can it happen that what is carried as a whole is not shaken as a whole if it is shaken by that which carries it? " But why do **4** waters break out? " First of all, there has often been an earthquake and yet no new liquid flowed. Second, if water did burst forth for this reason it would pour around the sides of the earth, as we see happens in the case of rivers and the sea; just as when boats sink the increase of water appears mainly over the sides. Finally, no such scanty eruption of water as *you* say would ever occur, nor would it seep in like bilge-water through a crack, but a huge deluge would be the result of liquid that is infinite and supports all that the earth consists of.

---

[1] Some readings in this sentence are uncertain.

1   7. Quidam motum terrarum aquae imputaverunt,
sed non ex eadem causa.   Per omnem, inquit, terram
multa aquarum genera decurrunt.   Aliubi perpetui
amnes, quorum navigabilis etiam sine adiutorio
imbrium magnitudo est; hinc Nilus per aestatem
ingentes aquas invehit; hinc, qui medius inter
pacata et hostilia fluit, Danuvius ac Rhenus, alter
Sarmaticos impetus cohibens et Europam Asiamque
disterminans, alter Germanos, avidam belli gentem,
2   repellens.   Adice nunc patentissimos lacus et stagna
populis inter se ignotis circumdata et ineluctabiles
navigio paludes, ne ipsis quidem inter se pervias
quibus incoluntur; deinde tot fontes, tot capita
fluminum subitos et ex occulto amnes vomentia,[1] tot
deinde ad tempus collectos torrentium impetus,
quorum vires quam repentinae tam breves.

3   Omnis aquarum et intra terram natura faciesque
est.   Illic quoque aliae vasto cursu [2] deferuntur et in
praeceps volutae cadunt; aliae languidiores in vadis
refunduntur et leniter ac quiete fluunt.   Quis autem
neget vastis illas receptaculis concipi et cessare multis
inertes locis?   Non est diu probandum ibi multas
aquas esse ubi omnes sunt; neque enim sufficeret

---

[1] Oltramare suggests *amne se evomentia*.
[2] *impetu* ABV.

---

[1] Aristotle 2.7.365b 1–5; Democritus' theory is that water
in cavities of the earth becomes blocked by additional rainwater and causes an earthquake when it forces its way out.
Also, Democritus believes that earthquakes are caused by the

7. Some other writers also attribute earthquakes **1**
to water but with different explanations. Throughout the entire earth, one of them says, run many
different kinds of water.[1] In some places there are
perpetual rivers large enough to be navigable, even
without the help of rains. For example, there is
the Nile, which carries great quantities of water all
summer. Elsewhere, rivers flow midway between
the pacified and the hostile; for example, the Danube
or the Rhine, one checking the attacks of Sarmatians
and marking a boundary between Europe and Asia,[2]
the other keeping back the Germans, a nation eager
for war. Consider now the very wide lakes and **2**
inland waters surrounded by people unknown to each
other, and swamps a boat cannot struggle through,
impassable even for those who live on the edges.
Then there are many springs, many sources of rivers
disgorging sudden streams from hidden places, many
rushing torrents that come together on an occasion,
whose force is as brief as it is sudden.

Also within the earth there is every type and variety **3**
of water. There also some are carried down with a
huge rush and fall tumbling headlong. Others,
more slow moving, back up in shallows and flow gently
and quietly. No one can deny that waters form in
vast reservoirs and lie motionless in many places
underground. There is no need of drawn-out proof
that many waters are there in the place where all
waters exist; for the earth would not be able to

movement of water in underground passages from land
saturated with water to parched land.

[2] The Danube was not usually regarded as a boundary
between Europe and Asia.

tellus ad tot flumina edenda, nisi ex reposito mul-
4 toque funderet. Si hoc verum est, necesse est aliquando illic amnis excrescat et relictis ripis violentus
in obstantia incurrat; sic fiet motus alicuius partis in
quam flumen impetum dedit et quam, donec de-
crescat, verberabit. Potest fieri ut aliquam regionem
rivus affluens exedat ac sic trahat aliquam molem,
qua lapsa superposita quatiantur.

5 Iam vero nimis oculis permittit nec ultra illos scit
producere animum, qui non credit esse in abdito
terrae sinus maris vasti. Nec enim video quid
prohibeat aut obstet quominus habeat aliquod etiam
in abdito litus per occultos aditus receptum mare,
quod illic quoque tantundem loci teneat aut fortassis
hoc amplius quod [1] superiora cum tot animalibus
erant dividenda; abstrusa enim et sine possessore
deserta liberius undis vacant.

6 Quas quid vetat illic fluctuare et ventis quos omne
intervallum terrarum et omnis aer creat impelli?
Potest ergo maior solito exorta tempestas aliquam
partem terrarum impulsam vehementius commovere.
Nam apud nos quoque multa quae procul a mari
fuerant subito eius accessu vapulaverunt et villas in
prospectu collocatas fluctus qui longe audiebatur
invasit. Illic quoque potest recedere ac resurgere [2]

---

[1] *quo* HPEAV.
[2] Haase, Gercke, Oltramare for *retegere* most MSS.; *reicere*
Z.

produce so many rivers unless it poured them out from a reservoir, and an ample one. If this is so, it must be 4 that sometimes under the earth a river becomes swollen and, leaving its banks, violently attacks anything in the way. Thus there will be a movement of the earth at some place which the river has attacked. The river will lash at it until the river decreases. It can happen that the flowing stream eats away some region and in so doing drags down a certain mass; at its collapse the surfaces above are shaken.

Now truly a man permits too much to his eyes and 5 does not know how to project his mind beyond them if he does not believe that bays of a vast sea exist in the hidden depths of the earth. I see nothing to prevent or oppose the sea from entering the earth through hidden openings, and from having some sort of coast even in the concealed depths. Also, there the sea occupies as much or perhaps more space than here because the upper regions had to be shared by so many living creatures. Whereas, the hidden regions are deserts without owners and are more freely accessible to water.

What prevents the underground water from fluctu- 6 ating and from being driven by winds which every opening in the earth and every part of the atmosphere creates? A storm rising greater than usual is able to move violently any part of the lands beaten by it. For on our surface also many places which have been far from the sea have been lashed by its sudden approach, and the tide which used to be heard in the distance has invaded villas located in sight of the sea. Down there also the sea below can rise up and

pelagus infernum, quorum neutrum fit sine motu superstantium.

1 8. Non quidem existimo diu te haesitaturum an credas esse subterraneos amnes et mare absconditum. Unde enim ista prorepunt, unde ad nos veniunt, nisi

2 quod origo umoris inclusa est? Age! Cum vides interruptum Tigrin in medio itinere siccari et non universum averti, sed paulatim non apparentibus damnis minui primum, deinde consumi, quo illum putas abire nisi in obscura terrarum, utique cum videas emergere iterum non minorem eo qui prius fluxerat?[1] Quid? Cum vides Alpheon, celebratum poetis, in Achaia mergi et in Sicilia rursus traiecto mari effundere amoenissimum fontem Arethusam?

3 Nescis autem inter opiniones quibus enarratur Nili aestiva[2] inundatio et hanc esse, e terra illum erumpere et augeri non supernis aquis sed ex intimo redditis? Ego quidem centuriones duos quos Nero Caesar (ut aliarum virtutum ita veritatis in primis amantissimus) ad investigandum caput Nili miserat, audivi narrantes longum ipsos iter peregisse, cum a rege Aethiopiae instructi auxilio commendatique

4 proximis regibus ad ulteriora penetrassent. "Post

[1] *fuerat* PABV.
[2] *inestimata* ABV.

recede, neither of which movements occur without shaking the earth above.

8. I do not suppose you will hesitate long about 1 whether you believe there are rivers and a hidden sea underground.   Where do rivers on the surface creep from, where do they come to us from, if the source of wetness is not shut up in the earth ?   Come on! 2 When you see the Tigris interrupted and dried up in mid-journey, not diverted as a whole, but gradually, with no apparent loss, first diminished and then wasted away, where do you think it goes if not to dim depths of the earth, especially since you see it emerge again no smaller than the size which flowed before ? What about this ?   When you see Alpheus, celebrated by poets, sink in Achaia and, crossing the sea, pour forth again in Sicily the very pleasant spring of Arethusa ?

Moreover, do you not know that among the theories 3 by which the summer inundation of the Nile is explained there is also this : it bursts forth from the earth and is swollen not by waters from above but by waters given out by the earth's interior ?   In fact, I have listened to two centurions whom Nero sent to investigate the source of the Nile [1] (just as he is very enthusiastic about the other virtues so he is especially devoted to the truth).   They said that when they had been supplied with help by the king of Ethiopia and had been recommended to the neighbouring kings they completed a long journey and penetrated to very distant parts. " After many 4

[1] Pliny 6.181 : Planning an attack on Ethiopia, Nero sent an exploring party of praetorians who reported nothing there but a desert.

155

multos dies," sicut illi [1] quidem aiebant, "pervenimus ad immensas paludes, quarum exitum nec incolae noverant nec sperare quisquam potest, ita implicatae aquis herbae sunt et aquae nec pediti eluctabiles nec navigio, quod nisi parvum et unius capax limosa et obsita palus non fert. Ibi," inquit, "vidimus duas petras, ex quibus ingens vis fluminis excidebat."

5 Sed sive caput illa, sive accessio est Nili, sive tunc nascitur, sive in terras ex priore recepta cursu redit— nonne tu credis illam, quicquid est, ex magno terrarum lacu ascendere? Habeant enim oportet pluribus locis sparsum umorem et in imo [2] coactum, ut eructare tanto impetu possint.

1 9. Ignem causam motus [3] quidam, et quidem non ignobiles,[4] iudicant, imprimis Anaxagoras, qui existimat simili paene ex causa et aera concuti et terram. Cum in inferiore parte spiritus crassum aera et in nubes coactum eadem vi [5] qua apud nos quoque nubila frangi solent rupit et ignis ex hoc collisu nubium cursuque elisi aeris emicuit, hic ipse in obvia

---

[1] *post multos dies, sicut illi* supplied by Oltramare; "*dein*" *ut quidem aiebant*, "*pervenimus*" Alexander; "*Et quidem, aiebant, pervenimus*" Haase.

[2] Gercke, Oltramare for *uno* MSS.

[3] *motus terrarum* ABV.

[4] supplied by Oltramare for *et quidem non* Z; *et quidem non* H; *et quidem sed non ob eandem causam* EST.

[5] Fortunatus for *eadem via* MSS.

---

[1] This vegetation is the "sudd," which is still a hindrance to boats going up the Nile.

days," so they said, " we came to huge swamps, the
way out of which neither the natives knew nor could
anyone hope to know; the vegetation [1] was so
entangled in water and the water impassable on foot
or by boat, because the muddy overgrown marsh
does not support anything except a small boat large
enough for only one man. There," he said, " we
saw two rocks from which a great quantity of river-
water fell." [2]

But whether that is the source [3] of the Nile or only 5
an addition to it, whether it is born there or merely
returns to the surface from an earlier passage underground—do *you* not think that, whatever the reason,
the water ascends from a great lake under the earth?
For it must be that the earth has moisture scattered in
many places and collected in the depths so as to be
able to disgorge it with such violence.

9. Some authorities, and indeed men of high 1
reputation, suppose that fire is the cause of earthquakes. Anaxagoras especially estimates that both
the atmosphere and the earth are shaken by just
about the same cause. Moving air in the lower region
inside the earth bursts the atmosphere, which is
thick and compacted into clouds, with the same force
that clouds in our part of the world are usually
broken open. Fire flashes out from this collision
of clouds and from the rush of air that is forced out.
This fire, seeking an exit, runs against anything it

[2] These two rocks may be the Veins of the Nile which Seneca
describes in Bk. 4.2.7.
[3] The real sources of the Nile were unknown until the early
part of the second century when one Diogenes found or heard
with some accuracy about the true sources.

incurrit exitum quaerens ac divellit repugnantia, donec per augustum aut nactus est viam exeundi ad caelum aut vi et iniuria fecit.

2 Alii in igne causam quidem esse, sed non ob hoc iudicant, sed quia pluribus obrutus locis ardeat et proxima quaeque consumat; quae si quando exesa ceciderint, tunc sequi motum earum partium quae subiectis adminiculis destitutae labant, donec corruerunt, nullo occurrente quod onus exciperet; tunc chasmata, tunc hiatus vasti aperiuntur, aut cum diu dubitaverunt super ea se quae supersunt stantque 3 componunt. Hoc apud nos quoque videmus accidere, quotiens incendio laborat pars civitatis; cum exustae trabes sunt aut corrupta quae superioribus firmamentum dabant, tunc diu agitata fastigia concidunt et tam diu deferuntur atque incerta sunt, donec in solido resederunt.

1 10. Anaximenes ait terram ipsam sibi causam esse motus nec extrinsecus incurrere quod illam impellat, sed intra ipsam et ex ipsa. Quasdam enim partes eius decidere, quas aut umor resolverit aut ignis exederit aut spiritus violentia excusserit; sed, his quoque cessantibus, non deesse propter quod ali-

---

[1] Aristotle 2.7.365a 20: Anaxagoras says that air, which naturally moves upward, causes earthquakes when it is trapped in cavities beneath the earth by rainwater clogging the upper parts of the earth. Aristotle objects to Anaxagoras' explanation and makes no mention of the fire that Seneca includes in the theory.

[2] Aristotle (2.7.365b 6–20) gives a different version: Anaximenes says that when the earth is in the process of becoming

meets and tears apart anything that resists it until either it finds a way out to the sky through narrow passages or makes a way out by force and destruction.[1]

Other authorities also conclude that the cause of earthquakes is fire, but for a different reason: buried fire breaks out in many places and as it blazes away it burns everything near it. If ever the places fall when they have been eaten away, then there follows a movement of those parts of the earth which are deprived of the support which lies underneath, and they slip until they collapse since nothing rushes in to receipt their weight. Then chasms, then vast gulfs are opened or, when they have hesitated a long time, they settle down over those things which are still standing under them. We see this happen also right in front of us when a section of a city suffers from fire. When beams are burned through or the members which gave support to the upper stories are destroyed, then the roofs, after trembling a long time, collapse, and waver for some time in their descent until they come to rest on something solid.

10. Anaximenes says that the earth itself is the cause of its earthquakes and that the earth does not encounter from outside something that shakes it but something within itself and of itself.[2] For, he says, certain parts of the earth fall in, which either moisture has dissolved or fire has eaten away or a blast of air has shattered; but even if these elements are not active, he says, there are other reasons that some

hot or dry it breaks up and is shaken by falling ground. Aristotle disagrees. Ammianus (17.7.12) ascribes this theory to Anaximander, the teacher of Anaximenes.

quid abscedat aut revellatur. Nam primum omnia
vetustate labuntur nec quicquam tutum a senectute
2 est; haec solida quoque et magni roboris carpit.
Itaque, quemadmodum in aedificiis veteribus
quaedam non percussa tamen decidunt, cum plus
ponderis habuere quam virium, ita in hoc universo
terrae corpore evenit ut partes eius vetustate sol-
vantur, solutae cadant et tremorem superioribus
afferant; primum, dum abscedunt, nihil enim utique
magnum sine motu eius cui haesit absciditur; deinde,
cum deciderunt, solido exceptae resiliunt pilae more,
quae, cum cecidit, exultat ac saepius pellitur, totiens
a solo in novum impetum missa. Si vero in stagnanti-
bus aquis delatae [1] sunt, hic ipse casus vicina concutit
fluctu, quem subitum vastumque illisum ex alto
pondus eiecit.

1   11. Quidam ignibus quidem assignant hunc tremorem, sed aliter. Nam, cum pluribus locis ferveant, necesse est ingentem vaporem sine exitu volvant, qui vi
sua spiritum intendit et, si acrius [2] institit, opposita
diffindit;[3] si vero remissior fuit, nihil amplius quam
movet. Videmus aquam spumare igne subiecto;
quod in hac aqua facit inclusa et angusta, multo magis
illum facere credamus, cum violentus ac vastus ingentes aquas excitat; tunc ille vaporatione fluc-
tuantium undarum quicquid pulsaverit agitatur.

---

[1] Gercke, Oltramare for *delata* HEZA; *demissa* P; *delapsa*
B.
[2] *arvis* ABV.
[3] *diffindit* E; *diffundit* most MSS.

part of the earth moves away or is torn away. In the first place, all things totter from length of time and nothing is safe from age; age wastes away even these very strong and solid objects. Accordingly, in old 2 buildings when some sections have more weight than strength they fall even though they are not knocked off. The same thing happens in this whole body of the earth: its parts are loosened by age, and once lossened they fall and cause a tremor to the parts above them. The parts first do this when they give way, for nothing big is cut away without moving whatever it adhered to; then when they fall they meet something solid and rebound like a ball. When a ball falls it leaps up and bounces repeatedly, as many times as it is sent back from the ground into a new flight. Moreover, if parts of the earth have been carried down in stagnant waters, this fall by itself shakes the vicinity with a wave ejected by the sudden mass which has been shot down from above.

11. Some, indeed, attribute earthquakes to fire but 1 give different explanations. When heat grows intense in many places it necessarily rolls up an enormous cloud of vapour that has no way out and causes strain on the air by its force. If the vapour exerts excessive pressure it breaks through all that opposes it; but if it is fairly moderate it causes nothing more than a movement of the earth. We see water foam up when fire is put under it. What happens in the case of a small quantity of enclosed water we may believe happens much more when violent, extensive fire stirs up great quantities of water. Then by the vaporization of the billowing water the fire causes whatever it strikes to shake.

SENECA

1   12. Spiritum esse qui moveat et plurimis et
maximis auctoribus placet. Archaelaus, antiquitatis
diligens,[1] ait ita: venti in concava terrarum deferuntur; deinde, ubi iam omnia spatia plena sunt
et in quantum aer potuit densatus est, is qui supervenit spiritus priorem premit et elidit ac frequentibus
2   plagis primo cogit, deinde proturbat. Tum ille
quaerens locum omnes angustias [2] dimovet et claustra
sua conatur effringere; sic evenit ut terrae, spiritu
luctante et fugam quaerente, moveantur. Itaque,
cum terrae motus futurus est, praecedit aeris tran-
quillitas et quies, videlicet quia vis spiritus quae
concitare ventos solet in inferna sede retinetur.
Nunc quoque, cum hic motus in Campania fuit,
quamvis hiberno tempore et inquieto, per superiores
dies caelo aer stetit.

3   Quid ergo? Numquam flante vento terra concussa
est? Admodum raro. Duo simul flavere venti;
fieri tamen et potest et solet. Quod si recepimus
et constat duos ventos rem simul gerere, quidni [3]

---

[1] *Archelaus, physicus, ut est captus antiquitatis, diligens*
Garrod, Oltramare; *Archelaus antiquus inquisitor satis diligens*
Alexander.
[2] *omnia obstacula* ABV.
[3] Fortunatus for *quidnam* HPEZ; *quid inde* ABV.

---

[1] Archelaus was closely associated with Anaxagoras.
Ammianus (17.7.11) ascribes this theory to Anaxagoras.

12. It is a favourite theory of most of the greatest **1**
authorities that it is moving air which causes earthquakes. Archelaus,[1] a scholar accurate in matters
of ancient times, says as follows: winds are carried
down into cavities of the earth; then, when all the
spaces are filled and the air is thickened as much as
it can be, the moving air which comes in on top of it
compresses the air that was there first and pushes it
and with frequent blows first packs it together then
forces it out. Then in seeking room the air unblocks **2**
all the narrow passageways and tries to break out of its
enclosure. In this way it comes about that the earth
is moved, when the moving air is struggling and
searching for a way out. And so, a calm and quiet
condition of the atmosphere precedes the period when
there will be an earthquake, obviously because the
force of air which usually stirs up the winds is retained
in the interior of the earth.[2] At this time too when
the earthquake occurred in Campania, even though
it was the restless season of the winter, the air
in space remained still throughout the preceding
days.

But what about this: has the earth never been **3**
shaken when the wind was blowing? Very rarely.
Two winds may blow at the same time; indeed, not
only can it happen but it is usual. If we accept this

[1] Pliny (2.192) says that earthquakes are unquestionably caused
by winds. The reading and meaning are doubtful. Archelaus
himself belonged to antiquity and to say that he was diligent
about ancient times seems idle here.

[2] Pliny 2.192: earth tremors never occur except when the
air is calm because all the air is withdrawn and shut up in
the veins and hidden cavities of the earth. Ammianus
(17.7.11) says the same.

accidere possit ut alter superiorem aera agitet, alter infernum?

1 13. In hac sententia licet ponas Aristotelem et discipulum eius Theophrastum, non, ut Graecis visum est, divini, tamen et dulcis eloquii virum et nitidi sine labore. Quid utrique placeat exponam. Semper aliqua evaporatio est e terra, quae modo arida est, modo umido mixta; haec ab infimo edita et in quantum potuit elata, cum ulteriorem locum in quem exeat non habet, retro fertur atque in se revolvitur; deinde rixa spiritus reciprocantis iactat obstantia et, sive interclusus sive per angusta enisus est, motum ac tumultum ciet.

2 Straton ex eadem schola est, qui hanc partem philosophiae maxime coluit et rerum naturae inquisitor fuit. Huius tale decretum est. Frigidum et calidum semper in contraria abeunt, una esse non possunt; eo frigidum confluit unde vis calidi [1] discessit, et invicem ibi calidum est unde frigus expulsum est. Hoc quod dico verum esse et [2] utrumque in contrarium agi ex hoc tibi appareat.

[1] Gercke, Oltramare for *calida* MSS.
[2] Haase, Gercke, Oltramare for *esse sed* B; *est sed* HEZ; *est si* P.

---

[1] Aristotle 2.8.366a 9–12: some earthquakes occur when the wind is blowing. Sometimes several winds are blowing at the same time, and when one of them plunges down into the earth the resultant earthquake is less violent because the force that causes it is divided.

[2] Aristotle 2.8.365b 21–29: there must be exhalations from both moist and dry, and earthquakes are a necessary result

and it is agreed that two winds act at the same time, why can it not happen that one agitates the upper atmosphere, the other the lower regions? [1]

13. In the same group you may place Aristotle [2] and his student Theophrastus, a man not of divine eloquence, as he seemed to the Greeks, but nevertheless of a smooth and clear eloquence without effort. I will set forth the theory they both liked; from the earth there is always some sort of evaporation which is sometimes dry sometimes mixed with moisture. This emanates from the depths of the earth; when it has risen as far as possible and does not have a higher place to go, it is carried back and is rolled up on itself. The conflict of air moving back and forth hurls aside all obstacles and, whether it is blocked or struggles out through narrow openings, it causes a movement and a disturbance of the earth.

Strato is of the same school.[3] He especially cultivated this branch of philosophy and was an investigator of the nature of the universe. His decision is this: cold and heat always change into opposites.[4] They cannot exist together. Cold flows into the place from which the force of heat has departed, and in turn heat exists in the place from which cold has been driven out. It will appear to you from the following that what I say is true and that both move contrary to each other.

of the existence of these exhalations. Aristotle also says (2.8.366b 5–15) that dry and moist exhalations along with wind and certain seasons are associated with earthquakes.

[3] The Peripatetic School. Strato succeeded Theophrastus as head of the Lyceum 287 B.C.

[4] Seneca is vague here and might mean "move away in opposite directions."

3   Hiberno tempore, cum supra terram frigus est,
calent putei nec minus specus atque omnes sub terra
recessus, quia illo se calor contulit superiora possi-
denti frigori cedens.   Qui, cum in inferiora pervenit
et eo se quantum poterat ingessit, quo densior, hoc
validior est.   Hic alii spiritui [1] supervenit; cui necessario congregatus ille iam et in angulum pressus loco
4   cedit.   Idem contrario evenit, cum vis maior frigidi
illata in cavernis est; quicquid illic calidi latet,
frigori cedens abit in angustum et magno impetu
agitur, quia non patitur utriusque natura concordiam
nec in uno moram.   Fugiens ergo et omni modo
cupiens excedere proxima quaeque remolitur ac
5   iactat.   Ideoque antequam terra moveatur, solet
mugitus audiri, ventis in abdito tumultuantibus.
Nec enim aliter posset, ut ait noster Vergilius:

Sub pedibus mugire solum et iuga celsa [2] moveri.

nisi hoc esset ventorum opus.

6   Vices deinde huius pugnae sunt eaedem: fit [3]
calidi congregatio ac rursus eruptio; tunc frigida

[1] *Hic alii spiritui* Oltramare for *huic alius* MSS.
[2] Virgil has *coepta.*
[3] *eaedem: fit* Gercke, Oltramare; *defit* ZLAV; *desit* PE;
deficit H.

---

[1] [Or: "This heat."   Section 4 deals with hot yielding to
cold; and 3 ends with cold yielding to hot.   The translation
here, based on Oltramare's conjectural emendation of *huic
alius* of the MSS., gives the sense required.   If *huic* is right,
alius wrong, Gercke's *frigus* for *alius* provides the right sort
of noun as subject to *supervenit.*   Another possibility is, not

In the wintertime, when there is cold on the sur- 3
face of the earth, wells are warm, and caves, and all
the recesses under the earth, because heat gathers
there yielding to the cold which possesses the upper
regions. When the heat penetrates to the lower
regions and accumulates there, as much as it can,
it becomes stronger as it becomes denser. Here it[1]
comes upon other air which necessarily yields to it,
packed as that cold air is and compressed into a
corner. The same thing happens in an opposite way 4
when a great quantity of cold is carried down into the
caverns. The heat that hides there gives way to the
cold and withdraws to the narrow passages and is
driven along with great impetus because the nature
of the two does not allow harmony or delay in the
same place. Therefore, the air in its flight and
desire to escape in any way pushes back and tosses
about all that is close to it. And so, before the 5
earthquake a roaring noise is usually heard from
winds that are creating a disturbance underground.
Otherwise it could not happen—as our Virgil says:

> The ground bellows under our feet
> And the high ridges move— [2]

unless this were the work of winds.

Then this conflict of the winds goes through the 6
same phases alternately. There is an accumulation of heat and again its eruption; then what is cold

algus, but *algor* " cold that is felt "; another, which assumes
the loss of a noun, is, not *alsus* but *alsius* (" feeling cold ").
However, *supervenit* looks as if its subject is heat, not cold.
So one goes back to Oltramare.—E.H.W.]

[2] Virgil *Aen.* 6.256.

compescuntur et succedunt, mox futura potentiora. Dum ergo alterna vis cursat et ultro citroque spiritus commeat, terra concutitur.

1 14. Sunt qui existiment spiritu quidem et nulla alia ratione tremere terram, sed ex alia causa quam Aristoteli placuit. Quid sit quod ab his dicatur audi. Corpus nostrum et sanguine irrigatur et spiritu, qui per sua itinera decurrit. Habemus autem quaedam angustiora receptacula animae per quae nihil amplius quam meat,[1] quaedam patentiora in quibus colligitur et unde dividitur in partes. Sic hoc totum terrarum omnium corpus et aquis, quae vicem sanguinis tenent, et ventis, quos nihil aliud quis quam animam vocaverit, pervium est. Haec duo aliubi 2 currunt, aliubi consistunt. Sed, quemadmodum in corpore nostro, dum bona valetudo est, venarum quoque imperturbata mobilitas modum servat; ubi aliquid adversi est, micat crebrius et suspiria atque anhelitus laborantis ac fessi signa sunt. Ita terrae quoque, dum illis positio naturalis est, inconcussae manent; cum aliquid peccatur, tunc velut aegri corporis motus est, spiritu illo qui modestius [2] perfluebat icto vehementius et quassante venas suas. (Nec ut illi paulo ante dicebant—quibus animal

---

[1] *commeat* AB (instead of *quam meat*).
[2] *molestius* PV; *molestus* AB.

is restrained and gives way but subsequently it will become more powerful. Therefore, while the force runs back and forth and the air moves here and there, the earth is shaken.

14. There are those who think that earthquakes 1 are indeed caused by air, and by no other cause, but for a different reason from Aristotle's theory. Listen to what they say: our body is irrigated by blood; also by air, which runs along by its own routes. However, we have some rather narrow receptacles for breath through which air does nothing more than pass, others wider in which the air is collected and from there distributed to the parts of the body. In the same way this whole body of the entire earth is a passageway both for water, which takes the place of blood, and for winds, which you might call simply respiration.[1] These two elements run together in some places, are stationary in other places. But in 2 our body the movement of the veins also preserves its rhythm undisturbed while there is good health but when there is something wrong the movement pulses more rapidly and inhaling and exhaling give signs of effort and exhaustion. In the same way the earth remains unshaken as long as its condition is normal. When something is wrong, then there is motion just like that of a sick body, because the air which was flowing through it in an even pattern is struck violently and causes its veins to shake. But not as they said a little above—those who are fond

[1] In Bk. 3.15.1–2 Seneca treats more fully the concept that the earth has veins and arteries similar to those in the human body. Also, in Bk. 5.4.2, he mentions the theory that winds are formed in a way analogous to flatulence in the human body.

placet esse terram. Nisi hoc est, quemadmodum animal, totum vexationem sentiet; neque enim in nobis febris alias aliis [1] partes moratius impellit, sed per omnes pari aequalitate discurrit).

3   Vide ergo ne [2] quid intret in illam spiritus ex circumfuso aere. Qui, quamdiu habet exitum, sine iniuria labitur; si offendit aliquid et incidit quod viam clauderet, tunc oneratur primo, infundente se a tergo aere, deinde per aliquam rimam maligne fugit et hoc acrius fertur, quo angustius. Id sine pugna

4   non potest fieri, nec pugna sine motu. At si ne rimam quidem per quam efflueret invenit, conglobatus illic furit et hoc atque illo circumagitur aliaque deicit, alia intercidit, cum tenuissimus idemque fortissimus et irrepat quamvis in obstructa et quicquid intravit vi sua diducat ac dissipet. Tunc terra iactatur; aut enim datura vento locum discedit, aut, cum dedit, in ipsam qua illum emisit cavernam fundamento spoliata considit.

1   15. Quidam ita existimant: terra multis locis perforata est nec tantum primos illos aditus habet quos velut spiramenta ab initio sui recepit, sed

---

[1] supplied by Madvig.
[2] Gercke, Oltramare for *nunc* most MSS.; *num* J[2].

---

[1] The Pythagorean theory that the earth is alive. Seneca's reference to a statement "a little above" (*paulo ante*) is unclear.

of the theory that the earth is a living creature.[1] Otherwise, the earth would feel the agitation all over, the way an animal does. For, in us a fever does not attack certain parts more slowly than others but spreads through all parts with the same uniformity.

Consider, therefore, whether some of the air from 3 the surrounding atmosphere enters into the earth. As long as it has a way out, it slips through without doing damage. If it stumbles against something or meets something which blocks its path, then at first it is loaded down with the atmosphere that flows upon it from behind, next it escapes with difficulty through some crack, and the narrower the crack the more violently the air spurts out. This cannot happen without a struggle, and a struggle cannot take place without causing movement. But if it does 4 not find even a crack to flow out of, the air becomes massed there and rages and is driven around this way and that, hurling some obstacles aside, cutting through others. It is very extenuated yet at the same time very strong. It pushes through obstructions, however large, and whatever it enters it splits by its force and scatters. Then the earth is tossed about. For it either opens to give room to the air or when it has given room it is deprived of its foundation and collapses into the very cavern from which it released the air.

15. Some think along the following lines:[2] the 1 earth is perforated in many places, and has not only those places of admission which it first received at its beginning and which it had as though for breathing

[2] Diogenes of Apollonia; Seneca gives his theory in Bk. 4.2.28.

multos illi casus imposuit. Aliubi deduxit quicquid
superne terreni erat aqua, alia torrentes cecidere,
alia aestibus magnis disrupta patuerunt. Per haec
intervalla intrat spiritus. Quem si inclusit mare et
altius adegit nec fluctus retro abire permisit, tunc
ille, exitu simul redituque praecluso, volutatur et,
quia in rectum non potest tendere, quod illi
naturale est, in sublime se intendit et terram pre-
mentem diverberat.

1   16. Etiamnunc dicendum est quod plerisque
auctoribus placet et in quod fortasse fiet discessio.[1]
Non esse terram sine spiritu palam est, non tantum
illo dico quo se tenet ac partes sui iungit, qui inest
etiam saxis mortuisque corporibus, sed illo dico vitali
et vegeto et alente omnia. Hunc nisi haberet,
quomodo tot arbustis spiritum infunderet non aliunde
viventibus et tot satis? Quemadmodum tam di-
versas radices aliter atque aliter in se mersas foveret,
quasdam summa receptas parte, quasdam altius
tractas, nisi multum haberet animae tam multa
tam varia generantis et haustu atque alimento sui
educantis?

2   Levibus adhuc argumentis ago. Totum hoc
caelum, quod igneus aether (mundi summa pars)

---

[1] *discessio* Z; *dissensio* HEPABV.

---

[1] Aristotle 2.8.366a 30–35: the sea drives the wind back
into the earth when ordinarily it would have been exhaled
from the earth.

but many others which violent chance has formed. In some places water washed away areas from the earth's surface; the torrents cut through some parts, other places were laid open because they were broken apart by great tides. Air enters through these openings. If the sea encloses the air and drives it deeper down and the water does not permit it to come back out,[1] then, when its way out and way back are at the same time blocked, the air is rolled about and, because it is not able to extend straight out, which is natural to it, it stretches itself upward and lashes apart the earth pressing down upon it.

16. And now I must state a theory which many 1 authorities favour and which will perhaps be voted for without dissent. It is obvious that the earth is not without air. I speak not only of the air by which it holds itself together and joins the parts of itself, which exists also in rocks and dead bodies, but I also speak of that air which is vital and active, nourishing all things.[2] Unless the earth has this, how does the earth infuse air into the many trees and plants which derive life from no other source? How does the earth nurture the many different roots plunged into herself in various ways, some penetrating only the upper part of the earth, others sunk deeper, unless the earth had an abundance of the breath which generates so many and such varied growths and nourishes them with food and drink?

Up to this point I am working with minor con- 2 siderations. This entire heaven, which fiery ether shuts in, the highest part of the universe, all those

[2] In Bk. 5.5.2; 5.6.1 Seneca speaks of a life-generating principle in water and fire.

claudit, omnes hae stellae, quarum iniri [1] non potest
numerus, omnis hic caelestium coetus (ut alia prae-
teream), hic tam prope a nobis agens cursum sol,
omni terrarum ambitu non semel maior—alimentum
ex terreno trahunt et inter se partiuntur nec ullo alio
scilicet quam halitu terrarum sustinentur; hoc illis
3 alimentum, hic pastus est.   Non posset autem tam
multa tantoque se ipsa maiora nutrire, nisi plena
esset animae, quam per diem ac noctem ab omnibus
partibus sui fundit.   Fieri enim non potest ut non
multum illi supersit ex qua tantum petitur ac sumitur.
Et ad tempus quidem quod exeat nascitur—nec enim
esset perennis illi copia suffecturi in tot caelestia
spiritus, nisi invicem ista recurrerent [2] et in aliud alia
solverentur—sed tamen necesse est abundet ac
4 plena sit et ex condito proferat.   Non est ergo
dubium quin multum spiritus intus lateat et caeca
sub terra spatia aer latus obtineat.   Quod si verum
est, necesse est id saepe moveatur quod re mobilissima
plenum est; numquid enim dubium esse cuiquam
potest quin nihil sit tam inquietum quam aer, tam
versabile et agitatione gaudens?

[1] *iniri* HZBV[1]; *inveniri* λV[2]; *diffiniri* ET.
[2] Reinhardt, Oltramare for *excurrerent* MSS.

stars whose number cannot begin to be counted, all this assembly of heavenly bodies (to omit other things), this sun which drives its course so near to us, much greater than the entire globe of the earth—all draw their nourishment from the earth's substance and share this nourishment among themselves and are obviously sustained by no other means than by the exhalations of the earth. This is their nourishment, this is their pasturage. Moreover, the earth **3** would not be able to nurture so many things and of such great size, even larger than the earth itself, unless earth were full of breath which it pours forth day and night from all its parts. For there must be a great super-abundance in an earth from which so much is sought and consumed. And, indeed, it is produced for the occasion when it must be sent forth —for the earth would not have a perennial supply of air to nurture so many celestial bodies [1] unless these bodies in turn came running back and various dues were paid one for one purpose, one for another—but none the less it is necessary that the earth abounds in air and is full of air and emits it from hidden reserves. Therefore, there is no doubt that a great **4** quantity of air lies within the earth and a widespread atmosphere occupies the hidden spaces underground. If this is true, it must needs be that that body (the earth) is often moved which is filled with an extremely movable substance. For surely no one can possibly doubt that nothing is more restless, more capricious and delighting in turbulence than air.

[1] Pliny 2.102: the whole seemingly empty space which some call sky (*caelum*) and others call atmosphere (*aer*) pours forth this life-giving air (*spiritus vitalis*).

1   17. Sequitur ergo ut naturam suam exerceat et
quod semper moveri vult aliquando et alia moveat.
Id quando fit? Quando illi cursus interdictus est.
Nam, quamdiu non impeditur, it placide; cum offen-
ditur et retinetur, insanit et moras suas abripit,
non aliter quam ille

> pontem indignatus Araxes.[1]

2   Quamdiu illi facilis et liber est alveus, primas quasque
aquas explicat; ubi saxa manu vel casu illata
repressere [1] venientem, tunc impetum mora quaerit
et, quo plura opposita sunt, plus invenit virium.
Omnis enim illa unda quae a tergo supervenit et in se
crescit, cum onus suum sustinere non potuit, vim
ruina parat et prona cum ipsis quae obiacebant fugit.
Idem spiritu fit, qui, quo valentior agiliorque est,
citius eripitur et vehementius saeptum omne distur-
bat; ex quo motus fit, scilicet eius partis sub qua
pugnatum est.

3   Quod dicitur verum esse et illo probatur. Saepe,
cum terrae motus fuit, si modo pars eius aliqua
disrupta est, inde ventus per multos dies fluxit, ut
traditur factum eo motu quo Chalcis laboravit; quod

---

[1] *inlata repressere* ET; *in latere pressere* HPZAB.

[1] Virgil *Aen.* 8.728.

17. It follows, therefore, that air exercises its 1
unique nature; whatever wants always to be in
motion will at times put other things in motion.
When does this happen? Whenever its path is
forbidden to it. For, whenever air is not impeded
it flows along calmly. When it is opposed and held
back it rages and tears apart its barriers, like the
River

> Araxes raging at its bridge.[1]

As long as a river has a smooth and open channel it 2
unfolds its waters in steady succession. When, by
man or chance, rocks are brought in to block its
flow, then it seeks force from the obstruction and
it finds more strength where more obstacles are opposed to it. For, when all the water that comes up
from behind accumulates upon itself, and is not able
to sustain its own weight, it acquires its force by
destruction and escapes in a forward rush with those
very obstacles which lay in its way. The same thing
happens in the case of air:[2] the stronger and more
mobile it is the more rapidly it is swept away and the
more violently it scatters every barrier. From this
an earthquake occurs, obviously of the part of the
earth under which the struggle was going on.

What is said is also proved to be true by this: often 3
when an earthquake occurs, if only some part of the
earth is broken open a wind blows from there for
several days, as happened—according to reports—
in the earthquake which Chalcis suffered. You will

[2] Seneca's description of a whirlwind, and of winds in
general, in Bk. 5.13.1-2 is very similar to his reasoning in this
chapter.

apud Asclepiodotum invenies, auditorem Posidonii,
in his ipsis quaestionum naturalium causis. Invenies et apud alios auctores hiasse uno loco terram
et inde non exiguo tempore spirasse ventum, qui
scilicet illud iter ipse sibi fecerat per quod ferebatur.

1 18. Maxima ergo causa est propter quam terra
moveatur spiritus natura citus et locum e loco mutans.
Hic, quamdiu non impellitur et in vacanti spatio
latet, iacet innoxius nec circumiectis molestus est.
2 Ubi illum extrinsecus superveniens causa sollicitat
compellitque et in artum [1] agit, si licet [2] adhuc, cedit
tantum et vagatur; ubi erepta discedendi facultas
est et undique obsistitur, tunc

> magno cum murmure montis
Circum claustra

---

[1] *in altum* Z.
[2] *scilicet* PλABV (instead of *si licet*).

---

[1] Seneca refers to Asclepiodotus also in 2.26.6, 2.30.1,
and 5.15.1. [There is a problem of interpretation (and reading?) in Seneca here: *in his ipsis quaestionum naturalium causis*.
If we accept this as right, what would *in ipsis causis* mean?
Probably " in regard to the very subjects of discussion with
which we are dealing." But what would *in . . . quaestionum
naturalium causis* mean? It is hard to see. Oltramare
suggests plausibly that Asclepiodotus' work had the title
Αἰτίαι Φυσικαὶ or Αἰτιῶν Φυσικῶν Ζητήσεις "Physical
Causes" or "Researches into Physical Causes." It is
hardly reasonable to think that Seneca misrendered it as if it

find this in a work of Asclepiodotus,[1] the pupil of Posidonius, where he deals with this very subject of phenomena in nature. Also, you will find in other writers that the earth has gaped open in some place and from there has puffed wind for a long time. Clearly the wind had made for itself the passageway through which it moved.

18. Accordingly, the principal cause of an earth- 1 quake is air, swift by nature and changing from place to place. As long as it is not shoved and it lurks in a vacant space, it lies harmless and is no trouble to surrounding areas. When a cause coming from 2 outside stirs it up and pushes it together and drives it into a narrow space it merely gives way and shifts about if it is still permitted to do so. When the chance of getting away is cut off and it is beset on all sides then

> With a mighty rumbling of the mountain
> Around the barriers [2]

were the unacceptable Ζητήσεων Φυσικῶν Αἰτίαι. I suggest (a) reading *ipsius* instead of *his ipsis*—that is, Seneca himself, while writing a work on *Naturales Quaestiones* speaks in it of a similar work by Asclepiodotus; and (b) that A. wrote a work entitled Φυσικῶν Αἰτίαι, "Causes of Natural Phenomena," with the same subject as Seneca's *Naturales Quaestiones*; that, in referring to A.'s work, S. called it in Latin *Naturalium Causae* or *Rerum Naturalium Causae*, "Causes of Natural Phenomena"; and that, not S., but a scribe in the early tradition of MSS., with S.'s own work in mind, inserted (or substituted for *Rerum*) *Quaestionum*, so that the text now reads, in error, *quaestionum naturalium causis*. However, if *quaestiones* can mean the same as *quaerenda* "phenomena to be examined into" (so Alexander), then in Latin such *quaerenda* could have *causae* without error.—E. H. Warmington.]

[2] Virgil *Aen.* 1.55–56.

fremit, quae diu pulsata convellit ac iactat eo acrior
3 quo cum mora valentiore luctatus est. Deinde, cum
circa perlustravit omne quo tenebatur nec potuit
evadere, inde, quo maxime impactus est, resilit et aut
per occulta dividitur ipso terrae motu raritate facta,
aut per novum vulnus emicuit; ita eius non potest
vis tanta cohiberi nec ventum tenet ulla compages.
Solvit enim quodcumque vinculum et onus omne
fert secum infususque per minima laxamentum sibi
parat[1] et indomita naturae potentia liberat se,[2]
utique cum concitatus sibi ius suum vindicat.
4   Spiritus vero invicta res est; nihil erit quod

Luctantes ventos tempestatesque sonoras
Imperio premat ac vinclis et carcere frenet.

5 Sine dubio poetae hunc voluerunt videri carcerem in
quo sub terra clausi laterent; sed hoc non intel-
lexerunt nec id quod clausum est esse adhuc ventum,
nec id quod ventus est posse iam claudi. Nam quod
in clauso est quiescit et aeris statio est; omnis in fuga
ventus est.
6   Etiamnunc et illud accedit his argumentis per
quod appareat motum effici spiritu,[3] quod corpora
quoque nostra non aliter tremunt quam si spiritum

---

[1] *sibi parat* Pincianus, Gercke, Oltramare for *superat* MSS.
[2] *se* added by Haase, Gercke, Oltramare; *liberat. Est utique
cum* HPAV.
[3] *effici spiritu* Z Oltramare; *efficit spiritus* HPEABV.

---

[1] Virgil *Aen.* 1.53-54.

it rages, and after beating against these barriers a
long time the air pulls them apart and hurls them
aside, becoming more violent the stronger the obstacles with which it has struggled.   Then when it   3
has wandered around all that restrains it and is still
unable to get out it rebounds from where it received
the greatest impact and is either dissipated through
hidden openings made here and there by the conse-
quent movement itself of the earth or erupts through
a new wound.   Thus the great force of air cannot be
checked, nor does any compact structure hold this
wind.   For it loosens any bond and carries every
weight away with it and makes a space for itself,
pouring through the smallest fissures.   By the in-
domitable force of its nature air frees itself, and
especially when agitated it asserts its rights for itself.

But moving air is an unconquerable thing; nothing   4
will exist which

> Represses by authority
> Or restrains by chains and prison
> The winds when they struggle
> And the storms when they roar.[1]

Undoubtedly the poets wanted this place where   5
the winds lie shut in under the ground to be considered a prison.   But they did not understand that
what is shut in is no longer wind and that which is
wind cannot be shut in.   For whatever is in an
enclosure is at rest and is stationary atmosphere;
all wind is in flight.

And now to these arguments is added an analogy   6
which makes it obvious that an earthquake is brought
about by moving air: our bodies also do not tremble

aliqua causa perturbat, cum timore contractus est,
cum senectute languescit et venis torpentibus marcet,
cum frigore inhibetur aut sub accessionem cursu
7 suo deicitur. Nam, quamdiu sine iniuria perfluit
et ex more procedit, nullus est tremor corpori; cum
aliquid occurrit quod inhibeat eius officium, tunc
parum potens in perferendis his quae suo vigore
tenebat,[1] deficiens concutit quicquid integer tulerat.

1   19. Metrodorum Chium, quia necesse est, audia-
mus quod vult sententiae loco dicentem.   Non enim
permitto mihi ne eas quidem opiniones praeterire
quas improbo, cum satius sit omnium copiam fieri
et quae improbamus damnare potius quam praeterire.

2   Quid ergo dicit ?   Quomodo, cum in dolio cantatur [2]
vox vibrat,[3] illa [4] per totum cum quadam discussione
percurrit ac resonat et tam leviter mota [5] tamen circumit non sine iactu [6] eius tumultuque quo inclusa
est, sic speluncarum sub terra pendentium vastitas
habet aera suum, quem, simul alius superne incidens
percussit, agitat, non aliter quam illa de quibus paulo
ante rettuli inania indito clamore sonuerunt.

----

[1] *tenebat* C; *tendebat* most MSS. Oltramare, Alexander;
tendebant P.
[2] Salmasius, Alexander for *cantantis* MSS.; *cantat quis*
Madvig.
[3] *vibrat* supplied by Oltramare.
[4] *illa* MSS; *illabitur* Haase; *ululat* Gercke; *fit illa* Castiglioni.
[5] *morata* ABV.
[6] *iactu* Warmington for *tactu* MSS.

----

[1] Cicero (*Academica* 2.73) quotes a few lines from the *On
Nature* of Metrodorus of Chios and refers to him as the " greatest
admirer of Democritus."

except when some cause disturbs the air inside, when it is contracted by fear, grows weak in old age, becomes feeble with sluggish veins, is paralysed by cold, or is thrown from its normal course under an attack of disease. For, as long as the air flows without 7 damage and proceeds in its usual way, there is no tremor in the body; when something happens which inhibits its function, then it no longer is strong enough to support what it had maintained in its vigour. As it fails it causes to collapse whatever it had sustained when it was intact.

19. Let us listen, because we must, to Metro- 1 dorus [1] of Chios stating what he prefers in giving *his* view. I do not permit myself to pass over even those opinions of which I disapprove, since it is better that there be an abundance of all views and to condemn the ones we disapprove of rather than omit them.

Well, what does he say? When someone sings 2 into a large jar his voice vibrates and runs through the whole jar and resonates with a kind of quavering. Even though the voice is projected only slightly it none the less travels around and causes a jolting [2] and disturbance in the surrounding jar. In the same way the vast caves hanging down under the earth have air of their own, which other air, as soon as it falls from above, strikes and agitates, the way those empty spaces I just mentioned vibrate when a shout is sent into them.

[2] The MSS have *tactu* which may well be right (" contact with "); but, in view of *tumultu*, Warmington's suggestion *iactu* (" jolting " rather than " vibration ") has been adopted here.

SENECA

1   20. Veniamus nunc ad eos qui omnia ista quae rettuli in causa esse dixerunt aut ex his plura. Democritus plura putat. Ait enim motum aliquando spiritu fieri, aliquando aqua, aliquando utroque, et id hoc modo prosequitur. Aliqua pars terrae concava est; in hanc aquae magna vis confluit. Ex hac est aliquid tenue et ceteris liquidius. Hoc, cum superveniente gravitate reiectum est, illiditur terris et illas movet, nec enim fluctuari potest sine motu eius in quod impingitur.

2   Etiamnunc, quomodo de spiritu dicebamus, de aqua quoque dicendum est. Ubi in unum locum congesta est et capere se desiit, aliquo incumbit et primo viam pondere aperit, deinde impetu; nec enim exire nisi per devexum potest diu inclusa, nec in directum cadere moderate aut sine concussione eorum

3 per quae vel in quae cadit. Si vero, cum iam rapi coepit, aliquo loco subsistit et illa vis fluminis in se revoluta est, in continentem[1] terram repellitur et illam, qua parte maxime pendet, exagitat. Praeterea aliquando madefacta tellus liquore penitus accepto altius sedit et fundus ipse vitiatur; tunc ea pars premitur in quam maxime aquarum vergentium pondus inclinat.

4   Spiritus vero nonnumquam impellit undas et,

---

[1] *concurrentem* PABV.

---

[1] Aristotle's account of Democritus' theories makes no mention of air (2.7.365b 1–5). Presumably, Seneca obtained his information from some source other than Aristotle's *Meteorologica*.

20. Now we come to those writers who have stated 1
as a cause of earthquakes either all the elements I
mentioned or several of them. Democritus thinks
several.[1] For he says that an earthquake is produced sometimes by moving air, sometimes by
water, sometimes by both. He follows through on
his theory in this way: some parts of the earth
are hollow. A large quantity of water flows into
them. Some of this water is thin and accordingly
more fluid than the rest. When it is driven back by
the heavy mass coming upon it, it strikes against
the earth and causes it to move, for water cannot
fluctuate without causing what it shoves against to
move.

And now we must speak about water also in the 2
same way as we spoke about air. When it is accumulated in one place and ceases to restrain itself it inclines
in one direction and opens a path, at first by its weight,
then by its impetus. Having been enclosed for a
long time, it cannot go out except down a slope, and
is not able to fall straight down moderately or without a concussion of those things through which or
into which it falls. But when it has already begun 3
to be swept along, if it is halted at some place and the
force of its current is rolled back upon itself, it is
driven back against the earth containing it and attacks
any part of the earth that is especially unstable. In
addition, at times the earth becomes so saturated
with moisture collected deep within it that it settles
lower and its very foundations are weakened; then
the earth is overwhelmed at that point against which
the weight of converging waters leans most heavily.

In fact, air sometimes drives water and if it 4

si vehementius institit, eam scilicet partem terrae
movet in quam coactas aquas intulit; nonnumquam
in terrena itinera coniectus et exitum quaerens
movet omnia. Terra autem penetrabilis ventis est
et spiritus subtilior est quam ut possit excludi,
vehementior quam ut sustineri concitatus ac rapidus.[1]

5   Omnes istas esse posse causas Epicurus ait plu-
resque alias temptat et illos [2] qui aliquid unum ex
istis esse affirmaverunt corripit, cum sit arduum de his
quae coniectura assequenda [3] sunt aliquid certi
6 promittere. Ergo, ut ait, potest terram movere
aqua, si partes aliquas eluit et adrosit,[4] quibus desiit
posse extenuatis sustineri quod integris ferebatur.
Potest terram movere impressio spiritus; fortasse
enim aer extrinsecus alio intrante aere agitatur,
fortasse aliqua parte subito decidente percutitur et
inde motum capit. Fortasse aliqua pars terrae velut
columnis quibusdam ac pilis sustinetur, quibus
vitiatis [5] ac recedentibus tremit pondus impositum.
7 Fortasse calida vis spiritus in ignem versa et fulmini
similis cum magna strage obstantium fertur. Fortasse palustres et iacentes aquas aliquis flatus impellit et inde aut ictus terram quatit aut spiritus
agitatio ipso motu crescens et se incitans ab imo in

---

[1] *rabidus* Z.
[2] Gercke, Oltramare for *alios* MSS.
[3] Kroll, Gercke, Oltramare for *sequenda* MSS.
[4] *abrasit* E; *arrosit* ABV.
[5] *impulsis* ABV.

pushes strongly it obviously moves that part of the earth against which it carries the collected water. Sometimes the air is massed into subterranean passageways and in seeking an exit moves everything. Moreover, the earth is infiltrated by winds, and moving air is too subtle to be excluded, too violent to be resisted when it is aroused and swift-moving.

Epicurus says that all these things can be causes 5 and he tries several other causes. Also, he criticizes those who insist that some single one of them is the cause, since it is difficult to promise anything certain about theories which are based on conjecture. Therefore, as he says, water can cause an earthquake 6 if it washes away and erodes some parts of the earth. When these parts are weakened they cease to be able to sustain what they supported when they were intact. The pressure of moving air can cause earthquakes; for perhaps the air inside the earth is agitated by other air entering, perhaps the earth receives a shock when some part of it suddenly falls and from this the earth takes on movement. Perhaps some part of the earth is sustained by a sort of column, and by a kind of piling, and when they receive flaws or give way the weight imposed on them trembles. Perhaps a warm quantity of moving air 7 is changed to fire and like lightning is carried along with great destruction to things that stand in its way. Perhaps some blast pushes the swampy and stagnant waters and consequently either the blow shakes the earth or the agitation of the air increases by its very motion and, stirring itself up, travels all the way from the depths to the surface of the earth.

187

summa usque perfertur. Nullam tamen illi placet
causam motus esse maiorem quam spiritum.

1   21. Nobis quoque placet hunc spiritum esse qui
possit tanta conari, quo [1] nihil est in rerum natura
potentius, nihil acrius,[2] sine quo ne illa quidem quae
vehementissima sunt valent.   Ignem spiritus concitat.   Aquae, si ventum detrahas, inertes sunt;
tunc demum impetum sumunt, cum illas agit flatus.
Et potest dissipare magna terrarum spatia et novos
montes subiectus [3] extollere et insulas non ante
visas in medio mari ponere.   Theren et Therasiam
et [4] hanc nostrae aetatis insulam spectantibus nobis
in Aegaeo mari natam quis dubitat quin in lucem
spiritus vexerit?

2   Duo genera sunt, ut Posidonio placet, quibus
movetur   terra.   Utrique   nomen   est   proprium.
Altera succussio est, cum terra quatitur et sursum ac
deorsum movetur;   altera inclinatio, qua in latera [5]
nutat [6] alternis navigii more.   Ego et tertium illud

[1] *quia* ABV.
[2] *vi aeris* AB (instead of *nihil acrius*).
[3] *subiectos* HABV.
[4] Muret and Gercke after him read ⟨*Inter*⟩ *Theren et
Therasiam* [*et*].
[5] *in latera* ET; *in altera* HPZ; *alterum* AV.
[6] *mutat* AB.

---

[1] Aristotle 2.8.365b 30–366a 5: wind is the substance that
has the greatest motive power.

[2] An apparent contradiction with Bk. 5.5.2 where Seneca says
water has its own motion even when there are no winds.

[3] The last island (*spectantibus nobis*) of the three is not the
same as that which Seneca, on the authority of Posidonius,

At any rate, Epicurus is satisfied that air is the main cause of earthquakes.

21. We also are satisfied that it is this moving air 1 which can accomplish such things. Nothing in nature is more powerful than air, nothing more energetic.[1] Without air not even the strongest elements have power. Air arouses fire. Waters are inert [2] if you take away the wind; they acquire movement only when a blast of air drives them. Also, air is able to scatter vast expanses of the earth and to lift new mountains up from beneath and to place in the middle of the sea new islands never seen before. Does anyone doubt that air brought Thera and Therasia into the light of day, as well as that island which in our own time was born before our very eyes in the Aegean Sea? [3]

There are two ways in which the earth is moved, 2 according to Posidonius.[4] Each way has its distinctive term. One is a " jolt underneath," when the earth is shaken by a jolt and moves up and down. The other is a " tilt," when the earth leans to one side or the other like a ship. I am of the opinion

says in 2.26.4 rose from the sea *maiorum nostrorum memoria*. Pliny (2.202) gives a list of islands that emerged from the sea, with dates (although the numbers in his text are uncertain) including Thera and Therasia among the Cyclades in 197 B.C. and Thia " in our age " (*in nostro aevo*) July 8, A.D. 19 (in fact, Dec. 31, A.D. 46). Seneca here in 6.21.1 may be referring to Thia.

[4] Aristotle 2.8.368b 23–30: there are two types of earthquakes, horizontal and vertical. Ammianus (17.7.13) distinguishes four types: upheaving, sidewise, gaping, and bellowing. Cf. Pseudo-Aristotle, *De Mundo*, 4. Pliny (2.198) gives a variety of motions among which the safest is the vibrating and the dangerous is the kind that resembles a wave.

existimo quod nostro vocabulo signatum est. Non
enim sine causa tremorem terrae dixere maiores, qui
utrique dissimilis est; nam nec succutiuntur tunc
omnia nec inclinantur sed vibrantur, res minime in
eiusmodi casu noxia. Sicut longe perniciosior est
inclinatio succussione;[1] nam, nisi celeriter ex altera
parte properabit motus qui inclinata restituat, ruina
necessario sequitur.

1   22. Cum dissimiles hi motus inter se sint, causae
quoque eorum[2] diversae sunt. Prius ergo de motu
quatiente dicamus. Si quando magna onera per
vices vehiculorum plurium tracta sunt et rotae maiore
nisu in salebras inciderunt, terram concuti senties.

2   Asclepiodotus tradit: cum petra e latere montis
abrupta cecidisset, aedificia vicina tremore collapsa
sunt. Idem sub terris fieri potest ut ex his quae
impendent rupibus aliqua resoluta magno pondere
ac sono in subiacentem cavernam cadat, eo vehementius quo aut plus ponderis venit aut altius; et sic
commovetur omne tectum cavatae vallis.

3   Nec tantum pondere suo abscindi saxa credibile
est sed, cum flumina supra ferantur, assiduus umor
commissuras lapidis extenuat et cotidie aliquid his ad
quae religatus est aufert et illam, ut ita dicam, cutem
qua continetur abradit. Deinde longa per aevum
deminutio usque eo infirmat illa quae cotidie atterit

----

[1] *succussione* ABV; *concussione* most MSS.
[2] *quoque eorum* Gronovius, Gercke, Oltramare for *quorum*
most MSS.

that there is also a third way, which is designated in our vocabulary. Our elders for good reason spoke about the earth's " tremor," which is unlike the other two, for at such a time things are neither jolted nor tilted but vibrated. In an event of this sort the result is minimal damage. In the same way, a tilt is far more destructive than a jolt, for unless a movement which restores the tilt rushes in quickly from the other side a collapse necessarily follows.

22. Since these movements are dissimilar among 1 themselves their causes are also different. First, therefore, let us talk about a jolting movement. If at any time heavy loads are drawn by a series of several vehicles, and their wheels, because of the greater strain, slip into ruts in the road, you will feel the ground quake.

Asclepiodotus reports: when rocks were torn from 2 the side of a mountain and fell the buildings in the vicinity collapsed because of the resulting shock. The same thing can happen under the earth with the result that from overhanging cliffs something may be loosened and fall with a great crash and noise into the cavern lying below. The greater the weight or the height the more violently it comes down. And thus the whole roof of the underground valley is moved.

It is credible that rocks are not only split off by their 3 own weight but also when liquid travels over them the continuous moisture weakens the joints in the stone and day by day carries away something of the mass to which the stone is attached and abrades the skin, so to speak, by which the stone is held in place. Finally, the prolonged attrition through the ages weakens those parts which it wears into day by day to

4 ut desinant esse oneri ferendo. Tunc saxa vasti
ponderis decidunt; tunc illa praecipitata rupes quicquid mobilis rei percussit [1] non passura consistere

Cum sonitu venit, et ruere omnia visa repente,

ut ait Vergilius noster.

1 23. Huius motus succutientis terras haec erit
causa; ad alteram transeo. Rara terrae natura est
multumque habens vacui; per has raritates spiritus
fertur, qui, ubi maior influxit nec emittitur, concutit
terram.

2 Haec placet et aliis, ut paulo ante rettuli, causa—
si quid apud te profectura testium turba est. Hanc
etiam Callisthenes probat, non contemptus vir; fuit
enim illi nobile ingenium et furibundi regis im-
patiens. Hic est Alexandri crimen aeternum, quod
nulla virtus, nulla bellorum felicitas redimet. Nam

3 quotiens quis dixerit, "Occidit Persarum multa
milia," opponetur ei: "Et Callisthenen." Quotiens
dictum erit, "Occidit Darium, penes quem tum
maximum regnum erat," opponetur ei: "Et
Callisthenen." Quotiens dictum erit, "Omnia

---

[1] *mobilis rei percussit* Oltramare for *ab illo repercussit*
most MSS.

---

[1] Lucretius 6.544–545: "the earth above trembles and
collapses in great ruin when age undermines the vast caverns
under the ground."

[2] Virgil *Aen.* 8.525.

[3] Seneca never gives an account of the third type, the
tremor.

the extent that they cease to function in supporting a burden.[1] Then rocks of vast weight fall down; then 4 the crag falling headlong will not permit any movable object it strikes to continue at rest.

> It comes with a roar
> And everything is seen
> To collapse suddenly,[2]

as our Virgil says.

23. This must be the cause of the motion that 1 makes the ground quake from beneath. Now I pass on to the second type.[3] The earth is naturally porous and has many voids. Air passes through these openings. When air in large quantities flows in and is not emitted it causes the earth to tilt.

This theory is accepted by others, as I mentioned 2 a little above—if a crowd of authorities will impress you—but is also approved by Callisthenes, and he is a man not to be looked down upon. For he had outstanding intelligence and did not submit to the rage of his king. The murder of Callisthenes [4] is the everlasting crime of Alexander, which no virtue, no success in war, will redeem. For when someone says, 3 " Alexander killed many thousands of Persians," the countering reply to him will be: " And Callisthenes, too." Whenever it is said: " Alexander killed Darius, who had the greatest kingdom at that time," the reply will be: " And he killed Callisthenes, too." Whenever it is said, " He conquered

[4] Because Callisthenes refused to prostrate himself before Alexander he was imprisoned until his death. Seneca may well be thinking of his own situation as a philosopher in the court of Nero.

Oceano tenus vicit, ipsum quoque temptavit novis classibus et imperium ex angulo Thraciae usque ad Orientis terminos protulit," dicetur: " Sed Callisthenen occidit." Omnia licet antiqua ducum regumque exempla transierit, ex his quae fecit nihil tam magnum erit quam scelus.

4   Hic Callisthenes in libris quibus describit quemadmodum Helice Burisque mersae sint—quis illas casus in mare vel in illas mare immiserit—dicit id quod in priore parte dictum est. Spiritus intrat terram per occulta foramina, quemadmodum ubique, ita et sub mari; deinde, cum obstructus ille est trames per quem descenderat, reditum autem illi a tergo resistens aqua abstulit, huc et illuc refertur et sibi ipse occurrens terram labefactat. Ideo frequentissime mari apposita vexantur et inde Neptuno haec assignata est maris [1] movendi potentia. Quisquis primas litteras [2] didicit [3] scit illum apud Homerum [4] Ἐνοσίχθονα [5] vocari.

1   24. Spiritum esse huius mali causam et ipse consentio. De illo disputabo quomodo intret hic spiritus, utrum per tenuia foramina nec oculis comprehensibilia an per maiora ac patentiora, et utrum ab imo an etiam per summa terrarum.

2   Hoc incredibile est. Nam in nostris quoque cor-

---

[1] *terras* Z.
[2] *litteras grecas* ET.
[3] *didicit Graecorum* ABV.
[4] *Homerum* ZJK; *horum* HP; *eos* AB.
[5] Fickert for *mesibipthona* HP; *sibi pthona* Z; *mesiptona* ABV.

everything all the way to the ocean and even made an attack on the ocean itself with ships unknown to that water; and he extended his empire from a corner of Thrace all the way to the farthest boundaries of the East," it will be said: "But he killed Callisthenes." Although he went beyond all the achievements in antiquity of generals and kings, of the things which he did nothing will be as great as his crime.

This Callisthenes, in books in which he describes 4 how Helice and Buris were inundated—what disaster sent the cities into the sea or the sea into the cities [1]—says what I said in an earlier section.[2] Air enters the earth through hidden openings as it does everywhere and so also under the sea. Then, when the path through which it had descended is obstructed and the waters standing at the rear have cut off its return it is carried here and there and running into itself causes the earth to totter. So, the regions close by the sea are the most frequently harassed. Accordingly, this power the sea has for moving the earth is assigned to Neptune. Anyone who has learned elementary literature knows that in Homer he is called the "Earthshaker."

24. And I myself agree that the cause of this 1 disaster is air. But I will argue about how this air enters the earth, whether through thin openings indetectable to the eyes or through larger and more extended openings, and whether it comes only from the depths or also through the surface of the earth.

This last is unbelievable. For even in our bodies 2

---

[1] Pliny 2.206: in the Gulf of Corinth traces of Helice and Buris are visible at the bottom of the water. (They were destroyed by earthquake in 373 B.C.)

[2] Above, in Chapter Four.

poribus cutis spiritum respuit nec est illi introitus nisi per quae trahitur, nec consistere quidem a nobis receptus potest nisi in laxiore corporis parte; non enim inter nervos pulpasve sed in visceribus et patulo
3 interioris partis recessu commoratur. Idem de terra suspicari licet vel ex hoc quod motus non in summa terra circave summam est sed subter et ab imo. Huius indicium est quod altitudinis profundae maria iactantur, motis scilicet his supra quae fusa sunt; ergo verisimile est terram ex alto moveri et illic spiritum in cavernis ingentibus concipi.

4 " Immo! " inquit.[1] " Ceu, cum frigore inhorruimus, tremor sequitur, sic terras quoque spiritus extrinsecus accidens quassat." Quod nullo modo potest fieri. Algere enim debet, ut idem illi accidat quod nobis, quos externa causa in horrorem agit. Accidere autem terrae simile quiddam nostrae affectioni, sed non ex simili causa concesserim. Illam interior et
5 altior iniuria debet impellere. Cuius rei argumentum vel maximum hoc potest esse quod, cum vehementi motu adapertum ingenti ruina solum est, totas nonnumquam urbes et recipit hiatus ille et abscondit.

6 Thucydides ait circa Peloponnesiaci belli tempus Atalanten insulam aut totam aut certe maxima ex parte suppressam. Idem Sidone accidisse Posidonio crede. Nec ad hoc testibus opus est; meminimus

[1] *inquis* E.

---

[1] Thucydides (3.89.3) refers to a tidal wave.

the skin keeps out the air, and air has no way in except by way of the parts through which it is breathed in, and even when it has been inhaled by us it cannot settle except in the relatively open part of the body. For it does not remain within the sinews or flesh but in the viscera and the wide cavity of the interior region. The same may be supposed about 3 the earth from the fact also that an earthquake is not in the earth's surface or around the surface but underneath, from the depths. An indication of this is that seas of great depth are tossed about obviously from the motion of the ground over which the seas spread. Accordingly, it is probable that the earth is moved from far below and that air is formed there in huge caverns.

" But no! " he says. " When we shiver with cold, 4 a trembling is the result. So also air coming from outside causes the earth to shake." This cannot happen to the earth at all. For the earth ought to feel cold so that the same thing happens to it as happens to us when an external cause produces a shuddering. I would agree that something similar to our condition occurs to the earth, but from a different cause. An interior injury has to afflict the earth deep inside. The greatest proof of my argument can be 5 this: when the ground is opened by the enormous destruction of an earthquake, that gaping hole sometimes takes in and buries entire cities.

Thucydides says that around the time of the 6 Peloponnesian War the island of Atalanta was either entirely submerged, or certainly most of it.[1] Believe Posidonius that the same thing happened at Sidon. Yet there is no need of authorities in regard to this,

enim terris interno motu divulsis loca disiecta et campos interisse.

Quod iam dicam quemadmodum existimem fieri.

1 25. Cum spiritus magna vi vacuum terrarum locum penitus opplevit coepitque rixari et de exitu cogitare, latera ipsa inter quae latet saepius percutit, supra quae urbes interdum sitae sunt. Haec nonnumquam adeo concutiuntur ut aedificia superposita procumbant, nonnumquam in tantum ut parietes quibus fertur omne tegimen[1] cavi decidant in illum subtervacantem locum totaeque urbes in immensam altitudinem vergant.

2 Si velis credere, aiunt aliquando Ossam Olympo cohaesisse, deinde terrarum motu recessisse et fissam unius magnitudinem montis in duas partes. Tunc effluxisse[2] Peneon, qui paludes quibus laborabat Thessalia siccavit, abductis in se quae sine exitu stagnaverant aquis. Ladon flumen inter Elin et Megalenpolin medius est, quem terrarum motus effudit.

3 Per haec quid probo? In laxos specus (quid enim aliud appellem loca vacua?) sub terras spiritum convenire; quod nisi esset, magna terrarum spatia commoverentur et una multa titubarent. Nunc exiguae partes laborant nec umquam per ducenta

---

[1] *regimen* A¹B.
[2] Fortunatus, Gercke, Oltramare for *effugisse* MSS.

for within our own memory lands have been torn apart by internal movement and regions have been separated and plains have disappeared.

Now I will explain how I believe that this happens.

25. When moving air with great force completely 1 fills an empty space under the earth and proceeds to struggle and think about a way out it repeatedly strikes the side-walls within which it lurks, over which cities are sometimes situated.[1] These " walls " are sometimes so shaken that buildings placed above them fall down, sometimes to such an extent that the walls which support the whole covering of the cave fall into the vacant space underground and entire cities collapse into the immense depths.

If you are willing to believe it, they say that at one 2 time Ossa was joined to Olympus; later they were separated by an earthquake and the whole of a single large mountain was split into two parts. Then the Peneus River flowed away and dried up the swamps (from which Thessaly used to suffer) by carrying off in itself the waters that had once formed stagnant pools, since they had no way out. An earthquake poured forth the Ladon River, which is midway between Elis and Megalepolis.

What do I prove by these things? That air 3 accumulates under the earth in vast caverns (for what else should I call empty places?). Unless this were so, great expanses of the earth would be shaken and many regions would be disturbed at the same time. As it is now, only small areas suffer and an earthquake

---

[1] Seneca attributes this theory to Archelaus, above, in Chapter 12.1. Lucan (3.459–461) describes the wind, seeking to break out, shaking the hollow caverns of the earth.

milia motus extenditur. Ecce hic, qui implevit
4 fabulis orbem, non transcendit Campaniam. Quid
dicam, cum Chalcis tremuit, Thebas stetisse; cum
laboravit Aegium, tam propinquas illi Patras de motu
solum [1] audisse? Illa vasta concussio quae duas
suppressit urbes, Helicen et Burin, circa Aegium
constitit. Apparet ergo in tantum spatium motum
pertendere quantum illa sub terris vacantis loci
inanitas pateat.

1   26. Poteram ad hoc probandum abuti auctoritate
magnorum virorum qui Aegyptum numquam tremuisse tradunt. Rationem autem huius rei hanc
reddunt quod ex limo tota concreverit. Tantum
enim, si Homero fides est, aberat a continenti Pharos
quantum navis diurno cursu metiri plenis lata velis
potest. Sed continenti ammota est. Turbidus
enim defluens Nilus multumque secum caeni trahens
et id subinde apponens prioribus terris Aegyptum
annuo incremento semper ultra tulit. Inde pinguis
et limosi soli est nec ulla intervalla in se habet, sed
crevit in solidum arescente limo, cuius pressa erat et
sedens structura, cum partes glutinarentur; nec
quicquam inane intervenire poterat, cum solido
liquidum ac molle semper accederet.

---

[1] de motu solum audisse ABV; audisse de motu Z; de motu
nihil audisse ET.

---

[1] Pliny 2.195: Egypt suffers very little from earthquakes
because of the summers there.
[2] *Odyssey* 4.354. Pliny 2.201: "the crossing from the

does not extend two hundred miles. That recent earthquake, which has filled the world with stories, did not travel beyond Campania. Why should I explain that when Chalcis trembled, Thebes stood firm; when Aegium suffered, Patrae, so near it, only heard about the earthquake? The vast shock which smashed two cities, Helice and Buris, stopped around Aegium. Therefore, it appears that an earthquake spreads over only as much area as the cavity of empty space extends under the earth. 4

26. In order to prove this I could have used, or misused, the authority of great men who report that Egypt has never had an earthquake.[1] They give the following explanation of this phenomenon: the fact that Egypt has grown entirely from mud. For, if there is any reliability in Homer, Pharos was as far away from the continent as a ship travelling with full sails could measure in one day's journey.[2] But Pharos has been moved up to the continent.[3] The swollen Nile as it flows down carries with it a great quantity of mud and adds it from time to time to the existing land and by annual increment always carries Egypt farther out. Hence the land is a rich, muddy soil and does not have within itself any openings but grows into a solid as the mud dries. Its structure was compressed sediment when the parts were glued together; nor can any empty space intervene since liquid and soft substance is always added to the solid material. 1

island of Pharos to the coast, if we believe Homer, formerly took a day and a night."

[3] In Caesar's time Pharos was connected with Alexandria by a narrow roadway like a bridge (*Bel. Civ.* 3.112).

2   Sed movetur et Aegyptus et Delos, quam Vergilius
stare iussit:

    Immotamque coli dedit et contemnere ventos.

Hanc philosophi quoque, credula natio, dixerunt non
moveri auctore Pindaro. Thucydides ait antea
quidem immotam fuisse sed circa Peloponnesiacum
3 bellum tremuisse. Callisthenes et alio tempore ait
hoc accidisse. " Inter multa," inquit, " prodigia
quibus denuntiata est duarum urbium, Helices et
Buris, eversio, fuere maxime notabilia columna ignis
immensi et Delos agitata." Quam ideo stabilem
videri vult, quia mari imposita sit habeatque con-
cavas rupes [1] et saxa pervia, quae dent deprehenso
aeri reditum; ob hoc et insulas esse certioris soli
urbesque eo tutiores quo propius ad mare accesserint.
4   Falsa haec esse Pompei et Herculaneum sensere.
Adice nunc quod omnis ora maris obnoxia est motibus.
Sic Paphos non semel corruit; sic nobilis [2] et huic
iam familiaris malo Nicopolis; Cyprum ambit altum

---

[1] *ripas* ABV.
[2] *mobilis* Z Alexander.

---

[1] Virgil *Aen.* 3.77. Virgil tells the story that Delos was a
floating island which Apollo bound fast and arranged to be
" unmoving " (*immotam*). Seneca gives *immotam* a different
meaning in order to suit his argument.

But Egypt does have earthquakes, and so does 2
Delos, which Virgil ordered to stand still:

> He arranged that it be tilled,
> A land without earthquake
> And scorning the winds.[1]

Philosophers, a credulous race, have also said, on
Pindar's authority,[2] that Delos did not have earthquakes. Thucydides says that Delos was previously
indeed stable but had an earthquake around the
time of the Peloponnesian War.[3] Callisthenes says 3
that this happened at another time, too. "Among
the many prodigies," he says, "by which the destruction of the two cities, Helice and Buris, was foretold,
especially notable were both the immense columns
of fire and the Delos earthquake." He wishes Delos
to be understood as stable because it is placed upon
the sea and has hollow cliffs and porous rocks to give
a way back for the air caught in them.[4] And for this
reason islands have firm ground and the closer cities
come to the sea the safer they are.

Pompeii and Herculaneum know that this is not 4
true. Now add that every seashore is subject to
earthquakes. For example, Paphos has collapsed
more than once. The famous Nicopolis has already
become familiar with this catastrophe also. Deep
sea surrounds Cyprus, and Cyprus has earthquakes.

---

[2] Pindar fr. 28 Christ. Herodotus (6.98) tells of an earthquake at Delos just before the Battle of Marathon.

[3] Thucydides (2.8) says Delos had not previously had an
earthquake within the memory of the Hellenes.

[4] Pliny (2.197) gives the remedy for earthquakes: wells,
caves, conduits for drainage, underground vaults—as in
Naples—which provide outlets for the confined air.

mare et agitatur;[1] Tyros et ipsa tam movetur quam diluitur.

Hae fere causae redduntur propter quas tremat terra.

1 27. Quaedam tamen propria in hoc Campano motu accidisse narrantur, quorum ratio reddenda est. Diximus [2] sexcentarum ovium gregem exanimatum in Pompeiana regione. Non est quare hoc putes 2 ovibus illis timore accidisse. Aiunt enim [3] solere post magnos terrarum motus pestilentiam fieri, nec id mirum est. Multa enim mortifera in alto latent. Aer ipse, qui vel terrarum culpa vel pigritia et aeterna nocte torpescit, gravis haurientibus est, vel corruptus internorum ignium vitio, cum e longo situ emissus est, purum hunc liquidumque maculat ac polluit insuetumque ducentibus spiritum affert nova genera morborum.

3 Quid quod aquae quoque inutiles pestilentesque in abdito latent, ut quas numquam usus exerceat, numquam aura liberior everberet? Crassae itaque et gravi caligine sempiternaque tectae nihil nisi pestiferum in se et corporibus nostris contrarium habent. Aer quoque, qui mixtus est illis quique inter illas paludes iacet, cum emersit, late vitium 4 suum spargit et haurientes necat. Facilius autem pecora sentiunt, in quae primum pestilentia incur-

---

[1] *agitatur* HPEABV; *agitata* Z; *agitat* Gercke, Oltramare.
[2] Gercke, Oltramare for *aiunt enim* MSS.
[3] Gercke, Oltramare for *diximus* MSS.

Tyre, too, is as much shaken by earthquakes as it is washed away by the sea.[1]

Such are the reasons generally given for why the earth trembles.

27. Yet certain things are said to have happened 1 peculiar to this Campanian earthquake, and they need to be explained. I have said [2] that a flock of hundreds of sheep was killed in the Pompeian district. There is no reason you should think this happened to those sheep because of fear. For they say that a plague 2 usually occurs after a great earthquake, and this is not surprising. For many death-carrying elements lie hidden in the depths. The very atmosphere there, which is stagnant either from some flaw in the earth or from inactivity and the eternal darkness, is harmful to those breathing it. Or, when it has been tainted by the poison of the internal fires and is sent out from its long stay it stains and pollutes this pure, clear atmosphere and offers new types of disease to those who breathe the unfamiliar air.

What about the fact that also unwholesome and 3 deadly waters lurk in hidden places, since use never exercises them, a fresh free breeze never stirs them up? As a consequence they are thick and covered by a heavy and eternal fog and contain only what is pestilential and contrary to our systems. Also, the atmosphere which is mixed with them and lies in those marshes, when it emerges, scatters its poison far and wide and kills those who breathe it. More- 4 over, the flocks, which the pestilence usually attacks

---

[1] Pliny 2.194: seaboard districts are more subject to earthquakes.

[2] Above, in Chapter 1.3.

rere solet, quo avidiora sunt; aperto caelo plurimum utuntur et aquis, quarum maxima in pestilentia culpa est. Oves vero mollioris naturae, quo propiora terris ferunt capita, correptas esse non miror, cum afflatus aeris diri circa ipsam humum exceperint. Nocuisset ille et hominibus, si maior exisset; sed illum sinceri aeris copia extinxit, antequam ut ab homine posset trahi surgeret.

1   28. Multas autem terras habere mortifera vel ex hoc intellege quod tot venena nascuntur non manu sparsa sed sponte, solo scilicet habente ut boni ita mali semina. Quid quod pluribus Italiae locis per quaedam foramina pestilens exhalatur vapor quem non homini ducere, non ferae tutum est? Aves quoque, si in illum inciderunt, antequam caelo meliore leniatur, in ipso volatu cadunt liventque corpora et non aliter quam per vim elisaé fauces tument.

2   Hic spiritus, quamdiu terra se continet,[1] tenui foramine fluens non plus potentiae habet quam ut despectantia et ultro sibi illata conficiat. Ubi per saecula conditus[2] tenebris ac tristitia loci crevit in vitium, ipsa ingravescit mora, peior quo segnior;

---

[1] *terra se continet* Z Oltramare; *terras continet* HPEV; *terra continetur* AB; *terra continet* Gercke.

[2] Haase, Gercke, Oltramare for *cónditis* MSS.

first, feel its effects more readily the greedier they are. Out in the open air they drink large amounts of water, in which there is the guilt of the greatest poison in time of pestilence. I am not surprised that sheep have been infected—sheep which have a delicate constitution—the closer they carried their heads to the ground, since they received the afflatus of the tainted air near the ground itself. If the air had come out in greater quantity it would have harmed people too; but the abundance of pure air extinguished it before it rose high enough to be breathed by people.

28. But you can understand that many lands have **1** death-dealing things from the fact that so many poisons grow spontaneously, not scattered by hand, soil obviously having seeds of sickness as well as of good health. What about this?—In several places in Italy a pestilential vapour is exhaled through certain openings, which is safe neither for people nor for wild animals to breathe.[1] Also, if birds encounter the vapour before it is softened by better weather they fall in mid-flight and their bodies are livid and their throats swollen as though they had been violently strangled.

As long as this air keeps itself inside the earth, **2** flowing out only from a narrow opening, it has power only to kill the creatures which look down into it and voluntarily enter it. When it has been hidden for ages in the dismal darkness underground it grows into poison, becomes more deadly by the very delay, becomes worse the more sluggish it is. When it

---

[1] Pliny (2.207–208) lists the places in Italy where deadly vapours are emitted, such as at Pozzuoli.

cum exitum nactus est, aeternum illud umbrosi
frigoris malum et infernam noctem volvit ac regionis [1]
nostrae aera infuscat. Vincuntur enim meliora
3 peioribus. Tunc etiam ille spiritus purior transit in
noxium;[2] inde subitae continuaeque mortes et mon-
struosa genera morborum, ut ex novis orta causis.
Brevis autem aut longa clades est, prout vitia valuere,
nec prius pestilentia desinit quam spiritum illum
gravem exercuit laxitas caeli ventorumque iactatio.

1   29. Nam quod[3] aliquos[4] insanis attonitisque similes
discurrere fecit metus. Qui excutit mentes, ubi
privatus ac modicus est. Quid? Ubi publice terret,
ubi cadunt urbes, populi opprimuntur, terra concutitur, quid mirum est animos inter dolorem et
2 metum destitutos aberrasse? Non est facile inter
magna mala consipere.[5] Itaque levissima fere
ingenia in tantum venere formidinis ut sibi exciderent.
Nemo quidem sine aliqua iactura sanitatis expavit,
similisque est furentis quisquis timet; sed alios cito
timor sibi reddit, alios vehementius perturbat et
3 in dementiam transfert. Inde inter bella erravere
lymphatici, nec usquam plura exempla vaticinantium
invenies quam ubi formido mentes religione mixta
percussit.

1   30. Statuam divisam non miror, cum dixerim

[1] *religionis* Z.
[2] *noxium* PKABV Gercke; *noxam* HE[2]Z Haase, Oltramare;
noxiam E[1]O.
[3] *quod* omitted OT.

has found a way out it lets fly the eternal evil and
infernal night of gloomy cold and stains darkly the
atmosphere of our region. For the better is conquered by the worse. Then even pure air changes 3
into noxious air; from it come sudden and continuous
deaths and monstrous types of disease arising from
unknown causes. Moreover, the disaster is brief
or long according to the strength of the poison, nor
does the pestilence stop before the clearing of the sky
and the tossing of the winds have purified that deadly
air.

29. Now, fear has made some people run around 1
as though insane or panic-stricken. Even when fear
is confined to individuals and is moderate it shatters
minds. What then? When there is public panic,
when cities fall, when populations are crushed, the
earth shaken, what wonder is it that minds wander
bereft between grief and fear? It is not easy to 2
keep one's wits during great disasters. As a result,
generally the most unstable personalities develop
such fear that they lose control of themselves. But
in fact, no one undergoes terror without a loss of
sanity and whoever is afraid is like a madman. Yet
fear brings some back to their senses quickly while it
disturbs others greatly and carries them over into
insanity. This is why during war people wander 3
about maddened, and you will never find more examples of prophecy than when fear mixed with religion strikes the mind.

30. I am not surprised that a statue was split apart 1

---

⁴ *aliquos* MSS; *aliquot* Erasmus, Oltramare, Alexander.
⁵ *concipere* ABV; *non desipere* ET.

montes a montibus recessisse et ipsum disruptum
esse ab imo solum.

Haec loca vi qondam et vasta convulsa ruina
(Tantum aevi longinqua valet mutare vetustas)
Dissiluisse ferunt, cum protinus utraque tellus
Una foret.   Venit ingenti [1] vi pontus et ingens [2]
Hesperium Siculo latus abscidit arvaque et urbes
Aequore [3] diductas angusto interluit aestu.

2   Vides totas regiones a suis sedibus revelli et trans
mare iacere quod in confinio fuerat; vides et urbium
fieri gentiumque discidium, cum pars naturae concita
est et aliquo mare, ignem, spiritum impegit.   Quorum
mira ut ex toto vis est; quamvis enim parte
3   saeviat, mundi tamen viribus saevit. Sic et
Hispanias a contextu Africae mare eripuit, sic per
hanc inundationem quam poetarum maximi cele-
brant ab Italia Sicilia reiecta est.   Aliquanto autem
plus impetus habent quae ex infimo veniunt; acriora
enim sunt quibus nisus est per angusta.

4   Quantas res hi terrarum tremores quamque mira

---

[1] *medio* Virgil.
[2] *undis* Virgil.
[3] *litore* Virgil.

---

[1] Virgil *Aen.* 3.414–419. Seneca has changed three words
in two lines of the quotation.
[2] Pliny 2.204: "nature" tore Sicily away from Italy.

in an earthquake since I have described how mountains were separated from mountains and the ground
itself was disrupted all the way from its depths.

> Once these lands were convulsed
> By vast destructive forces.
> So much
> Is the long duration of time
> Able to change things.
> They say the lands leaped apart,
> Although from the very first
> Both had been one.
> The great sea came with enormous violence
> And split Italy from Sicily
> And flowed with its narrow channel
> Between fields and cities
> Which had been separated
> By the sea.[1]

You see entire regions torn from their places and 2
what had been close by lying on the other side of the
sea. You see cities and nations split asunder when
part of nature is aroused and has driven the sea, or
fire, or air forwards to some point. Their strength is
astounding since it comes from the whole; for although it rages only in one section it none the less
rages with the force of the universe. For example, 3
the sea also ripped Spain from its connection to
Africa. Also, Sicily was cut off from Italy [2] by that
flood which the greatest poets celebrate. But the
currents which come from underground have considerably greater force, for a struggle through narrow
areas makes things more violent.

Enough has been said about what marvels these 4

spectacula ediderint, satis dictum est; cur ergo aliquis ad hoc stupet quod aes unius statuae, ne solidum quidem sed concavum ac tenue, disruptum est, cum fortasse in illud se spiritus quaerens fugam incluserit? Illud vero quis nescit? Diductis aedificia angulis vidimus moveri iterumque componi. Quaedam vero parum aptata positu suo et a fabris neglegentius solutiusque composita terrae motus saepius agitata compegit.

5 Quod si totos parietes et totas findit domos et latera magnarum turrium, quamvis solida sint, scindit et pilas operibus subditas dissipat, quid est quare quisquam dignum adnotari putet sectam esse aequaliter ab imo ad caput in partes duas statuam?

1 31. Quare tamen per plures dies motus fuit? Non desiit enim assidue tremere Campania, clementius quidem, sed cum ingenti damno, quia quassa quatiebat, quibus ad cadendum male stantibus opus [1] non erat impelli sed agitari. Nondum videlicet spiritus omnis exierat, sed adhuc, emissa sui parte maiore, oberrabat. Inter argumenta quibus probatur spiritu ista fieri non est quod dubites et hoc 2 ponere: cum maximus editus tremor est, quo in

---

[1] *opus* added by Madvig, Gercke, Oltramare.

---

[1] Pliny 2.198: earthquakes stop when the wind has found an outlet. If they go on they do not stop for forty days, usually longer, and some have gone on for one or two years.

tremors of the earth do and how they produce
amazing sights.   Then why is anyone astonished that
the bronze of a single statue, not even solid but hollow
and thin, has been shattered, when perhaps moving
air in seeking a way out has shut itself up inside that
statue? But who does not know this? We have
seen buildings with their corners split move apart
and come back together again.   Moreover, some
things that were not fitted in their place and were
made rather carelessly and loosely by artisans have
been fastened together by the repeated shaking
of an earthquake.

But if an earthquake cracks whole walls and entire   5
homes and splits the sides of great towers, however
solid they might be, and scatters pilings that support
great structures, what reason is there that anyone
should think it worth noting that a statue has been
cut equally in two from top to bottom?

31. Yet why has an earthquake lasted for several   1
days?[1]   For Campania did not cease its continuous
trembling; the earthquake became milder but still
caused great damage because it shook things already
shaken, and since they were scarcely standing, and
were ready to fall, they did not need to be pushed
but only to be shaken.   Obviously all the air had not
yet left but was still wandering around, even though
the greater part of it had been emitted.   Among
the arguments that prove earthquakes happen because of moving air this is one you should not hesitate
to propose also: when the greatest tremor to spend   2

Aristotle (2.8.367b 31) says they frequently continue for forty
days or so, and symptoms appear subsequently for one or two
years in the same district.

urbes terrasque saevitum est, non potest par illi
subsequi alius, sed post maximum lenes motus sunt,
quia iam vehementius exitum ventis luctantibus
fecit; reliquiae deinde residui spiritus non idem
possunt, nec illis pugna opus est, cum iam viam in-
venerint sequanturque ea qua prima vis ac maxima
evasit.[1]

3   Hoc quoque dignum memoria iudico ab eruditissimo
et gravissimo viro cognitum.   Forte enim, cum hoc
evenit, lavabatur.   Vidisse se affirmat in balneo
tessellas quibus solum erat stratum alteram ab altera
separari itemque committi et aquam modo recipi in
commissuras pavimento recedente, modo compresso
bullire et elidi.   Eundem audivi narrantem vidisse
se macerias [2] mollius crebriusque tremere quam natura
duri sinit.

1   32. Haec, Lucili, virorum optime, quantum ad
ipsas causas; illa nunc quae ad confirmationem
animorum pertinent.   Quos magis refert nostra
fortiores fieri quam doctiores.   Sed alterum sine
altero non fit; non enim aliunde animo venit robur
quam a bonis artibus, quam a contemplatione
2   naturae. Quem enim non hic ipse casus adversus
omnes firmaverit et erexerit?   Quid est enim cur ego
hominem aut feram, quid est cur sagittam aut lan-
ceam tremam? Maiora me pericula expectant:

----

[1] *impellit* ABV.
[2] Kroll, Gercke, Oltramare for *materias* MSS.

its rage against cities and countries has been produced, another equal to it cannot follow. After the largest shock there are only gentle quakes because the first tremor, acting with greater vehemence, has created an exit for the struggling air. The remains of the air that is left do not have the same force, nor do they have any need to struggle, since already they have found a path and follow the route by which the first and largest force of air escaped.

I consider this also worth recording, since it was 3 observed by a very wise and respected man. He happened to be taking a bath when this earthquake occurred. He affirms that while in the bath he saw the tiles with which the floor was paved separate one from the other and come back together again, and that when the floor opened up water was taken into the joints and when it closed back together the water bubbled and was forced out. I have heard the same person telling that he saw earthen walls vibrating more gently and rhythmically than the nature of a hard substance permits.

32. So much for these explanations, Lucilius, my 1 good friend, concerning the causes of earthquakes; now to those things which pertain to the reassurance of the mind. It is more important for us to be brave than to be learned. But the one does not occur without the other, for strength comes to the mind only from the liberal arts and the study of nature. For 2 example, has not this very disaster in Campania made every man strengthened and resolute against all catastrophes? Why should I fear man or wild beast, why should I fear arrow or spear? Greater dangers lie in wait for me: we are attacked by

fulminibus [1] et terris et magnis naturae apparatibus [2]
3 petimur. Ingenti itaque animo mors provocanda
est, sive nos aequo vastoque impetu aggreditur, sive
cotidiano et vulgari exitu. Nihil refert quam minax
veniat quantumque sit quod in nos trahat; quod a
nobis petit minimum est. Hoc senectus a nobis
ablatura est, hoc auriculae dolor, hoc umoris in
nobis corrupti abundantia, hoc cibus parum obse-
quens stomacho, hoc pes leviter offensus.

4 Pusilla res est hominis anima, sed ingens res
contemptus animae. Hanc qui contempsit securus
videbit maria turbari, etiamsi illa omnes excitaverunt
venti, etiamsi aestus aliqua perturbatione mundi
totum in terras vertet oceanum; securus aspiciet
fulminantis caeli trucem atque horridam faciem,
frangatur licet caelum et ignes suos in exitium
omnium, in primis suum misceat; securus aspiciet
ruptis compagibus dehiscens solum, illa licet infero-
rum regna retegantur. Stabit super illam voraginem
intrepidus et fortasse quo debebit cadere desiliet.

5 Quid ad me quam magna sint quibus pereo?
Ipsum perire non magnum est. Proinde, si volumus
esse felices, si nec hominum nec deorum nec rerum
timore versari, si despicere fortunam supervacua
promittentem, levia minitantem, si volumus tran-
quille degere et ipsis diis de felicitate controversiam

---

[1] *fluminibus* J²ABV Alexander.
[2] Oltramare for *partibus* MSS.

lightning bolts, earthquakes, and the vast prepared equipment of nature. Therefore, death must be 3 challenged with great courage whether it assails us with a great attack which is universal, or with a death which is a daily and common occurrence. It does not matter how threateningly it comes or how great the disaster to which it drags us. What it seeks from us is insignificant. Old age will likely take it away from us, an earache, an abundance of corrupt moisture in our bodies, food poorly suited to the stomach, a foot lightly injured.

The life of man is an insignificant thing, but con- 4 tempt for life is a great thing. The man who has contempt for life will gaze secure upon the raging sea, even though all the winds stir it up, even though the tide, because of some upheaval of the world, turns the entire ocean against the land. Secure, he will look upon the fierce and horrid face of a thundering heaven, although heaven bursts apart and unites its fires for the destruction of all things, especially itself. Secure, he will view the ground gaping open with its framework broken, even though the regions of the dead are uncovered. Without fear he will stand at the edge of that abyss and perhaps he will jump into the place where he will have to fall.

What does it matter to me how great the means by 5 which I die? To die itself is not great. Accordingly, if we want to be happy and not torn by fear of men, or of gods, or of circumstances; to despise fortune which promises needless things, threatens unimportant things; if we want to live tranquilly and vie with the gods themselves in happiness—life must be

agere, anima in expedito est habenda. Sive illam
insidiae, sive morbi petent, sive hostium gladii,
sive insularum cadentium fragor, sive ipsarum ruina
terrarum, sive vasta vis ignium urbes agrosque pari
clade complexa, qui volet illam accipiat.

6   Quid aliud debeo quam exeuntem hortari et cum
bonis ominibus [1] emittere? " Vade fortiter, vade
feliciter! Nihil dubitaveris; redderis. Non de re,
sed de tempore est quaestio; facis [2] quod quandoque
faciendum est. Nec rogaveris,[3] nec timueris, nec
te velut in aliquod malum exituram [4] tuleris retro;
rerum natura te, quae genuit, expectat et locus melior
7   ac tutior. Illic non tremunt terrae, nec inter se
venti cum magno nubium fragore concurrunt,
non incendia regiones urbesque vastant, non nauf-
ragiorum totas classes sorbentium metus est, non
arma contrariis disposita vexillis et in mutuam perniciem multorum milium par furor, non pestilentia
et ardentes promiscue communes populis cadentibus
rogi."

Istud leve est; quod [5] timemus grave est. Potius
8   semel incidat quam semper impendeat. Ego autem
perire timeam, cum terra ante me pereat, cum ista
quatiantur quae quatiunt et in iniuriam nostram non
sine sua veniant? Helicen Burinque totas mare

---

[1] *ominibus* H²A; *hominibus* H¹P¹ZF; *omnibus* ΛBV¹.
[2] *fac* ABV¹.
[3] *negaveris* AB; *cogitaveris* V.

considered as held in readiness. Whether treacheries or diseases attack it, or the swords of enemies, or the crash of falling tenements, or the collapse of the earth itself, or the enormous force of fire embracing cities and fields with equal devastation, let life be taken by whoever or whatever wants it.

What do I owe life other than to encourage it 6 as it leaves and to dispatch it with good wishes? " Go bravely, go happily! Do not hesitate at all; you are being given back to Nature. The question is not one of fact but of time. You do what must be done some time. Do not beg, nor be afraid, nor turn back as though you were about to pass away towards something bad. The nature which produced you is waiting for you, and a better and safer place. No 7 earthquakes are there, no winds running into each other with a great crash of clouds, nor do conflagrations devastate regions and cities, nor is there fear of shipwrecks swallowing entire fleets, nor armies arranged with opposing banners and the equal madness of many thousands of soldiers for mutual destruction; no pestilence and communal funeral pyres burning for nations falling, without distinction."

Death is unimportant; only the fear we have of it is serious. It is better for death to happen once rather than threaten constantly. Therefore, why 8 should I fear to die when the earth perishes before I do, when the forces which do the shaking are shaken and bring about our destruction only by destroying themselves? The sea received Helice and Buris

---

[4] *exituram* ZV Oltramare; *exiturum* most MSS.
[5] Haase, Oltramare for *quid* MSS.

accepit; ego de uno corpusculo timeam? Supra
oppida duo navigatur—duo autem quae novimus,
quae in nostram notitiam memoria litteris servata
perduxit; quam multa alia aliis locis mersa sunt, quot
populos aut terra, aut infra se mare inclusit? Ego
recusem mei finem, cum sciam me sine fine non esse?
Immo, cum sciam omnia esse finita, ego ultimum
suspirium timeam?

9 Quantum potes itaque ipse te cohortare, Lucili,
contra metum mortis. Hic est qui nos humiles facit;
hic est qui vitam ipsam cui parcit inquietat ac perdit;
hic omnia ista dilatat, terrarum motus et fulmina.
Quae omnia feres constanter, si cogitaveris nihil
10 interesse inter exiguum tempus et longum. Horae
sunt quas perdimus. Puta dies esse, puta menses,
puta annos; perdimus illos nempe perituros. Quid,
oro te, refert num perveniam ad illos? Fluit tempus
et avidissimos sui deserit. Nec quod futurum est
meum est, nec quod fuit; in puncto fugientis tem-
11 poris pendeo, et magni est modicum fuisse. Ele-
ganter ille Laelius sapiens dicenti cuidam, " Sexaginta
annos habeo," " Hos," inquit, " dicis sexaginta quos
non habes." Ne ex hoc quidem intellegimus in-
comprehensibilis vitae condicionem et sortem temporis semper alieni quod annos numeramus amissos.
12 Hoc affigamus animo, hoc nobis subinde dicamus:

entire. Should *I* fear for my one little body?
Ships sail over two towns—two towns indeed which
we know, which memory preserved in letters has
brought to our knowledge. How many others have
been submerged in other places, how many peoples
has either the land or the sea enclosed within itself?
Am *I* to refuse an end to myself when I know that I
am not without an end? Indeed, when I know that
all things are finite am I to fear a final breath?

And so, Lucilius, brace yourself, as much as you 9
can, against the fear of death. This is the fear which
makes us lowly; this is what disquiets and destroys
the very life it spares; this magnifies all those things,
such as earthquakes and lightning. You will endure all these courageously if you reflect that there
is no difference between a long and short period of
living. They are only hours which we lose. Suppose 10
it is a matter of days, months, years; we lose only
what is going to be lost anyway. What difference
does it make, I ask you, whether *I* reach them or
not? Time flows on and leaves behind those who are
most avid for it. Neither what will be is mine nor
what was. I am suspended on a point of fleeting time;
and to have been a restrained man is of great importance. When someone said, " Sixty years of age 11
are mine," the wise Laelius replied, fittingly: " You
are talking about sixty years which are *not* yours."
We do not understand the terms of an incomprehensible life and the allotment of a time that is never
our own, even from the fact that we count the number of years that have been lost.

Let us fix this in the mind, let us repeatedly say 12
this to ourselves: we must die. When? What

moriendum est. Quando? Quid tua? Mors
naturae lex est, mors tributum officiumque mortalium malorumque omnium remedium est. Optavit
illam quisquis timet. Omnibus omissis, hoc unum,
Lucili, meditare, ne mortis nomen reformides; effice
illam tibi cogitatione multa familiarem, ut, si ita
tulerit, possis illi et obviam exire.

concern of yours is that? Death is a law of nature. Death is something due and an obligation for mortals, and is the cure for all ills. Whoever is afraid has been longing for death. Giving up all else, Lucilius, meditate upon this one thing: so that you may not fear the name of death. By long reflection make death familiar to you so that, if necessity arises, you can also go out and meet it.

BOOK VII
COMETS

LIBER SEPTIMUS [1]

DE COMETIS [2]

1   1. Nemo usque eo tardus et hebes et demissus in terram est ut ad divina non erigatur ac tota mente consurgat, utique ubi novum aliquod e caelo miraculum fulsit.   Nam, quamdiu solita decurrunt, magnitudinem rerum consuetudo subducit.   Ita enim compositi sumus ut nos cotidiana, etiamsi admiratione digna sunt, transeant, contra minimarum quoque rerum, si insolitae prodierunt, spectaculum dulce

2   fiat.   Hic itaque coetus astrorum, quibus immensi corporis pulchritudo distinguitur, populum non convocat; at, cum aliquid ex more mutatum est, omnium vultus in caelo est.   Sol spectatorem, nisi deficit, non habet.   Nemo observat lunam nisi laborantem; tunc urbes conclamant, tunc pro se quisque superstitione vana strepitat.[3]

3   Quanto illa maiora sunt quod sol totidem, ut ita dicam, gradus quot dies habet et annum circuitu suo claudit, quod a solstitio ad minuendos dies vertitur,

---

[1] *liber quartus* PKTU; *l. sextus* EZLGMV; *explicit septimus incipit l. octavus* H; [*Liber Septimus*] *Liber Quartus* Oltramare.
[2] *de cometis* PEZ.

BOOK VII

COMETS

1. No one is so completely slow and dull and 1
stooping to the earth that he is not aroused by celestial
phenomena but rises erect with his whole mind,
especially when some new marvel flashes in the sky.
For, as long as things run along in their ordinary
way our familiarity with them robs them of their
importance. For we are so constructed that daily
occurrences, although they are worthy of admiration,
pass us by; on the other hand the spectacle of even
minor events affords pleasure if they appear unusual. Accordingly, the usual collection of stars which 2
distinguishes the immense firmament does not attract
people's attention, but when something is changed
from the ordinary the eyes of all are on the sky.
The sun does not have a spectator unless it is in
eclipse, no one watches the moon if it is not in eclipse,
but then cities cry out and each person makes a din
in accordance with inane superstition.

How much more important are the following con- 3
siderations. The sun has as many steps, so to speak,
as it has days and it closes the year by its own
circuit; from the summer-solstice it turns to make the

---

³ *strepitat* HZF Oltramare; *trepidat* P²ABV Gercke; *strepit.*
At Axelson, Alexander.

quod ab aequinoctio [1] statim [2] inclinat et dat noctibus
spatium, quod sidera abscondit, quod terras, cum
tanto maior sit illis, non urit sed calorem suum
intensionibus ac remissionibus temperando fovet,
quod lunam numquam implet nisi adversam sibi,

4 nec obscurat nisi obliquam? [3] Haec tamen non
adnotamus, quamdiu ordo servatur. Si quid tur-
batum est aut praeter consuetudinem emicuit, spec-
tamus [4] interrogamus ostendimus; adeo naturale est
magis nova quam magna mirari.

5 Idem in cometis fit: si rarus et insolitae figurae
ignis apparuit, nemo non scire quid sit cupit et,
oblitus aliorum, de adventicio quaerit, ignarus utrum
debeat mirari an timere. Non enim desunt qui
terreant, qui significationes eius graves praedicent.
Sciscitantur itaque et cognoscere volunt prodigium

6 sit an sidus. At mehercules non aliud quis aut mag-
nificentius quaesierit aut didicerit utilius quam de
stellarum siderumque natura, utrum flamma con-
tracta, quod et visus noster affirmat et ipsum ab illis
fluens lumen et calor inde descendens, an non sint
flammei orbes, sed solida quaedam terrenaque corpora, quae per igneos tractus [5] labentia inde splen-
dorem trahant caloremque, non de suo clara.

7 In qua opinione magni fuerunt viri, qui sidera
crediderunt ex duro concreta et ignem alienum

---

[1] *aequinoctio* Z Oltramare; *solstitio* HPEABV.
[2] *statim* HPZABV Oltramare; *statum* E Gercke.
[3] *nisi obliquam* supplied by Oltramare; *nisi vicinam* Gercke.
[4] *expectamus* HPEZ.
[5] *cursus* ABV.

days shorter; for, from the equinox it immediately inclines and gives more space to the night. It hides the stars. Although the sun is much larger than the earth it does not burn it up but fosters it by controlling its heat in an alternately more intense and more subdued degree. It never causes the moon to be full unless it is opposite, nor dims it by phases unless it is oblique. Yet we do not note these things as long 4 as the usual order is preserved. If something is disturbed or flashes out beyond the customary we look at it, ask about it, point it out—so natural it is to marvel more at the new than at the great.

The same thing happens in the case of comets. 5 If a rare fire, and one of unusual shape, appears everyone wants to know what it is and, ignoring the other celestial phenomena, asks about the new-comer, uncertain whether he ought to admire or fear it. For there is no lack of people who create terror and predict dire meanings of it. And so, people ask again and again and want to know whether it is an omen or a star. But, by Hercules, no one 6 could study anything more magnificent or learn anything more useful than the nature of the stars and planets, whether they are of concentrated flame, which our eyes and the light itself flowing from them and the heat descending from them attests, or whether they are not flaming orbs at all but solid and sort of earthy bodies which slip through fiery tracks and take from them brightness and heat, and are not bright on their own account.

There have been many great men of this opinion; 7 they believe that stars are packed together from a hard substance and feed on fire that is not their own.

pascentia. Nam per se, inquiunt, flamma diffugeret, nisi aliquid haberet quod teneret et a quo teneretur, conglobatamque nec stabili inditam corpori profecto iam mundus turbine suo dissipasset.

1 2. Ad haec investiganda proderit quaerere num [1] cometae condicionis eiusdem sint cuius superiora. Videntur enim cum illis quaedam habere communia: ortus et occasus, ipsam quoque, quamvis spargatur et longius exeat, faciem; aeque enim ignei splen-

2 didique sunt. Itaque, si omnia terrena sidera sunt, his quoque eadem sors erit; si vero nihil aliud sunt quam purus ignis manensque mensibus senis nec illos conversio mundi solvit et velocitas, illa quoque possunt et tenui constare materia nec ob hoc discuti assiduo caeli circumactu.

3 Illo quoque pertinebit haec excussisse ut sciamus utrum mundus terra stante circumeat an mundo stante terra vertatur. Fuerunt enim qui dicerent nos esse quos rerum natura nescientes ferat, nec caeli motu fieri ortus et occasus, nos ipsos [2] oriri et occidere. Digna res contemplatione, ut sciamus in quo rerum statu simus, pigerrimam sortiti an velocissimam sedem, circa nos deus omnia an nos agat.

1 3. Necessarium est autem veteres ortus cometarum habere collectos; deprehendi enim propter raritatem

---

[1] *non* P^{1}Z.

[2] *nos ipsos* Z Oltramare; most MSS. omit *nos*.

---

[1] E.g. Aristarchus of Samos (c. 300 B.C.) suggested that the earth moves round the sun.

For, they say, flame by itself would scatter unless it had something to hold to and by which it was held; and if flame were merely massed together and not set within a stable body, then surely the universe by its own whirling motion would already have scattered it.

2. It will be worth while in this investigation to 1 inquire whether comets have the same nature as the planets and stars I spoke about above. A comet seems to have certain things in common with them: rising and setting, the same appearance, although a comet is scattered and extends farther. It is also fiery and bright. And so, if all planets are earthy 2 bodies, comets will also have the same condition. But if comets are nothing but a pure fire which remains for six months at a time and they are not broken up by the turning and speed of the universe, then stars, too, can consist of thin matter and are not scattered by this continuous rotation of the sky.

Also, it will be relevant to investigate these matters 3 so that we may know whether the universe travels around while the earth stands still or whether the earth turns while the universe stands still. For there have been people [1] who say that we are the ones whom nature causes to move, even though we are unaware of it, and that rising and setting does not happen from a motion of the sky but we ourselves rise and set. The subject deserves study so that we may know what our status is, whether we possess the most inactive abode or a very swift one, whether god causes all things to move around us or causes us to move around.

3. However, it is necessary to have a record of the 1 rising of comets in times past. Because of their

eorum cursus adhuc non potest, nec explorari an
vices servent et illos ad suum diem certus ordo pro-
ducat.

Nova haec caelestium observatio est et nuper in
2 Graeciam invecta. Democritus quoque, substilis-
simus antiquorum omnium, suspicari se ait plures
stellas esse quae currant, sed nec numerum illarum
posuit nec nomina, nondum comprehensis quinque
siderum cursibus. Eudoxus primus ab Aegypto
hos motus in Graeciam transtulit. Hic tamen de
cometis nihil dicit; ex quo apparet ne apud Aegyptios
quidem, quibus maior caeli cura fuit, hanc partem
3 elaboratam. Conon postea, diligens et ipse inquisitor, defectiones quidem solis servatas [1] ab Aegyp-
tiis collegit, nullam autem mentionem feci
cometarum, non praetermissurus, si quid explorati
apud illos comperisset.

1   4. Duo certe, qui apud Chaldaeos studuisse se
dicunt, Epigenes et Apollonius Myndius,[2] peritissimus
inspiciendorum natalium,[3] inter se dissident. Hic

---

[1] *observatas* Gercke.
[2] *Myndius* Z Oltramare; *mindius* HFT; *mundius* Eλ;
medicus ABV.
[3] *natalium* Schott, Gercke, Oltramare for *naturalium* MSS.

---

[1] Aristotle (1.6.342b 27–29) credits Democritus (and Anaxagoras) with the theory that a comet is the result of light coming
from planets in conjunction, which Seneca rejects (below,
Chapter Twelve) partly by insisting that the number of planets
is limited to five.
[2] Eudoxus of Cnidus was a pupil of Plato.
[3] Catullus (66) says that Conon discovered the Lock of

rarity their path cannot yet be understood, nor can it be determined whether they maintain sequences and whether a definite pattern causes them to reappear at a particular time.

This observation of celestial bodies has been recently brought into Greece and is new. Demo- 2 critus, the most accurate of all the ancients, says that he suspects there are more stars on the move, but he does not give their number or their names, since the orbits of the five planets had not yet been comprehended.[1] Eudoxus was the first one to bring knowledge of these orbits from Egypt into Greece.[2] Yet he says nothing about comets, from which it appears that this part of astronomy had not been worked on even by the Egyptians, who had a very great interest in the sky. Later, Conon, himself a diligent 3 inquirer, actually collected the eclipses of the sun recorded by the Egyptians.[3] However, he made no mention of comets, and yet he would not likely have passed them by if he had learned anything definite among the Egyptians.

4. Certainly, two authorities, who say they studied 1 among the Chaldaeans, disagree with each other, Epigenes and Apollonius of Myndus,[4] the latter highly skilled in casting horoscopes. Apollonius says

Berenice transformed into a constellation. Conon of Samos belongs to the first half of the third century.

[4] Epigenes and Apollonius of Myndos cannot be dated. All we know of Apollonius is what Seneca tells us. Epigenes is cited by Pliny, Aetius, and Plutarch. Oltramare believes they were contemporaries of Seneca rather than predecessors of Posidonius, others believe that Seneca knew their theories only from Posidonius' works. Pliny (7.193) speaks well of Epigenes as an " authority of the first rank."

enim ait cometas in numero stellarum errantium poni a Chaldaeis tenerique cursus eorum. Epigenes contra ait Chaldaeos [1] nihil de cometis habere comprensi, sed videri illos accendi turbine quodam aeris concitati et intorti. Primum ergo, si tibi videtur, opiniones huius ponamus ac refellamus.

2 Huic videtur plurimum virium habere ad omnes sublimium motus stella Saturni. Haec, cum proxima signa Marti premit aut in lunae viciniam transit aut in solis incidit radios, natura ventosa et frigida contrahit pluribus locis aera conglobatque; deinde, si radios solis assumpsit, tonat fulguratque; si Martem 3 quoque consentientem habet, fulminat. Praeterea, inquit, aliam materiam habent fulmina, aliam fulgurationes. Aquarum enim et omnis umidi evaporatio splendores tantum caeli citra [2] ictum minaces movet; illa autem calidior sicciorque terrarum exhalatio fulmina extundit. Trabes vero et faces, quae nullo alio inter se quam magnitudine distant, hoc 4 modo fiunt: cum umida terrenaque in se globus aliquis aeris clausit, quem turbinem dicimus, quacumque fertur, praebet speciem ignis extenti, quae tam diu durat quam diu mansit aeris illa complexio umidi intra se terrenique multum vehens.

1 5. Ut a proximis mendaciis incipiam, falsum est faces et trabes exprimi turbine. Turbo enim circa

---

[1] *ait Chaldaeos* HPZ Oltramare; *ait se a Chaldaeis* ABV Gercke.
[2] *contra* H; *circa* B.

that the Chaldaeans place comets in the category
of planets and have determined their orbits; Epigenes, on the contrary, says that the Chaldaeans
have no understanding of comets but that to them
comets seem to be on fire from some sort of turbulence
in aroused and twisted atmosphere. Therefore,
first of all, if it seems all right to you, let us set forth
Epigenes' theories and refute them.

The planet Saturn seems to Epigenes to exert the 2
greatest power on all the motions of the celestial
bodies. When it presses upon the constellation
closest to Mars or passes into the moon's vicinity or
encounters the rays of the sun, since it is windy and
cold by nature, it attracts and collects air in many
places. Then, if Saturn absorbs the rays of the sun
there is thunder and lightning flashes. If it also has
Mars in conjunction there are lightning bolts. In 3
addition, he says, lightning bolts have one material,
lightning flashes another. For the evaporation of
water and of all moisture produces only flashes in the
sky, threatening but not actually delivering a blow.
However, the warmer and drier exhalation of the
earth forces out lightning bolts. But Beams and
Torches, which differ from each other only in size
occur this way: when some globe of air, which we 4
call a whirlwind, shuts up moist and earthy elements
within itself, wherever it travels it presents the
appearance of an extended fire which lasts as long as
that tangle of air remains, carrying within itself a
great quantity of moist and earthy elements.

5. To begin with the most obvious falsehoods: it 1
is untrue that Torches and Beams are squeezed out by
a whirlwind. For a whirlwind is conceived and carried

terras concipitur ac fertur ideoque arbusta radicitus
vellit et, quacumque incubuit, solum nudat, silvas
interim et tecta corripiens, inferior fere [1] nubibus,
utique numquam altior. At contra trabes editior
caeli pars ostentat; itaque numquam nubibus ob-
2 stiterunt. Praeterea turbo omni nube velocius
rapitur et in orbem vertitur; super ista velociter
desinit et ipse se vi sua rumpit. Trabes autem non
transcurrunt nec praetervolant ut faces, sed com-
morantur et in eadem caeli parte collucent.

3   Charmander quoque, in eo libro quem de cometis
composuit, ait Anaxagorae visum grande insolitum-
que caelo lumen magnitudine amplae trabis et id
per multos dies fulsisse. Talem effigiem ignis longi
fuisse Callisthenes tradit, antequam Burin et Helicen
4 mare absconderet. Aristoteles ait non trabem illam
sed cometen fuisse; ceterum ob nimium ardorem
non apparuisse sparsum ignem sed, procedente
tempore, cum iam minus flagraret, redditam suetam [2]
cometis faciem.[3] In quo igne multa quidem fuerunt
digna quae notarentur, nihil tamen magis quam
quod, ut ille fulsit in caelo, statim supra Burin et
Helicen mare fuit.

5   Numquid ergo Aristoteles non illam tantum sed
omnes trabes cometas esse credebat hanc habentes [4]

---

[1] *fertur* ABV.
[2] *suetam* Garrod, Oltramare for *suam* MSS.
[3] *cometae facem* Gercke.
[4] *credebat? Hanc habetis* HPZ.

along near the earth. Thus it tears up trees by the roots, and wherever it has pressed hard it lays bare the ground, meanwhile carrying off forests and houses. It is generally lower than the clouds, certainly never higher. But on the contrary the higher part of the sky displays Beams. And so, Beams never stood so as to block off the clouds. Besides, a whirl-wind is carried along more rapidly than any cloud and spins in a circle; in addition it ceases suddenly and breaks itself apart by its own force. But beams do not run or fly across the way Torches do, but stay and shine in one part of the sky.

Also, Charmander [1] says, in that book he wrote on comets, that a large and unusual light of the size of a great Beam was seen in the sky by Anaxagoras and shone for many days. Callisthenes reports that a similar likeness of an extended fire appeared just before the sea covered Buris and Helice. Aristotle says that this was not a Beam but a comet.[2] More-over, he says that because of its excessive brightness the fire did not appear scattered but as time went on and it blazed less it recovered the usual appearance of a comet. In that fire there were many worthy things which should be noted, but nothing more so than the fact that when it flashed in the sky the sea immediately covered Buris and Helice.

Did Aristotle believe, then, that not only this one but all Beams are comets, with this difference, that

---

[1] Only Seneca mentions Charmander.

[2] According to Aristotle (1.6.343b 18) the " great comet," as he calls it (cf. 1.6.343b 1; 1.7.344b 34), occurred in the archonship of Asteius (373–372 B.C.). He makes no mention of the comet's change of appearance.

differentiam quod his continuus ignis est, ceteris sparsus? Trabes enim flammam aequalem habent nec ullo loco [1] intermissam aut languidam, in ultimis vero partibus coactam, qualem fuisse in illa de qua modo rettuli Callisthenes tradit.

1 6. Duo, inquit Epigenes, cometarum genera sunt. Alii ardorem undique effundunt nec locum mutant; alii in unam partem ignem vagum in modum comae porrigunt et stellas praetermeant, quales duo aetate nostra visi sunt. Illi priores criniti undique et immoti humiles fere sunt et isdem causis quibus trabes facesque conflantur ex intemperie aeris turbidi multa secum arida umidaque terris exhalata versantis.

2 Potest enim spiritus per angusta elisus accendere [2] supra se positum aera plenum alimentis idoneis igni, deinde propellere et [3] niti donec [4] ex aliqua causa refluat rursus ac remittatur, deinde iterum proximo die ac sequentibus consurgere et eundem locum inflammare. Videmus enim ventos per complures dies ad constitutum redire; pluviae quoque et alia tempestatum genera ad praescriptum revertuntur.

3 Ut breviter autem voluntatem eius exprimam, eadem fieri ratione hos cometas existimat qua fiunt ignes turbine eiecti; hoc unum interest quod illi

[1] *modo* E.   [2] *ascendere* OABV.

Beams have a continuous fire, comets a scattered fire? For Beams have an even flame, not interrupted at any point or dull but collected in the end parts like the fire Callisthenes reported was in the one which I just mentioned.

6. There are, Epigenes says, two types of comets. 1 Some pour out fire in all directions and do not change position. Others extend a vague fire like hair in one direction and travel among the stars, like the two seen in our own time. The first type has hair on all sides, is motionless, generally low, and is produced by the same causes as Beams or Torches; that is, blown into flame by the intemperance of disturbed air which rolls about within itself many dry and wet exhalations from the earth. For moving air, driven through 2 narrow openings, is able to set fire to the atmosphere which is located above it and is full of nourishment suitable for fire. Then the air is able to drive the atmosphere forward, and shove it until, for some reason or another, the air flows backwards and loses its force; then it can rise on the next and the following days and set fire to the same place. For we see winds return at a fixed time for several days. Rains, also, and other kinds of inclement weather return at a prescribed period.

However, to express his idea briefly, Epigenes 3 supposes that these comets occur for the same reason that fires occur when they are ejected by a whirlwind. There is this one difference, namely that

---

[3] Oltramare for *ex* MSS.; *ea* Madvig; *eum* Gercke.
[4] *niti donec* Madvig, Oltramare for *nitido nec* Z; *nitido ne* in most of the MSS.

turbines ex superiore parte in terras deprimuntur, hi de terra in superiora eluctantur.

1   7. Adversus haec multa dicuntur. Primum, si ventus in causa esset, numquam cometes sine vento appareret; nunc autem et quietissimo aere apparet. Deinde, si vento fieret, cum vento caderet; et, si vento inciperet, cresceret vento eoque esset ardentior quo ille incitatior. His accedit illud quoque quod ventus multas aeris partes impellit, cometes uno loco apparet; et ventus in sublime non pervenit, cometae autem visuntur [1] supra quam ire ventis licet.

2   Transit deinde ad illos quos ait certiorem habere stellarum speciem, qui [2] et procedunt et signa praetereunt. Hos ait ex isdem causis fieri quibus illos quos dixit humiliores; hoc tamen interesse quod terrarum exhalationes multa secum arida ferentes celsiorem petant partem et in editiora caeli aquilone pellantur.

3   At [3] si illos aquilo propelleret, ad meridiem semper agerentur, quo ventus hic nititur. Atqui varie cucurrerunt, alii in ortum, alii in occasum, omnes in flexum; quod iter non daret ventus. Deinde, si aquilonis illos impetus a terris in altum levaret, aliis ventis non orirentur cometae. Atqui oriuntur.

---

[1] *nascuntur* A^{1}B.
[2] *quia* Z.
[3] *at* supplied by Gercke, Oltramare.

whirlwinds are pressed down to the earth from the upper regions while comets struggle up from earth to the upper regions.

7. Many arguments are stated against these views 1 of Epigenes. First, if wind existed as a cause a comet would never appear without wind; whereas, a comet appears in a very quiet atmosphere also. Second, if a comet came from wind it would fall with the wind; and, if it began with the wind it would grow with the wind and would be brighter the more aroused the wind is. To these refutations add this also: the fact that a wind pushes forward many sections of the atmosphere while comets appear in only one spot. Also, wind does not come into the upper regions, but comets are seen higher than winds are permitted to reach.

Epigenes then crosses over to those comets which 2 he says have a more definite resemblance to stars and which move forward in the sky and pass by the constellations. These, he says, occur from the same causes as those which he called the lower comets. Yet they have this difference, namely that the exhalations from the earth carrying with them many dry elements seek the higher region and are driven by the North Wind into the more elevated parts of the sky.

But if the North Wind propelled them they would 3 always be driven towards the south in the direction the wind strikes. Yet comets run in various directions, some to the east, others to the west, all in a curve; a path which the wind would not provide. Finally, if the impetus of the North Wind lifted them from earth to the upper regions comets would not rise with other winds. Yet they do.

1   8. Illam nunc rationem eius (utraque enim utitur)
refellamus. Quicquid umidi aridique terra efflavit,
cum in unum coit, ipsa discordia corporum spiritum
versat in turbinem; tunc illa vis venti circumeuntis,
quicquid intra se comprehendit, cursu suo accendit
et levat in altum ac tam diu manet splendor ignis
expressi quamdiu alimenta sufficiunt; quibus desinen-
tibus et ipse subsidit.

2   Qui hoc dicit, non notat qualis sit turbinum cursus
et qualis cometarum. Illorum rapidus ac violentus
et ipsis ventis citatior est, cometarum lenis et qui per
diem noctemque quantum transierit abscondat.
Deinde turbinum motus vagus est et disiectus et,
ut Salustii verbis utar, verticosus, cometarum autem
compositus et destinatum iter carpens.

3   Num quis nostrum crederet lunam aut quinque
sidera rapi vento aut turbine rotari? Non, ut puto.
Quare? Quia non est illis perturbatus et impotens
cursus. Ad cometas idem transferamus: non con-
fuse nec tumultuose eunt, ut aliquis credat illos causis
4 turbulentis et inconstantibus pelli. Deinde, etiamsi
vertices isti comprehendere terrena umidaque et ex
humili in altum exprimere possent, non tamen supra
lunam efferrent; omnis illis usque in nubilum vis est.
Cometas autem immixtos stellis videmus per superiora labentes. Ergo veri simile non est in tantum

8. Now let us refute the following theory of his 1
(for he uses both theories). The earth exhales dry
and humid elements; when they combine, the very
discord of the elements turns the air into a whirlwind. Then that force of revolving wind sets on
fire by its very motion whatever it catches within
itself and lifts it on high, and the gleam of the fire
that is forced out remains as long as the nutriments
last. But when the fuel fails the fire itself also subsides.

Whoever says this sort of thing does not notice 2
what kind of movement whirlwinds and comets have.
The motion of whirlwinds is rapid and violent and
swifter than winds themselves, that of comets is slow
and one which conceals how much they have traversed
in a day and a night. Finally, the movement of
whirlwinds is unpredictable and erratic and—to use a
word of Sallust's—eddying, but that of comets is
regular and sticks to a route which has a destination.

Would any one of us believe that the moon or 3
the five planets are carried along by the wind or
revolved by a whirlwind? No, I think. Why?
Because their motion is not irregular and uncontrolled.
Let us transfer this same observation to comets.
They do not move confusedly or chaotically to such an
extent that someone might believe they are driven
by turbulent and irregular forces. Besides, even if 4
those air turbulences could contain earthy and humid
substances and could force them from below to the
heights they still could not carry them above the
moon. All their force is on this side of the clouds.
But indeed, we see comets mixed in with the stars,
gliding through the upper regions. Therefore, it is

243

spatium perseverare turbinem, qui, quo maior est,
maturius corrumpitur.

1 9. Utrumlibet itaque eligat; aut levis vis tam
alte [1] pervenire non poterit, aut magna et concitata
citius ipsa se franget.

Praeterea humiliores illi cometae ob hoc, ut putat,
non exeunt altius quia plus terreni habent; gravitas
illos sua in proximo tenet. Atqui necesse est in his
cometis diuturnioribus celsioribusque plenior materia
sit; neque enim diutius apparerent, nisi maioribus
nutrimentis sustinerentur.

2 Dicebam modo non posse diu verticem permanere
nec supra lunam aut usque in stellarum locum crescere.
Nempe efficit turbinem plurium ventorum inter ipsos
luctatio. Haec diu non potest esse. Nam cum
vagus et incertus spiritus convolutatus est, novissime
3 uni vis omnium cedit. Nulla autem tempestas magna
perdurat. Procellae, quanto plus habent virium,
tanto minus temporis. Venti, cum ad summum
venerunt, remittuntur. Omnis [2] violentia necesse
est ipsa concitatione in exitium [3] sui tendat.[4] Nemo
itaque turbinem toto die vidit, ne hora quidem; mira
velocitas eius et mira brevitas est. Praeterea vio-
lentius celeriusque in terra circaque eam volvitur;
quo excelsior, eo solutior laxiorque est, et ob hoc

---

[1] *tam alte* Muret, Oltramare; *iam alte* Z; *tantum* BV;
tamen HP; *in altum* Gercke.
[2] *omnis* Oltramare; *omni* MSS.; *omnia violenta* Madvig,
Gercke.
[3] *exitium* HPV; *exitum* most MSS.
[4] *tendat* Z Oltramare for *tendant* in most MSS.

improbable that a whirlwind continues over such a great space, for the larger a whirlwind is the more quickly it is broken up.

9. Let Epigenes, then, choose whichever alter- 1 native he wants: either a light force will be unable to rise very high, or a large and disturbed force will break itself up quickly.

Furthermore, as Epigenes thinks, these lower comets do not travel very high because they have too much earthy substance. Their own weight keeps them close to the proximity of the earth. And yet in those other comets, the ones that are longer lasting and higher, there must be more plentiful material. For they would not appear for such a long time unless they were sustained by a greater nourishment.

I was saying recently that turbulent air cannot 2 continue very long nor rise above the moon or grow up to the place of the stars. Obviously, it is the struggling of many winds among themselves which produces a whirlwind. Such a struggle cannot last long. For when wandering and irregular moving air has become convoluted the force of all the winds eventually yields to one wind. Moreover, a large 3 storm does not last. The more strength squalls have, the less time they have. Winds diminish when they reach their maximum. It needs be that all violence by its very impetuosity tends towards its own destruction. Consequently, no one has seen a whirlwind last an entire day or even an hour; its speed is startling and its brevity is amazing. Besides, on the earth and around it a whirlwind flies more violently and swiftly. The higher it is the less co-hesive and compact it is, and for this reason it is

4 diffunditur.[1] Adice nunc quod, etiamsi in summum
pertenderet, ubi sideribus iter est,[2] utique ab eo
motu qui universum trahit solveretur. Quid enim
est illa conversione mundi citatius? Hac omnium
ventorum in unum congesta vis dissiparetur et
terrae solida fortisque compages, nedum particula
aeris torti.

1 10. Praeterea manere in alto non potest ignis
turbine illatus, nisi ipse quoque permanet turbo.
Quid porro tam incredibile est quam in turbine
longior mora, utique ubi[3] motus motu contrario
vincitur? Habet enim suam locus ille vertiginem,
quae rapit caelum

　　Sideraque alta trahit celerique volumine torquet.

Et ut des ei aliquam advocationem, quod fieri nullo
modo potest, quid de his cometis dicetur qui senis
mensibus apparuerunt?

2 Deinde duo debent esse motus eodem loco, alter
ille divinus et assiduus, suum sine intermissione pera-
gens opus, alter novus et recens et turbine illatus;
necesse est ergo alter alteri impedimento sit. Atqui
quia[4] lunaris illa orbita ceterorumque supra lunam
meantium motus irrevocabilis est nec haesitat usquam

---

[1] Gercke adds *citius* before *diffunditur*.
[2] *interest* HP (instead of *iter est*).
[3] *utique ubi* Z Oltramare for simply *ut* in most MSS.
[4] *quia* supplied by Gercke, Oltramare.

dissipated. Add now the fact that even if it reached 4
the highest region, where the stars have their path,
a whirlwind would be especially broken up by the
motion which carries along the universe. For what
is more rapid than the turning of the world? By
means of this rotation the force of all winds, even if
gathered in one place, would be dissipated, and so
would the solid and powerful structure of the earth,
to say nothing of a little bit of twisted air.

10. Besides, fire carried there in a whirlwind 1
cannot remain on high unless the whirlwind itself
also remains. What further is so unbelievable as
a whirlwind of long duration, especially when the
motion of the whirlwind is overcome by the contrary motion of the sky? For that region has its
own whirling, which carries the sky along:

> And pulls the high stars
> And spins them
> In a rapid whirl.[1]

And even though you grant to that whirling some
delay of action (which is totally impossible), what will
be said of those comets which have appeared for six
months at a time?

Then there must be two motions in the same place, 2
one divine and continuous, performing its task without interruption, the other a new, recent motion
carried by the whirlwind. So one motion must
necessarily impede the other. And yet the lunar
orbit, and the movements of the other bodies travelling above the moon, is invariable. It nowhere

[1] Ovid *Met.* 2.71.

nec resistit nec dat ullam nobis suspicionem obiectae sibi morae, fidem non habet turbinem, violentissimum et perturbatissimum tempestatis genus, in medios siderum ordines pervenire et inter disposita ac tran-

3 quilla versari. Credamus ignem circumacto turbine accendi et hunc expulsum in sublime praebere nobis opinionem speciemque sideris longi; puto, talis esse debet quale est id quod ignem efficit; turbinis autem rotunda facies est (in eodem enim vestigio versatur et columnae modo circumagentis se volvitur); ergo ignem quoque qui inclusus est similem esse illi oportet. Atqui longus est et disiectus minimeque similis in orbem coacto.

1 11. Epigenem relinquamus et aliorum opiniones persequamur. Quas antequam exponere incipiam, illud imprimis praesumendum est cometas non in una parte caeli aspici nec in signifero tantum orbe sed tam in ortu quam in occasu, frequentissime tamen

2 circa septentrionem. Forma eis,[1] ut nomen,[2] est una. Quamvis enim Graeci discrimina fecerint eorum quibus in morem barbae flamma dependet et eorum qui undique circa se velut comam spargunt et eorum quibus fusus quidem est ignis sed in verticem tendens, tamen omnes isti eiusdem notae sunt come-

3 taeque recte dicuntur. Quorum cum post longum

[1] Leo, Oltramare for *eius* in most MSS.
[2] *ut nomen* Leo, Oltramare for *non* MSS.

hesitates or stops, nor does it give us any indication of an obstacle delaying it. Therefore it is unbelievable that a whirlwind, the most violent and turbulent type of storm, reaches right into the groups of stars and is active among ordered and tranquil bodies. Let us suppose that fire is kindled by the whirlwind 3 as it is driven around and that this fire is expelled to the heights and gives us the impression and appearance of an elongated star. I think the shape of the fire ought to be the same sort as that which produces the fire. However, the shape of a whirlwind is round. For, it moves in the same track and revolves like a column that is turning round and round. Therefore, the fire which is enclosed ought to be like a whirlwind. And yet the fire is elongated and scattered and not at all like something round-shaped.

11. Let us leave Epigenes and go on to the 1 theories of others. Before I undertake to describe them I must first state that comets are seen not in one part only of the sky or only in the one area of the zodiac but they are seen as much in the east as in the west; most frequently, however, towards the north. The shape is the same for all of them, just as the 2 name is. It is true that the Greeks distinguish three types of comets: [1] those from which the flame hangs down like a beard, those which scatter a sort of hair around them on all sides, and those which have indeed a kind of dispersed fire but stretching to a point. None the less, they all have the same characteristics and are correctly called comets. Since their shapes 3

---

[1] Aristotle gives only two types of comets, the *cometes* and the *pogonias* (1.7.344a 23–24). Pliny (2.89) ascribes to the Greeks only Aristotle's two terms.

tempus appareant formae, inter se eos comparare
difficile est. Illo ipso tempore quo apparent inter
spectantes de habitu illorum non convenit sed, prout
cuique acrior acies aut hebetior est, ita ait aut luci-
diorem esse aut rubicundiorem et crines aut in interiora reductos aut in latera demissos. Sed, sive
sunt aliquae differentiae illorum sive non sunt, eadem
fiant ratione necesse est cometae. Illud unum constare debet praeter solitum aspici novam sideris
faciem circa se dissipatum ignem trahentis.

1 12. Quibusdam antiquorum haec placet ratio.
Cum ex stellis errantibus altera se alteri applicuit,
confuso in unum duarum lumine facies longioris
sideris redditur; nec hoc tunc tantum evenit, cum
stella stellam attigit, sed etiam cum appropinquavit;
intervallum enim quod inter duas est illustratur ab
utraque inflammaturque et longum ignem efficit.

2 His illud respondebimus certum esse numerum
stellarum mobilium, solere autem eodem tempore
et has apparere et cometen, ex quo manifestum fit
non illarum coitu fieri cometen sed proprium esse et
3 sui iuris. Etiamnunc frequenter stella sub altioris
stellae vestigium venit; et Saturnus aliquando supra
Iovem est et Mars Venerem aut Mercurium recta
linea despicit, nec tamen propter hunc illorum con-
cursum, cum alter alterum subit, cometes fit. Alio-

---

[1] Aristotle (1.6.342b 27–29) credits this theory to Anaxagoras
and Democritus.

appear only after long intervals it is difficult to compare them. Even at the time of their appearance there is no agreement among observers regarding their looks. According to whether an observer's eyesight is sharp or weak he asserts that the comet is bright or red and its hair is compressed within the interior or flowing on the sides. But whether or not there are any differences in them, comets are necessarily produced in the same explainable way. This one description ought to be generally agreed upon: an unusual star of strange appearance is seen trailing fire streaming around it.

12. Some of the ancient scholars[1] favour this explanation: when one of the planets has come into conjunction with another the light of both blends into one and presents the appearance of an elongated star. This happens not only when planet touches planet but even when they only come close. For the space between the two planets lights up and is set aflame by both planets and produces a train of fire.

We will give this answer[2] to their theory: the number of planets is fixed. Moreover, planets are usually visible when a comet also is seen to appear. Consequently it is obvious that a comet is not produced by a conjunction of planets but has its own existence and in its own right. Besides, frequently a planet passes under the track of a higher planet. Saturn is often above Jupiter, and Mars looks vertically down on Venus or Mercury. And yet no comet is produced as a result of this coming together of planets, when one passes under the other. Otherwise, a comet

[2] Seneca follows Aristotle's refutation of the theory (1.6.343a 22–26).

quin annis omnibus fieret; omnibus enim aliquae
stellae in eodem signo simul sunt.

4   Si cometen faceret stella stellae superveniens,
momento esse desineret. Summa enim velocitas
transeuntium est, ideoque omnis defectio siderum
brevis est quia cito illa idem cursus qui admoverat
abstrahit. Videmus solem et lunam intra exiguum
tempus, cum obscurari coeperunt, liberari: quanto
celerior debet fieri in stellis digressio tanto minori-
bus? Atqui cometae senis mensibus manent, quod
non accideret, si duarum stellarum conventu gig-
nerentur; illae enim diu cohaerere non possunt et
5   necesse est illas lex celeritatis suae separet.[1] Praeterea ista nobis vicina videntur, ceterum intervallis
ingentibus dissident; quomodo ergo potest altera
stella usque ad alteram stellam ignem mittere, ita
ut utraque iuncta videatur, cum sint ingenti regione
diductae?

6   Stellarum, inquit, duarum lumen miscetur et
praebet unius speciem, nempe sic quemadmodum
rubicunda fit nubes solis incursu, quemadmodum
vespertina aut matutina flavescunt, quemadmodum
arcus alterve sol visitur.[2]

7   Haec omnia primum magna vi efficiuntur; sol enim
est qui ista succendit; stellarum non est eadem potentia. Deinde nihil horum nisi infra lunam in terrarum
vicinia nascitur; superiora pura et sincera sunt et
8   coloris sui semper. Praeterea, si quid tale accideret,

---

[1] *semper agat* ABV.
[2] *vincitur* AV.

would be produced every year, for every year some planets are in the same constellation simultaneously.

If a star made a comet by approaching another 4 star the comet would cease to exist in a moment. For, the velocity of stars in transit is very great. Consequently, every eclipse of stars is brief because the same motion that brought them rapidly together separates them rapidly. We see the sun and the moon separate within a very short time after the eclipse has begun. The separation ought to be much quicker in the case of stars, which are much smaller. And yet comets remain for six months, which would not happen if they were produced by the conjunction of two planets. Planets are not able to stay together very long. The law of their own speed necessarily separates them. Besides, 5 those stars only appear to us to be close. In fact, they are divided by immense distances. Therefore, how could one star transmit fire all the way to another star, in such a way that they both seemed joined, when they are separated by vast space ?

The light of two planets, it is said, is mingled and 6 gives the appearance of one; in the same way, to be sure, that a cloud turns pink from the rays of the sun, or as a cloud in the evening or morning sky turns orange, or as a rainbow or a second sun is seen.

First, all these phenomena are produced by a great 7 force. It is the sun which illuminates them. Planets do not have that same power. Second, all these phenomena occur below the moon, in the vicinity of the earth. The upper regions are pure and without admixtures, always keeping their own colour. Besides, if any such phenomenon did occur 8

non haberet moram sed extingueretur cito, sicut
coronae quae solem lunamve cingunt intra brevissimum spatium exolescunt; ne arcus quidem diu
perseverat. Si quid esset tale quo medium inter
duas stellas spatium confunderetur, aeque cito dila-
beretur; utique non in tantum maneret quantum
morari cometae solent. Stellis intra signiferum
cursus est; hunc premunt gyrum. At cometae
ubique cernuntur; non magis certum est illis tempus
quo appareant quam locus ullus ultra quem non
exeant.

1   13. Adversus haec ab Artemidoro illa dicuntur:
non has tantum stellas quinque discurrere, sed has
solas observatas esse; ceterum innumerabiles ferri
per occultum aut propter obscuritatem luminis
nobis ignotas aut propter circulorum positionem
talem ut tunc demum cum ad extrema eorum venere
visantur. Ergo intercurrunt quaedam stellae, ut ait,
nobis novae, quae lumen suum constantibus misceant
et maiorem quam stellis mos est porrigant ignem.

2   Hoc ex his quae mentitur levissimum est. Tota
eius enarratio mundi mendacium impudens est.
Nam, si illi credimus, summa caeli ora solidissima est,
in modum tecti durata et alti crassique corporis,
3   quod atomi congesti coacervatique [1] fecerunt. Huic
proxima superficies ignea est, ita compacta ut solvi
vitiarique non possit; habet tamen spiramenta
quaedam et quasi fenestras per quas ex parte

---

[1] *congestae coacervataeque* Z Oltramare.

it would not last; it would be quickly extinguished the way halos which encircle the sun or the moon fade within a very short space of time. Not even a rainbow lasts very long. If there were any such phenomena by which the space midway between two planets might be united it would disappear with equal rapidity. Certainly it would not remain as long as comets ordinarily do. The planets have their orbits within the zodiac; they influence this circle. But comets are observed everywhere. The time when they appear is no more fixed than the limits of space beyond which they may not pass.

13. Against such theories Artemidorus gives the following arguments: not these five planets only have erratic movements but these five are the only ones seen. However, innumerable planets move in secret, unknown to us either on account of the dimness of their light or because the position of their orbits is such that they are eventually seen only when they reach the extremities of those orbits. Therefore, as he says, certain planets appear, new to us, which mingle their light with the permanent stars and project a brighter fire than is usual in stars.

This is the least of the things he lies about. His whole account of the universe is a shameless falsehood. For example, if we believe him, the highest region of the sky is completely solid, hardened in the manner of a roof and of a deep and thick material formed by massed and accumulated atoms. The surface next to this is fiery and so compact that it cannot be disintegrated or flawed. Yet it has certain ventilators and windows, so to speak, through which fires flow in from the outer regions of the

exteriore mundi influant ignes, non tam magni ut interiora [1] conturbent, qui rursus ex mundo in exteriora labuntur; itaque haec quae praeter consuetudinem apparent influxerunt ex illa ultra [2] mundum iacente materia.

1 14. Solvere ista quid aliud est quam manum exercere [3] et in ventum iactare bracchia? Velim tamen mihi dicat iste, qui mundo tam firma lacunaria imposuit, quid sit quare credamus illi tantam esse crassitudinem caeli. Quid fuit quod illo tam solida 2 corpora adduceret et ibi detineret? Deinde, quod tantae crassitudinis est, necesse est et magni ponderis sit; quomodo ergo in summo manent gravia? Quomodo illa moles non descendit et se onere suo frangit? Fieri enim non potest ut tanta vis ponderis quantam ille substituit pendeat et levibus innixa sit. 3 Ne illud quidem potest dici extrinsecus esse aliqua retinacula quibus cadere prohibeatur, nec rursus de medio aliquid esse oppositi quod imminens corpus excipiat ac fulciat. Illud etiamnunc nemo dicere audebit mundum ferri per immensum et cadere quidem, sed non apparere an cadat, quia praecipitatio eius aeterna est, nihil habens [4] novissimum 4 in quod incurrat. Hoc quidam de terra dixerunt, cum rationem nullam invenirent propter quam pondus in aere staret; fertur, inquiunt, semper, sed

---

[1] *inferiora* λ.

[2] *ultra* Opsipoeus, Oltramare; *utraque* in the MSS.

[3] *exerere* B² Gercke, Alexander.

[4] *habentis* Z supported by Oltramare; Alexander thinks *habens* may be Seneca's error.

universe. The fires are not so great that they disturb the inner region, and they slip back out again from the world to the outer regions. And so, stars that appear in an unusual way have streamed in from that matter which lies outside the universe.

14. To refute these theories is like exercising by throwing arm-length punches into the wind. None the less, I could wish the person who has placed so solid a panelled ceiling on the world would tell me what reason we have for believing him, that the sky is so thick. What was it that took such solid bodies up there and kept them there? Then, also, whatever has such great thickness must also have great weight. Therefore, how do heavy things stay in the uppermost region? Why does that mass not fall and break itself apart by its own weight? For it cannot happen that such a force of weight as Artemidorus perched up there could be hanging down and supported by light supports. It cannot even be said that there are some sort of cables outside which prevent it from falling. Nor, again, is there any opposing structure in the middle which might receive and support the threatening mass. Moreover, no one will dare to say that the world is moving through immense space and is actually falling, and that it is not apparent whether it falls or not because its headlong rush is eternal and it has nothing at the end with which it might collide. Some say this about the earth, when they find no explanation of why a weight stands poised in air.[1] It is always moving, they say, but it

[1] Pliny (2.162), in dealing with the concept of the earth as a sphere, is struck by the miracle that the " earth hangs suspended and does not fall."

non apparet an cadat, quia infinitum est in quod
cadit.

Quid est deinde quo probes non quinque tantum
stellas moveri sed multas esse [1] et in multis mundi
regionibus? Aut, si hoc sine ullo probabili argumento
licet respondere,[2] quid est quare non aliquis aut omnes
stellas moveri aut nullam dicat?[3] Praeterea nihil
te adiuvat ista stellarum passim euntium turba.
Nam, quo plures fuerint, saepius in aliquas incident;
rari autem cometae, et ob hoc mirabiles sunt.

1   15. Quid quod testimonium dicet contra te omnis
aetas, quae talium stellarum exortus et adnotavit et
posteris tradidit? Post mortem Demetrii Syriae
regis, cuius Demetrius et Antiochus liberi fuere,
paulo ante Achaicum bellum cometes effulsit non
minor sole. Primo igneus ac rubicundus orbis fuit
clarumque lumen emittens, quanto vinceret noctem;
deinde paulatim magnitudo eius districta [4] est et
evanuit claritas; novissime totus [5] intercidit. Quot [6]
ergo coire stellas oportet, ut tantum corpus efficiant?
Mille in unum licet congreges, numquam hunc
2   habitum solis aequabunt. Attalo regnante initio
cometes modicus apparuit; deinde sustulit se diffu-
ditque et usque in aequinoctialem circulum venit,
ita ut illam plagam caeli cui lactea nomen est in

[1] *esse* omitted by Gercke.
[2] *responde* Alexander. Warmington suggests *spondere.*
[3] *dicas* V.
[4] *destructa* λ; *adstricta* EZJ[2].
[5] *motus* λ.
[6] *quid* HPEZBV.

is not noticeable that it is falling because it falls into something which has no perceptible limit.

How next can you prove that not only the five planets move but that there are also many planets in many regions of the universe? Or, if it is permitted to make such a statement without any believable proof why should not someone say that either all the stars move or that none moves? Besides, that crowd of stars of yours going here and there helps your argument not at all. For, the more they are the more frequently they will run into some. Yet comets are remarkable just because they are so rare.

15. What about the fact that all past ages which 1 have noted the appearance of such celestial bodies and recorded them for posterity will give evidence against you? After the death of Demetrius [1] the king of Syria, whose sons were Demetrius and Antiochus, a little before the Achaean War, a comet appeared as big as the sun. At first it was a fiery red disc, emitting a light so bright that it dispelled the night. Then gradually its size diminished and its brightness faded. Finally it disappeared entirely. How many stars then would have to come together in order to produce a body of such size? Although you pack a thousand of them together in one place they would never equal the size of our sun. In the reign of Attalus [2] a comet appeared, of 2 moderate size at first. Then it rose up and spread out and went all the way to the equator, so that its vast extent equalled the region of the sky which is

[1] This is Demetrius Soter, who died in 151 B.C.
[2] Attalus III of Pergamum, who bequeathed his kingdom to Rome in 133 B.C.

immensum extentus aequaret. Quot[1] ergo convenisse debent erraticae, ut tam longum caeli tractum occuparent igne continuo?

1 16. Contra argumenta dictum est, contra testes dicendum est. Nec magna molitione detrahenda est auctoritas Ephoro: historicus est. Quidam incredibilium relatu commendationem parant et lectorem, aliud acturum si per cotidiana ducetur, miraculo excitant; quidam creduli,[2] quidam neglegentes sunt; quibusdam mendacium obrepit, qui-
2 busdam placet; illi non evitant, hi appetunt. Haec in commune de tota natione, quae approbari opus suum et fieri populare non putat posse, nisi illud mendacio aspersit. Ephorus vero non est religiosissimae fidei; saepe decipitur, saepe [3] decipit. Sicut hunc cometen, qui omnium mortalium oculis custoditus est, quia ingentis rei traxit eventum, cum Helicen et Burin ortu suo merserit, ait illum [4] discessisse in duas stellas,
3 quod praeter illum nemo tradidit. Quis enim posset observare illud momentum quo cometes solutus et in duas partes redactus est? Quomodo autem, si est qui viderit cometen in duas dirimi, nemo vidit fieri ex duabus? Quare autem non adiecit in quas stellas

---

[1] Fortunatus, Oltramare for *quid* HPABV; *quod* Z.
[2] *increduli* Z.
[3] *saepius* Z Alexander.
[4] *illum* HPEZBV Axelson, Alexander; *ilico* Gercke, Oltramare.

---

[1] Ephorus was born about the middle of the fourth century B.C. at Cyme in Aeolia and was author of a history of the

called the Milky Way. So how many planets would need to come together to occupy with a continuous fire such a long tract of the sky?

16. I have refuted the statements; now I must discredit the witnesses. It is not great effort to destroy the authority of Ephorus:[1] he is an historian. Some historians get praise for their works by relating incredibile stories, and by means of the marvellous they arouse a reader who would likely go and do something else if he were led through ordinary incidents. Some historians are credulous; others are negligent. On some, falsehood creeps unawares; some it pleases. The former do not avoid falsehood, the latter actively seek it. So much then for the whole tribe of them in common. They do not think their works can be approved and become popular unless they sprinkle them with lies. Ephorus indeed is not a man of very strict reliability. He is often deceived; he often tries to deceive. For example, the comet which was observed carefully by the eyes of all mankind because it dragged with it an event of great importance, since at its rising it sunk Helice and Buris, he says split up into two planets, a fact which no one except him reports. For who could observe that moment when the comet broke up and was reduced to two parts? Moreover, if there is anyone who saw a comet separate into two, how did nobody ever see one formed from two? And why did he not add the names of the planets into which

ancient world down to 340 B.C. Only fragments of his work survive. It was much used by later historians. No doubt Seneca is unjust to Ephorus, whom Polybius (6.45.1) considers the most learned of ancient historical writers.

divisus sit, cum aliquae ex quinque stellis debuerint? [1]

1   17. Apollonius Myndius [2] in diversa opinione est.
Ait enim cometen non unum ex multis erraticis
effici, sed multos cometas erraticos esse. Non est,
inquit, species falsa [3] nec duarum stellarum confinio
ignis extentus, sed proprium sidus cometae est, sicut
solis ac lunae. Talis [4] illi forma est, non in rotundum
restricta, sed procerior et in longum producta.

2 Ceterum non est illi palam cursus; altiora mundi
secat et tunc demum apparet cum in imum cursus
sui venit. Nec est quod putemus eundem visum
esse sub Claudio quem sub Augusto vidimus, nec
hunc qui sub Nerone Caesare apparuit et cometis
detraxit infamiam illi similem fuisse qui post exces-
sum divi Iulii ludis Veneris Genetricis circa undecimam

3 horam diei emersit. Multi variique sunt, dispares
magnitudine, dissimiles colore; aliis rubor est sine
ulla luce, aliis candor et purum liquidumque lumen,
aliis flamma et haec non sincera nec tenuis sed multum
circa se volvens fumidi ardoris. Cruenti quidam,

---

[1] *aliquae . . . debuerint* Alexander for *aliqua . . . debuerit.*
[2] *Mydius* P; *mundius* λ; *mindius* J²; *mitidius* ET;
medicus ABV.
[3] *fissa* AB; *scissa* V.
[4] Warmington suggests *tali* "It has the shape of a
knuckle-bone." But there is no manuscript authority.

the comet was split, since they must be two of the five planets?

17. Apollonius of Myndos has a theory different 1 from Epigenes. He says that a comet is not one body composed of many planets but that many comets are planets. A comet, he says, is not an illusion or fire extending from the edges of two planets but is a celestial body on its own, like the sun and the moon. It has a distinct shape thus: not limited to a disc, but extended and elongated lengthwise. On 2 the other hand, its orbit is not clear. A comet cuts through the upper regions of the universe and then finally becomes visible when it reaches the lowest point of its orbit. There is no reason to think that the same comet was seen in the time of Claudius that we saw in the time of Augustus, nor that the one which appeared in the reign of Nero Caesar (and took away the bad reputation of comets) was similar to the one which burst forth after the death of the deified Julius, about sunset on the day of the games for Venus Genetrix.[1] Comets are many and 3 various, different in size, unlike in colour. Some are red without any light, others are white and have a pure, clear light. Others have a flame, yet this is not clear or thin but rolls around itself much smoky fire. Some are bloody, menacing—they carry

[1] The comet of Julius Caesar was in 44 B.C. More than one comet appeared in the time of Augustus. The Claudius comet was in A.D. 54. Two occurred in the reign of Nero: one in A.D. 60, which resulted in the exile of Plautus (Tacitus *Ann.* 14.22), and another at the end of A.D. 64, which was followed by the Conspiracy of Piso in A.D. 65 (Tacitus *Ann.* 15.47; Suetonius *Nero* 36). Seneca's remarks about the Nero comet here and below (Chapter 21.2) are ironic.

minaces, qui omen prae [1] se futuri sanguinis ferunt. Hi minuunt augentque lumen suum, quemadmodum alia sidera, quae clariora, cum descendere, sunt maioraque, quia ex loco propiore visuntur, minora, cum redeunt, et obscuriora, quia abducunt se longius.

1   18. Adversus haec protinus respondetur non idem accidere in cometis quod in ceteris. Cometae enim, quo primum die apparuerunt, maximi sunt. Atqui deberent crescere, quo propius accederent; nunc autem manet illis prima facies, donec incipiant extingui. Deinde, quod adversus priores, etiam adversus hunc dicitur: si erraret cometes essetque sidus, intra signiferi terminos moveretur, intra quos omne sidus cursus suos colligit.

2   Numquam apparet stella per [2] stellam; acies nostra non potest per medium sidus exire, ut per illud superiora perspiciat. Per cometen autem non aliter quam per nubem ulteriora cernuntur; ex quo apparet illum non esse sidus sed levem ignem ac tumultuarium.

1   19. Zenon noster in illa sententia est. Congruere iudicat stellas et radios inter se committere; hac societate luminis existere imaginem stellae longioris. Ergo quidam nullos esse cometas existimant sed speciem illorum per repercussionem vicinorum siderum aut per coniunctionem cohaerentium reddi.

[1] *post* Gercke and most MSS.
[2] *super* PBV; *supra* A.

---

[1] Or: "a fire like a light-armed soldier levied in a hurry."—E.H.W.
[2] Zeno of Citium, who lived about 336–264 B.C.

before them the omen of bloodshed to come. Others diminish and increase their light, just as the other stars do which are brighter and larger when they descend because they are seen from a closer position, and are smaller and dimmer when they recede because they are withdrawing far away.

18. Against this statement the response will be 1 immediately that the same thing does not happen in the case of comets which happens in the case of the other celestial bodies. For comets are largest on the day on which they first appear. And yet they would be bound to increase in size the closer they approach. As it is, however, their original appearance remains until they begin to be extinguished. Then, what is said against previous theorists is also said against this one : if a comet were a planet—that is, if it were a celestial body—it would move within the limits of the zodiac, within which all celestial bodies restrict their orbits.

A star never appears through another star ; our 2 eyesight is not able to pass through the middle of a celestial body to see through it to the things on the other side. But through a comet the things beyond are seen as though through a cloud. Accordingly it is obvious that a comet is not a celestial body but a light or irregular fire.[1]

19. Our Stoic Zeno [2] has the following theory : he 1 judges that stars come together and combine their rays, and from this union of light there comes into existence the image of a rather long star. Therefore, some suppose that comets do not exist but that only the appearance of comets is rendered through the reflection of neighbouring celestial bodies or through the conjunction of stars clinging together.

2   Quidam aiunt esse quidem, sed habere cursus suos
et post certa lustra in conspectum mortalium exire;
quidam esse quidem, sed non quibus siderum nomen
imponas, quia dilabuntur nec diu durant et exigui
temporis [1] mora dissipantur.

1   20. In hac sententia sunt plerique nostrorum nec
id putant veritati repugnare. Videmus enim in
sublimi varia ignium concipi genera et modo caelum
ardere, modo

Longos a tergo flammarum albescere tractus,[2]

modo faces cum igne vasto rapi. Iam ipsa fulmina,
etiamsi velocitate mira simul et praestringunt
aciem et relinquunt, ignes sunt aeris triti et impetu
inter se maiore collisi; ideo ne resistunt quidem,
sed expressi fluunt et protinus pereunt.

2   Alii vero ignes diu manent nec ante discedunt quam
consumptum est omne quo pascebantur alimentum.
Hoc loco sunt illa a Posidonio scripta miracula,
columnae clipeique flagrantes aliaeque insigni novi-
tate flammae. Quae non adverterent animos,[3] si ex
consuetudine et lege decurrerent; ad haec stupent
omnes quae repentinum ex alto ignem efferunt, sive

---

[1] *operis* A¹BV.
[2] Virgil has *flammarum longos a tergo albescere tractus.*
See above, Bk. 1.14.2, where Seneca gets the word order correct
but uses *stellarum* instead of *flammarum.*
[3] *omnes* Z.

Yet some say that comets do exist, but that they **2**
have their own orbits and after fixed periods of time
they come into men's view. Others say that they
exist but that one should not give them the name of
celestial bodies because they slip away and do not
last long and are dissipated in a brief period of time.

20. Most of our Stoics have the preceding theory, **1**
and they think it is not contrary to the facts: for
we see various kinds of fires conceived on high, sometimes the heaven blazing, sometimes

> Long trails of flame
> Glowing white behind,[1]

sometimes great fiery Torches hurtling by. Lightning bolts themselves—even though they have remarkable speed and dazzle the eyesight and at the
same time leave it unhurt—are fires of air that have
been subjected to friction and collision among themselves from a rather violent pressure. For this reason
lightning does not last long but once released it
flows away and immediately dies out.

But other fires remain a long time and do not **2**
disperse until all the fuel on which they feed has been
consumed. In this group are those marvellous sights
described by Posidonius: blazing Columns and
Shields, and other flames remarkable for their novelty.
They would not attract attention if they ran along
in accordance with the usual laws. All men are
amazed at those phenomena which carry sudden fire
down from on high, whether something flashes and

---

[1] Virgil *Georg.* 1.367. The line is incorrectly quoted here.
See above 1.14.2 and note.

emicuit aliquid et fugit, sive compresso aere et in ardorem coacto loco miraculi stetit.

3 Quid ergo? Non [1] aliquando lacuna secedentis [2] retro aetheris patuit et vastum in concavo lumen? Exclamare posset: [3] " Quid hoc est? "

> medium video discedere caelum
> Palantesque polo stellas,

quae aliquando non expectata nocte fulserunt et per medium eruperunt diem. Sed alia huius rei ratio est. Quare alieno tempore appareant in aere, quas esse, etiam cum latent, constat?

4 Multos cometas non videmus, quia obscurantur radiis solis; quo deficiente quondam cometen apparuisse, quem sol vicinus obtexerat, Posidonius tradit. Saepe autem, cum occidit sol, sparsi ignes non procul ab eo videntur. Videlicet ipsa stella sole perfunditur et ideo aspici non potest; comae [4] autem radios solis effugiunt.

1 21. Placet ergo nostris cometas, sicut faces, sicut tubas trabesque et alia ostenta caeli, denso aere creari. Ideo circa septentrionem frequentissime apparent quia illic plurimum est aeris pigri.

2 " Quare ergo non stat cometes sed procedit? " Dicam. Ignium modo alimentum suum sequitur;

---

[1] *non* HPZ Oltramare, Alexander; *num* ABV Gercke.

[2] *secedentis* Gercke, Oltramare, Alexander instead of *si cedentis* HPEZ; *descendentis* V.

[3] *posset* Z Oltramare; *posses* Gercke, Alexander and most MSS. [*posset* sc. Posidonius or an imaginary interlocutor.]

[4] Gronovius, Gercke, Oltramare for *cometae* MSS.

disappears, or the atmosphere is compressed and forced into glowing, and it is taken as a miracle.

What then about this? Sometimes a gap extends 3 in the atmosphere which recedes backward and a great light appears in the hollow. A person might cry out, " What is this? "

> I see the middle of heaven gape open
> And the stars
> Wandering in the sky,[1]

stars which sometimes do not wait for night but burst out and shine well within daytime. But this involves quite another problem: Why do they appear at a time not their own? It is generally agreed that stars exist even when hidden.

We do not see many comets because they are 4 obscured by the rays of the sun. Posidonius reports that once during an eclipse a comet appeared [2] which the nearness of the sun had concealed. Moreover, often when the sun has set, scattered fires are seen not far from it. Obviously the comet itself is blanketed by the light of the sun and so cannot be seen, but the tail escapes the sun's rays.

21. Accordingly, our Stoics are pleased to believe 1 that comets, like Torches, Trumpets, and Beams, and other displays of the sky, are created from condensed air. So, they appear most frequently in the north because most of the thick air is there.

" Therefore, why does a comet not stand still but 2 moves? " I will tell you. A comet follows its fuel the way fire does; for even though it struggles to-

---

[1] Virgil *Aen.* 9.20.   [2] This happened in 94 B.C.

quamvis enim illi ad superiora nisus sit, tamen deficiente materia retro iens ipse descendit. In aere quoque non dextram laevamque premit partem—nulla est enim illi via—sed, qua illum vena pabuli sui duxit, illa repit nec ut stella procedit sed ut ignis pascitur.

3   " Quare ergo per longum tempus apparet et non cito extinguitur? " Sex enim mensibus hic quem nos Neronis principatu laetissimo vidimus spectandum se praebuit, in diversum illi Claudiano circumactus. Ille enim a septentrione in verticem surgens orientem petiit semper obscurior; hic ab eadem parte coepit sed in occidentem tendens ad meridiem flexit

4   et ibi se subduxit oculis. Videlicet ille fumidiora[1] habuit et aptiora[2] ignibus, quae persecutus est; huic rursus uberior fuit et plenior regio, huc itaque descendit invitante materia, non itinere. Quod apparet duobus quos spectavimus fuisse diversum, cum hic in dextrum motus sit, ille in sinistrum. Omnibus autem quinque[3] stellis in eandem partem cursus est, id est contrarius mundo. Hic enim ab orto volvitur in occasum, illae ab occasu in ortum eunt, et ob hoc duplex iis motus est, ille quo eunt et hic quo auferuntur.

---

[1] Oltramare for *humidiora* in most MSS.; *humiliora* P[1].
[2] *altiora* ABV.
[3] *quinque* added by Gercke, Oltramare.

wards the upper regions, none the less when the fuel becomes insufficient a comet goes backward and sinks down by itself. Also, in the atmosphere it does not press to the right or left side—for it has no route— but it crawls wherever a vein of its food leads it. It does not proceed as a star does but feeds as a fire does.

" Why, then, does it appear for a long time and is **3** not quickly extinguished? " The comet we have seen in the very happy principate of Nero displayed itself to our view for six months, moving in a direction opposite to the comet of Claudius' time. The Claudius comet rose from the north into the zenith and moved east, always growing dimmer. The Nero comet began in the same place but as it started moving towards the west it turned south and there withdrew from sight. Obviously the Claudius comet found **4** smokier elements, and elements more suited to its fires, which it followed. The Nero comet, on the other hand, found a richer and more abundant region, and so it descended to it, lured by its food not by its route. It is apparent that the two comets we saw had different routes since the Nero one moved towards the right, the other one towards the left. Moreover, all five planets have motion in the same direction, that is, contrary to the motion of the universe. For the universe revolves from east to west, the planets travel from west to east, and for this reason they have a double motion: one the direction in which they move and the other the direction in which they are carried away.[1]

---

[1] Pliny 2.32: the motion of all the planets, and among them the sun and the moon, follows a course contrary to that of the universe.

1   22. Ego nostris non assentior.   Non enim existimo
cometen subitaneum ignem sed esse [1] inter aeterna
opera naturae.

Primum, quaecumque aer creat, brevia sunt;
nascuntur enim in re fugaci et mutabili.   Quomodo
potest aliquid in aere idem diu permanere, cum ipse
aer numquam idem diu maneat?   Fluit semper et
brevis illi quies est; intra exiguum momentum in
alium quam in quo fuerat statum vertitur, nunc
pluvius, nunc serenus, nunc inter utrumque varius.
Nubes, quae illi familiarissimae sunt, in quas coit et
ex quibus solvitur, modo congregantur, modo diger-
untur, numquam immotae [2] iacent.   Fieri non potest
ut ignis certus in corpore vago sedeat et tam perti-
naciter haereat quam quem natura, ne umquam
excuteretur, aptavit.

2   Deinde, si alimento suo haereret, semper descen-
deret (eo enim crassior est aer quo terris propior);
numquam cometes in imum usque demittitur neque
appropinquat solo.

1   23. Etiamnunc ignis aut it quo illum natura sua
ducit, id est sursum, aut eo quo trahit materia cui
adhaesit et quam depascitur; nullis ignibus ordinariis
et caelestibus iter flexum est.   Sideris proprium
est ducere orbem.   Atqui hoc an cometae alii fece-
2   runt?   Nescio; duo nostra aetate fecerunt.   Deinde
omne quod causa temporalis accendit cito intercidit;

---

[1] *esse* added by Gercke.
[2] *in morte* LZ.

22. *I* do not agree with our Stoics.   For I do not 1
think that a comet is just a sudden fire but that it is
among the eternal works of nature.

First of all, all things the atmosphere creates are
short-lived, for they are produced in an unstable and
changeable element.   How can anything remain the
same for long in atmosphere when atmosphere itself
never remains the same for very long?   It is always
flowing and its periods of rest are short.   Within a
brief moment it changes into a condition other than
the one in which it had been; now rainy, now clear,
now a varied mixture between the two.   Clouds—
which are closely associated with atmosphere, into
which atmosphere congeals and from which it is
dissolved—sometimes gather, sometimes disperse,
never remain motionless.   It cannot happen that fire
may reside securely in an unstable milieu and cling
as pertinaciously as something which nature has
designed so that it might never be shaken loose.

Second, if fire clings to its fuel it should always 2
descend, for the atmosphere is thicker the closer it is
to the earth.   A comet never descends all the way
to the lowest regions of the atmosphere and does not
approach the ground.

23. Furthermore, fire either goes where its own 1
nature leads it, that is, upwards, or in the direction
that its fuel attracts it, to which it clings and on which
it feeds.   None of the ordinary fires in the sky has a
curved path.   It is characteristic of a planet to follow
a curve.   And yet did other comets do this?   I do not
know.   The two in our time did.   Next, everything 2
which a temporary cause sets afire quickly dies out.
Thus Torches gleam only while they pass across the

sic faces ardent, dum transeunt; sic fulmina in unum
valent ictum; sic quae transversae dicuntur stellae
cadentes praetervolant et secant aera. Nullis
ignibus nisi in suo mora est, illis dico divinis quos
habet mundus aeternos, quia partes eius sunt et
opera. His autem agunt aliquid et vadunt et teno-
rem suum servant paresque sunt. Non alternis
diebus maiores minoresve fierent, si ignis esset collec-
ticius [1] et ex aliqua causa repentinus? Minor enim
esset ac maior, prout plenius aleretur aut malignius.

3   Dicebam modo nihil diuturnum esse quod exarsit
aeris vitio. Nunc amplius adicio: morari ac stare
nullo modo potest. Nam et fax et fulmen et stella
transcurrens et quisquis alius est ignis aere expressus
in fuga est nec apparet, nisi dum cadit. Cometes
habet suam sedem et ideo non cito expellitur sed
emetitur spatium suum, nec extinguitur sed excedit.

1   24. " Si erratica," inquit, " stella esset, in signifero
esset." Quis unum stellis limitem ponit? Quis
in angustum divina compellit? Nempe haec ipsa
sidera quae sola moveri creditis alios et alios circulos
habent; quare ergo non aliqua sint quae in proprium
iter et ab istis remotum secesserint? Quid est quare
in aliqua parte caeli pervium non sit?

2   Quod si iudicas non posse ullam stellam, nisi signi-

1 *collectus* ABOT.

sky; a lightning bolt is able to strike only once; so-called shooting stars flit past and, falling, cut through the atmosphere. No fires have any duration except in their own element. I refer to those divine fires which the universe maintains as eternal fires because they are parts and works of it. Comets, however, do something: they move, preserve their continuity, and are uniform. If their fires were merely collected, the sudden occurrence of some accidental cause, they would become larger or smaller on alternate days. For such a fire would be lesser or greater according to whether it were fed less or more abundantly.

I was saying recently that no fire is eternal which 3 bursts into flame from a defect in the atmosphere. Now I am adding more to that: it cannot be lasting and stable in any way. For, a Torch and lightning bolt and a shooting star, and whatever other thing is fire forced out of the atmosphere, is in flight and appears only while it is falling. A comet has its own position and so is not quickly expelled but measures out its own space. It is not extinguished but simply departs.

24. " If a comet were a planet," someone said, " it 1 would be in the zodiac." Who places one boundary for planets? Who confines divine things in a narrow space? Yet those very stars which you believe are the only ones that move obviously have orbits that are different from one another. Why, then, should there not be other stars which have entered on their own route far removed from them? What reason is there that in some part or other of the sky there should not be a passageway?

But if you are convinced that no planet can have an 2

ferum attigit, vadere, cometes potest sic alium habere
circulum ut in hunc tamen parte aliqua sui incidat;
quod fieri non est necessarium, sed potest. Vide ne
hoc magis deceat magnitudinem mundi ut in multa
itinera divisus est[1] nec unam deterat semitam,
3 ceteris partibus torpeat. Credis autem in hoc
maximo et pulcherrimo corpore,[2] inter innumerabiles
stellas quae noctem decore vario distinguunt, quae
minime vacuam et inertem esse patiuntur, quinque
solas esse quibus exercere se liceat, ceteras stare
fixum et immobilem populum?

1 25. Si quis hoc loco me interrogaverit: "Quare
ergo non, quemadmodum quinque stellarum, ita
harum observatus est cursus?" Huic ego respon-
debo: multa sunt quae esse concedimus; qualia
2 sunt? ignoramus. Habere nos animum, cuius imperio et impellimur et revocamur, omnes fatebuntur;[3]
quid tamen sit animus ille rector dominusque nostri,
non magis tibi quisquam expediet quam ubi sit.
Alius illum dicet spiritum esse, alius concentum
quendam, alius vim divinam et dei partem, alius
tenuissimum animae,[4] alius incorporalem potentiam;
non deerit qui sanguinem dicat, qui calorem. Adeo

---

[1] *hinc et* in most MSS.; *vigeat* Leo, Oltramare; *vices det*
Gercke; *micet* Madvig; *migret* Schultess; *est, sic* Alexander.
[2] *opere* ABV.
[3] *fatemur* ABV.
[4] *aerem* EJ[2]T; *aera* Haase.

orbit unless it touches the zodiac, a comet can have
such an unusual orbit that it still comes into the zodiac
at some point of it.   This does not necessarily happen,
but it is possible.   Consider whether this concept is
not more in keeping with the size of the universe:
that the universe, divided as it is into many routes,
does not wear away just one path while it is inactive
in other sections.   Moreover, do you believe that in   3
this great and beautiful structure among the innumerable stars which decorate the night with their
varied beauty, which do not allow the night to have
any void and inactivity, there are only five celestial
bodies which are permitted to move and that the
others stand by as a fixed and immobile crowd?

25. If at this point anyone should ask me, " Why   1
then has the course of comets not been observed in
the same way as the five planets? "   I shall reply to
him: there are many things that we concede exist;
what their qualities are we do not know.   All will   2
agree that we have a mind, by whose orders we are
impelled forward and summoned back; but what
the mind is, that director and ruler of ourselves, no
one can explain to you any more than where it is.
One person [1] will say that it is a spirit, another some
sort of harmony, another will call it a divine power
or a part of god, another the thinnest part of life's
breath, another an incorporeal force.   Someone will
be found who calls it blood or heat.   It is so impossible

---

[1] Seneca gives in succession the theories of some Stoics; of
Plato, Aristoxenus, and Dicaearchus; of other Stoics (*dei
partem*); of Epicurus; of Anaximenes and Diogenes of Apollonia; of Aristotle (*incorporalem potentiam*); of Empedocles and
Critias; and of Zeno and Posidonius.

animo non potest liquere de ceteris rebus ut adhuc
ipse se quaerat.

3 Quid ergo miramur cometas, tam rarum mundi
spectaculum, nondum teneri legibus certis nec initia
illorum finesque notescere, quorum ex ingentibus
intervallis recursus est? Nondum sunt anni mille
quingenti ex quo Graecia

> stellis numeros et nomina fecit,

multaeque hodie sunt gentes quae facie tantum
noverunt caelum, quae nondum sciunt cur luna
deficiat, quare obumbretur. Haec apud nos quoque
4 nuper ratio ad certum perduxit. Veniet tempus quo
ista quae nunc latent in lucem dies extrahat et
longioris aevi diligentia. Ad inquisitionem tan-
torum aetas una non sufficit, ut tota caelo vacet; quid
quod tam paucos annos inter studia ac vitia non aequa
portione dividimus? Itaque per successiones ista
5 longas explicabuntur. Veniet tempus quo posteri
nostri tam aperta nos nescisse mirentur. Harum
quinque stellarum quae se ingerunt nobis, quae alio
atque alio occurrentes loco curiosos nos esse cogunt,
qui matutini vespertinique ortus sint, quae stationes,
quando in rectum ferantur, quare agantur retro,
modo coepimus scire; utrum mergeretur Iupiter an

for the mind to be clear concerning other subjects that it is still searching for itself.

Why, then, are we surprised that comets, such a 3 rare spectacle in the universe, are not yet grasped by fixed laws and that their beginning and end are not known, when their return is at vast intervals? It has not yet been fifteen hundred years since Greece

> Numbered the stars
> And gave them names.[1]

And yet there are many nations today that know the sky only by its face and do not yet understand why the moon lacks fulness and why it is obscured in an eclipse. Among us, too, only recently did science produce definite knowledge in these matters.[2] The 4 time will come when diligent research over very long periods will bring to light things which now lie hidden. A single lifetime, even though entirely devoted to the sky, would not be enough for the investigation of so vast a subject. What about the fact that we do not divide our few years in an equal portion at least between study and vice? And so this knowledge will be unfolded only through long successive ages. There 5 will come a time when our descendants will be amazed that we did not know things that are so plain to them. The five planets force themselves upon our attention. Occurring in one place or another they compel us to be curious. Recently we have begun to understand what their morning and evening risings mean, their positions, the time of their movement straight forwards, why they move backward. Whether Jupiter

---

[1] Virgil *Georg.* 1.137.
[2] In the second century B.C.

occideret an retrogradus esset (nam hoc illi nomen
imposuere cedenti) ante paucos annos didicimus.

6   Inventi sunt qui nobis dicerent: " Erratis, quod
ullam stellam aut supprimere cursum iudicatis aut
vertere.   Non licet stare caelestibus nec averti;
prodeunt omnia; ut semel missa[1] sunt, vadunt;
idem erit illis cursus qui sui finis.   Opus hoc aeternum irrevocabiles habet motus; qui si quando con-
stiterint, alia aliis incident, quae nunc tenor et
aequalitas servat."

7   Quid est ergo cur aliqua redire videantur? Solis
occursus speciem illis tarditatis imponit et natura
viarum circulorumque sic positorum ut certo tempore intuentes fallant;[2] sic naves, quamvis plenis velis
eant, videntur tamen stare.   Erit qui demonstret
aliquando in quibus cometae partibus currant, cur
tam seducti a ceteris errent, quanti qualesque sint.
Contenti simus inventis; aliquid veritati et posteri
conferant.

1   26. " Per stellas," inquit, " ulteriora non cernimus;
per cometas aciem transmittimus." Primum si
fit istud, non in ea parte fit qua sidus ipsum est spissi
ignis ac solidi, sed qua rarus splendor excurrit et in

---

[1] *missa* HEZV Oltramare; *iussa* Gercke.
[2] Fortunatus, Gercke, Oltramare for *afflant* HPEZ; *afficiat*
ABV.

was rising or whether it was setting or retrograde (for that is the term they have given to it when it recedes)—we learned only a few years ago.

People have been found who would say to us: 6 " You are wrong if you judge that any star either stops or alters its orbit. It is not possible for celestial bodies to stand still or turn away. They all move forward. Once they are set in motion they advance. The end of their orbital motion will be the same as their own end. This eternal creation has irrevocable movements. If they stop at any time it means that the bodies which are now maintained by a constancy and equilibrium will collide with one another."

What is the reason, then, that some celestial bodies 7 appear to move backward? The encounter with the sun imposes upon them the appearance of slowness, as well as the nature of their paths and their orbits which are so placed that at a fixed period they deceive observers. In the same way ships seem to be standing still even though they are moving under full sail. Some day there will be a man who will show in what regions comets have their orbit, why they travel so remote from other celestial bodies, how large they are and what sort they are. Let us be satisfied with what we have found out, and let our descendants also contribute something to the truth.

26. Someone says, " We do not see through stars 1 to objects on the other side, yet our vision passes through comets." First of all, if this does happen, it does not happen in that part where the celestial body itself is a thick and solid fire but only where a scattered glow extends and is dispersed into hair.

crines dispergitur; per intervalla ignium, non per ipsos vides.

2   " Stellae," inquit, " omnes rotundae sunt, cometae porrecti; ex quo apparet stellas non esse." Quis enim tibi concedit cometas longos esse? Quorum natura quidem, ut ceterorum siderum, globus est, ceterum fulgor extenditur. Quemadmodum sol radios suos longe lateque dimittit, ceterum ipsi alia est forma, alia ei quod ex ipso fluit lumini, sic cometarum corpus ipsum corrotundatur, splendor autem longior quam ceterorum siderum apparet.

1   27. " Quare? " inquis. Dic tu mihi prius quare luna dissimillimum soli lumen accipiat, cum accipiat a sole; quare modo rubeat, modo palleat; quare lividus illi et ater color sit, cum conspectu solis excluditur.

2   Dic mihi quare omnes stellae inter se dissimilem habeant aliquatenus faciem, diversissimam soli. Quomodo nihil prohibet ista sidera esse, quamvis similia non sint, sic nihil prohibet cometas aeternos esse et sortis eiusdem cuius cetera, etiamsi faciem illis non habent similem.

3   Quid porro? Mundus ipse, si consideres illum, nonne ex diversis compositus est? Quid est quare in Leone sol semper ardeat et terras aestibus torreat, in Aquario astringat hiemem, flumina gelu claudat? Et hoc tamen et illud sidus eiusdem condicionis est, cum effectu et natura dissimile sit. Intra brevissimum tempus Aries extollitur, Libra tardissime emergit; et hoc tamen sidus et illud eiusdem naturae

You see through the gaps in the fire not through the fire itself.

"Stars," he says, "are all round, comets are ex- 2 tended; from which it is apparent that they are not stars." But who will concede to you that comets are elongated? In fact, their nature is a globe shape, as is that of the other celestial bodies, only their glow is extended. Just as the sun sends out rays far and wide but itself has a different shape, different from the light which flows from it, so the body itself of comets is rounded but their glow appears more lengthened than that of other celestial bodies.

27. "Why?" you ask. Tell me first why the 1 moon receives light totally unlike the sun although she receives it from the sun. Why does the moon sometimes grow red, sometimes pale? Why is her colour blue or black when she is cut off from the sun's view? Tell me why all stars have an appearance 2 unlike each other to some extent and very unlike the sun. It in no way prevents them from being true celestial bodies, even though they are not alike. In the same way nothing prevents comets from being eternal and in the same category as that of the other stars, though comets do not have a similar appearance.

What more is there to say? Is not the universe, 3 if you examine it, composed of contrasts? Why is it that in Leo the sun is always blazing and scorches the earth with its heat, in Aquarius it clamps winter down, closes the rivers with ice? Yet both constellations are of the same class even though they are unlike in influence and characteristics. Aries rises within a very short time, Libra emerges quite slowly; and yet both these constellations are of the

est, cum illud exiguo tempore ascendat, hoc diu
4 proferatur. Non vides quam contraria inter se ele-
menta sint? Gravia et levia sunt, frigida et calida,
umida et sicca; tota haec mundi concordia ex dis-
cordibus constat. Negas cometen stellam esse, quia
forma eius non respondeat ad exemplar nec sit ceteris
similis? Vides enim: simillima est illa quae tri-
cesimo anno revertitur ad locum suum huic quae
5 intra annum revisit sedem suam. Non ad unam
natura formam opus suum praestat, sed ipsa varietate
se iactat. Alia maiora,[1] alia velociora aliis fecit, alia
validiora,[2] alia temperatiora; quaedam eduxit a
turba, ut singula et conspicua procederent, quaedam
in gregem misit. Ignorat naturae potentiam qui
illi non putat aliquando licere, nisi quod saepius fecit.
6 Cometas non frequenter ostendit, attribuit illis
alium locum, alia tempora, dissimiles ceteris motus;
voluit et his magnitudinem operis sui colere. Quorum
formosior facies est quam ut fortuitam putes, sive
amplitudinem eorum consideres, sive fulgorem qui
maior est ardentiorque quam ceteris. Facies vero
habet insigne quiddam et singulare, non in angustum
coniecta et artata, sed dimissa liberius et multarum
stellarum amplexa regionem.
1 28. Aristoteles ait cometas significare tempestatem

---

[1] *minora* ABVT.   [2] *calidiora* Z.

same character, although one ascends in a short time and the other appears slowly. Do you not see how 4 opposite the elements are among themselves? They are heavy and light, cold and hot, wet and dry; all the harmony of this universe is formed out of discordant elements. You say that a comet is not a star because its form does not correspond to a type and it is not just like other stars. Consider: a body that returns to its position every thirty years is very similar to a body that revisits its place in a year. Nature 5 does not present her work in only one form but prides herself on her variety. She has made some things larger, some swifter than others, some stronger, some more moderate; she has separated some from the crowd, so that they might move as unique and conspicuous things; some she has consigned to the herd. Anyone who thinks that nature is not occasionally able to do something she has not done frequently, simply does not understand the power of nature.

Nature does not often display comets. She has 6 assigned to them a different place, different periods, movements unlike the other celestial bodies. Also, she wished by means of comets to honour the magnitude of her work. The appearance of comets is too beautiful for you to consider an accident, whether you examine their size or their brightness, which is greater and more brilliant than the other celestial bodies. In fact, their appearance has a kind of exceptional distinction. They are not bound and confined to a narrow spot but are let loose and freely cover the region of many celestial bodies.

28. Aristotle says that comets indicate a storm 1

et ventorum intemperantiam atque imbrium. Quid ergo ? Non iudicas sidus esse quod futura denuntiat ? Non enim sic hoc tempestatis signum est quomodo futurae pluviae

Scintillare oleum et putres concrescere fungos,

aut quomodo indicium est saevituri maris, si

marinae
In sicco ludunt fulicae notasque paludes
Deserit atque altam supra volat ardea nubem,

sed sic quomodo aequinoctium in calorem frigusque flectentis anni, quomodo illa quae Chaldaei canunt, quid stella nascentibus triste laetumve constituat.

2 Hoc ut scias ita esse, non statim cometes ortus ventos et pluvias minatur, ut Aristoteles ait, sed annum totum suspectum facit; ex quo apparet illum non ex proximo quae in proximum daret signa traxisse, sed habere reposita et comprensa [1] legibus 3 mundi. Fecit hic cometes qui Paterculo et Vopisco consulibus apparuit, quae ab Aristotele Theophrastoque sunt praedicta; fuerunt enim maximae et

[1] *comprehensa* ABT; *compressa* HZ; *compulsa* V.

---

[1] Aristotle 1.7.344b 20–345a 5.
[2] Virgil *Georg.* 1.392.
[3] Virgil *Georg.* 1.362. The sea-" coots " would be black sea-birds of some kind.

and undue excess wind and rain.[1] Well, what of it? Do you not judge that that which foretells the future is a celestial body? Indeed, a comet is not a sign of storm in the same way that there is a sign of coming rain when

> The oil in the lamp sputters
> And a crumbling excrescence
> Grows on the wick,[2]

or in the same way that it is a forecast of rough sea if

> The sea-coots play on dry land,
> And the heron deserts her familiar swamp
> And flies above the high cloud,[3]

but in the way that the equinox is a sign of the year turning to hot or to cold, or as the things the Chaldaeans predict, the sorrow or joy that is established at people's birth by a star.

In order that you may understand that this is true: 2 the rising of a comet does not immediately threaten wind or rain, as Aristotle says it does, but makes the entire year suspect.[4] From which it is clear that the comet has not drawn from its close neighbourhood the signs which it gives for the immediate future but that it has them stored up and linked to the laws of the universe. The comet which appeared in the consul- 3 ship of Paterculus and Vopiscus [5] did what was predicted by Aristotle and Theophrastus: for there were

---

[4] Aristotle 1.7.344b 27.
[5] L. Julius Paterculus and Vopiscus were *consules suffecti* in A.D. 60. On the chronological relationship between this comet, the earthquake in Achaia, and Macedonia, and the earthquake at Pompeii, see above 6.1.2 and note.

continuae tempestates ubique, at in Achaia Macedoniaque urbes terrarum motibus prorutae sunt.

1 29. "Tarditas," inquit, "illorum argumentum est graviores esse multumque in se habere terreni. Ipse praeterea cursus; fere enim compelluntur in cardines." Utrumque falsum est. De priore dicam prius. Omnia [1] quae tardius feruntur gravia sunt. Quid ergo? Stella Saturni, quae ex omnibus iter suum lentissime efficit, gravis est? Atqui levitatis

2 argumentum habet quod supra ceteras est. "Sed maiore," inquis, "ambitu circuit nec tardius it quam ceterae sed longius." Succurrat tibi idem me de cometis posse dicere, etiamsi segnior illis cursus sit. Sed mendacium est ire eos tardius, nam intra sextum mensem dimidiam partem caeli transcurrit hic proximus, prior intra pauciores menses recepit se.

3 "Sed quia graves sunt, inferius deferuntur." Primum non defertur quod circumfertur. Deinde hic proximus a septentrione motus sui initium fecit et per occidentem in meridiana pervenit erigensque cursum suum oblituit, alter ille Claudianus, a septentrione primum visus, non desiit in rectum assidue celsior ferri,[2] donec excessit.

Haec sunt quae aut alios movere ad cometas pertinentia aut me. Quae an vera sint, dii sciunt, qui-

---

[1] Gercke, Oltramare for *quia* HPEZAV.
[2] *fieri* OBV.

---

[1] Pliny 2.112: fires falling from above into the clouds produce storms.

very violent and continuous storms everywhere,[1] and in Achaia and Macedonia cities were destroyed by earthquake.

29. " The slowness of comets is proof," someone **1** says, " that they are rather heavy and contain much earth-matter. Besides, their very orbit is proof of this, for generally they are driven towards cardinal points." Both ideas are wrong. I will speak first about the former. All bodies are heavy that move rather slowly. What about this? Is the planet Saturn heavy, which completes its orbit the slowest of all planets? And yet the fact that it is higher than the others holds proof of its lightness. " But," you **2** say, " it circles by a greater orbit and does not move more slowly than the others but over a longer distance." It should occur to you that I could make the same statement about comets, even if their orbit were slow. But it is not true that they move slowly, for this last comet ran across half the sky in only six months. The previous comet withdrew in fewer months.

" But because they are heavier they are carried **3** lower." In the first place, a thing is not carried down, if it is carried around. In the second place, this recent comet started its motion in the north and passing through the west it arrived in the southern region and its orbit passed out of sight as it was rising. The other comet, the one in the time of Claudius, was first seen in the north, and was carried continuously straight up and did not stop until it disappeared.

These are the matters pertaining to comets which have impressed me and others. Whether or not they

bus est scientia veri. Nobis rimari illa et coniectura ire in occulta tantum licet, nec cum fiducia inveniendi nec sine spe.

1   30. Egregie Aristoteles ait numquam nos vere-cundiores esse debere quam cum de diis agitur. Si intramus templa compositi, si ad sacrificium accessuri vultum submittimus, togam adducimus, si in omne argumentum modestiae fingimur,[1] quanto hoc magis facere debemus, cum de sideribus de stellis de deorum natura disputamus, ne quid temere, ne quid impu-denter[2] aut ignorantes affirmemus, aut scientes

2   mentiamur! Nec miremur tam tarde erui quae tam alte iacent. Panaetio et his qui videri volunt cometen non esse ordinarium sidus sed falsam sideris faciem diligenter tractandum est an aeque omnis pars anni edendis cometis satis apta sit, an omnis caeli regio idonea in qua creentur, an, quacumque ire, ibi etiam concipi possint, et cetera. Quae universa tolluntur, cum dico illos non fortuitos esse ignes sed intextos mundo, quos non frequenter educit sed in occulto movet.

3   Quam multa praeter hos per secretum eunt num-quam humanis oculis orientia! Neque enim omnia deus homini fecit.[3] Quota pars operis tanti nobis

---

[1] *fungimur* ABVT.
[2] *imprudenter* HZE.
[3] *patefecit* Gercke.

---

[1] This passage of Aristotle is otherwise unknown.

are true only the gods know, who have knowledge of the truth. We can only investigate these things and grope into the dark with hypotheses, not with the assurance of discovering the truth, and yet not without hope.

30. Aristotle has said excellently that we should 1 never be more reverent than when a subject deals with the gods.[1] If we enter temples with composure, if, when we are about to approach a sacrifice, we lower our eyes, draw in our toga, if we assume every sign of modesty, how much more ought we to do so when we discuss the planets, the stars, the nature of the gods, lest in our ignorance we assert something rashly, impudently, or even lie knowingly! Let us 2 not be surprised that things which are so deeply hidden are dug out so slowly. Panaetius [2] and others who wish it to be the view that a comet is not an ordinary celestial body but only the false appearance of one, must investigate diligently whether all seasons of the year are equally enough suited for producing comets, whether all regions of the sky are suitable for comets to be created there, whether they can also be formed in any place wherever they might pass, etc. All these investigations are dismissed when I say that comets are not accidental fires but are interwoven in a universe that produces them infrequently and causes them in an unknown way to move.

How many other bodies besides these comets 3 move in secret, never rising before the eyes of men! For god has not made all things for man. How much a part of god's immense work is entrusted to

[2] Panaetius of Rhodes, a Stoic, was the teacher of Posidonius.

committitur? Ipse qui ista tractat, qui condidit,
qui totum hoc fundavit [1] deditque circa se, maiorque
est pars sui operis ac melior, effugit oculos; cogita-
4 tione visendus est.   Multa praeterea cognata numini
summo et vicinam sortita potentiam obscura sunt aut
fortasse, quod magis mireris, oculos nostros et im-
plent et effugiunt, sive illis tanta subtilitas est
quantam consequi acies humana non possit, sive in
sanctiore secessu maiestas tanta delituit et regnum
suum, id est se, regit, nec ulli dat aditum nisi animo.
Quid sit hoc sine quo nihil est scire non possumus,
et miramur si quos igniculos parum novimus, cum
maxima pars mundi, deus, lateat!
5   Quam multa animalia [2] hoc primum cognovimus
saeculo, quam multa ne hoc quidem! [3]   Multa veni-
entis aevi populus ignota nobis sciet; multa saeculis
tunc futuris cum memoria nostri exoleverit reser-
vantur.   Pusilla res mundus est, nisi in illo quod
6 quaerat omnis aetas [4] habeat.   Non semel quaedam
sacra traduntur: Eleusin servat quod ostendat
revisentibus; rerum natura sacra sua non semel
tradit.   Initiatos nos credimus, in vestibulo eius
haeremus.   Illa arcana non promiscue nec omnibus
patent; reducta et interiore sacrario clausa sunt, ex

[1] *firmavit* ABV; *formavit* T.
[2] *venalia* Gercke.
[3] *quam multa negotia ne hoc* MSS. Oltramare; *negotia* excised
by Alexander.
[4] *aetas* Z Alexander; *mundus* MSS. Oltramare.

us? The very one who handles this universe, who established it, who laid the foundations of all that is and placed it around himself, and who is the greater and better part of his work, has escaped our sight; he has to be perceived in thought. Moreover, many 4 things related to the highest divinity or allotted a neighbouring power are obscure. Or perhaps—which may surprise you more—they both fill and elude our vision. Either their subtlety is greater than the human eye-sight is able to follow or such a great majesty conceals itself in too holy a seclusion. It rules its kingdom—that is, itself—and grants no admission to any except the mind. What this is, without which nothing exists, we are not able to know. And yet we are surprised if we imperfectly understand some little bits of fire, even though the greatest part of the universe, god, remains hidden!

How many animals we have learned about for the 5 first time in this age; how many are not known even now! Many things that are unknown to us the people of a coming age will know. Many discoveries are reserved for ages still to come, when memory of us will have been effaced. Our universe is a sorry little affair unless it has in it something for every age to investigate. Some sacred 6 things are not revealed once and for all. Eleusis keeps in reserve something to show to those who revisit there. Nature does not reveal her mysteries once and for all. We believe that we are her initiates but we are only hanging around the forecourt. Those secrets are not open to all indiscriminately. They are withdrawn and closed up in the inner sanctum. This age will glimpse one of the

quibus aliud haec aetas, aliud quae post nost subibit aspiciet.

1   31. Quando ergo ista in notitiam nostram perducentur? Tarde magna proveniunt, utique si labor cessat. Id quod unum toto agimus animo, nondum perfecimus ut pessimi essemus; adhuc in processu vitia sunt. Invenit luxuria aliquid novi, in quod insaniat; invenit impudicitia novam contumeliam sibi; invenit deliciarum dissolutio et tabes aliquid

2 adhuc tenerius molliusque, quo pereat. Nondum satis robur omne proiecimus; adhuc quicquid est boni moris extinguimus. Levitate et politura corporum muliebres munditias antecessimus, colores meretricios matronis quidem non induendos viri sumimus, tenero et molli ingressu suspendimus gradum (non ambulamus sed incedimus), exornamus anulis digitos, in omni articulo gemma disponitur.

3 Cotidie comminiscimur per quae virilitati fiat iniuria, ut traducatur, quia non potest exui; alius genitalia excidit, alius in obscenam ludi partem fugit et, locatus ad mortem, infame armaturae genus [1] in quo morbum suum exerceat legit.

1   32. Miraris si nondum sapientia omne opus suum implevit! Nondum tota se nequitia protulit; adhuc

---

[1] *armaturae genus* Housman, Gercke, Oltramare for *armatur. egenus* HPEZ; *armatur et genus* ABV.

---

[1] [We may accept Housman's emendation without his belief that the *tunica* (i.e. the *armaturae genus*) of a " net-fighting " gladiator (*retiarius*) is meant. Housman (*Class. Rev.* XVIII

secrets; the age which comes after us will glimpse another.

31. " When, then, will these things be brought to 1
our knowledge?" Great works come forward only
slowly, especially if effort lags. The one thing we
strive for with our entire mind—to be as full of evil
as possible—we have not yet achieved. Vices are
still making progress. Luxury still discovers some
new fad in which it may carry on foolishly. Indecency
finds a new insult to itself. The dissolution and
corruption of soft living finds something still more
refined and delicate for its own destruction. We have 2
not yet done enough throwing away of all our
strength. We go on stifling whatever is left of
morality. By the smoothness and polish of our
bodies we men have surpassed a woman's refinements.
We men have taken over the cosmetics of whores,
which would not indeed be worn by decent women.
With a delicate soft gait we swing our steps high—
we do not walk, we strut. We adorn our fingers with
rings; a gem is arranged on every joint. Daily we 3
invent ways whereby an indignity may be done to
manliness, to ridicule it, because it cannot be cast off.
One man cuts of his genitals, another flees to an
indecent part of a gladiators' school; and, hired for
death, he chooses a disgraceful type of armament to
practise his sickness in.[1]

32. You are surprised that wisdom has not yet 1
achieved all its work! Depravation has not yet
displayed itself entirely; it is still being born. And

1904, 395 ff.) was answered by S. G. Owen (*Class. Rev.* XIX
1905, 354 ff.). I feel that Seneca does not mean to indicate
any particular gladiator or weapon.—E.H.W.]

nascitur. Et huic omnes operam damus, huic oculi
nostri, huic manus serviunt. Ad sapientiam quis
accedit? Quis dignam iudicat nisi quam in transitu
noverit? Quis philosophum aut ullum liberale
respicit studium, nisi cum ludi intercalantur, cum
aliquis pluvius intervenit dies quem perdere libet?
2 Itaque tot familiae philosophorum sine successore
deficiunt. Academici et veteres et minores nullum
antistitem reliquerunt. Quis est qui tradat prae-
cepta Pyrrhonis?[1] Pythagorica illa invidiosa turbae
schola praeceptorem non invenit. Sextiorum nova
et Romani roboris secta inter initia sua, cum magno
3 impetu coepisset, extincta est. At quanta cura
laboratur, ne cuius pantomimi nomen intercidat!
Stat per successores Pyladis et Bathylli domus;
harum artium multi discipuli sunt multique doctores.
Privatum urbe tota sonat pulpitum; in hoc viri, in
hoc feminae tripudiant; mares[2] inter se uxoresque
contendunt uter det latus mollius.[3] Deinde, sub
persona cum diu trita frons est, transitur ad galeam.
4   Philosophiae nulla cura est. Itaque adeo nihil
invenitur ex his quae parum investigata antiqui
reliquerunt ut multa quae inventa erant oblitteren-

---

[1] *Platonis* ABV.
[2] *maris* Z; *maritus* Leo; *mariti* Gercke.
[3] Madvig, Oltramare for *illius* MSS; *mimis* Alexander.

---

[1] Pyrrho of Elis founded the Sceptic School. He died about
275 B.C.
[2] During the first century B.C. Q. Sextius and his son Sex-

we all give our energy to vice; our eyes and our hands
are in its service. Who comes near wisdom? Who
judges wisdom worthy of more than learning about in
passing? Who respects a philosopher or any liberal
study except when the games are called off for a time
or there is some rainy day which he is willing to
waste? And so the many schools of philosophy are 2
dying without a successor. The Academy, both the
Old and the New, has no professor left. Who is then
to teach the precepts of Pyrrho?[1] That famous
school of Pythagoras, hated by the rabble, has not
found a teacher. The new sect of the Sextii,[2] made
up of truly Roman vigour, was extinct at its very
beginning although it started with great energy.
But how much worry is suffered lest the name of some 3
pantomime actor be lost for ever! The House of
Pylades and of Bathyllus[3] continues through a long
line of successors. For their arts there are many
students and many teachers. The acting-stage
resounds in private homes throughout the entire
city. On it both men and women dance. Husbands
and wives contend over which of the two may bare
the flank more voluptuously. Finally, when the
brow is worn smooth long under the mask a
transition is made to the helmet of the gladiator.

There is no interest in philosophy. Accordingly, 4
so little is found out from those subjects which the
ancients left partially investigated that many things
which were discovered are being forgotten. But,

tius Niger advocated a moral system based on a knowledge of
nature.

[3] Pylades and Bathyllus were rival pantomime performers
in the time of Tiberius.

tur. At mehercule, si hoc totis membris premere-
mus, si in hoc iuventus sobria incumberet, hoc
maiores docerent, hoc minores addiscerent, vix ad
fundum veniretur in quo veritas posita est, quam
nunc in summa terra et levi manu quaerimus.

by Hercules, if we applied ourselves to this with all our might—if youth soberly applied itself to it, if the elders taught it and the younger generation learned it—we would scarcely reach to the bottom where truth is located, which we now seek on the surface of the earth and with slack effort.

INDEX OF SENECA'S SOURCES

(A brief identification of the lesser known authorities is given in the footnotes at the first occurrence of the name.)

INDEX OF PROPER NAMES

(Other than those of Seneca's sources)

INDEX OF PROPER NAMES

INDEX OF PROPER NAMES

INDEX OF PROPER NAMES

INDEX OF SUBJECTS

compiled by S. Naughton

INDEX OF SUBJECTS

INDEX OF SUBJECTS

INDEX OF SUBJECTS

NOTE ON WINDS

Scientific writers in Graeco-Roman times preferred exact divisions of the sky and an exact direction-source for each wind; but natural lack of precision in most people caused some wind-names to be applied vaguely each to more than one wind, and direction-names to be applied with like vagueness; just as one says, as if it were always true, that " the sun rises in the east (*oriens*, ἀνατολή) and sets in the west " (*occasus, occidens*, δύσις ἡλίου), whereas the sun does these things twice only during every year. So we have:—Ἄρκτος the " Bear ", *Septemtrio(nes)* the " Seven-Star Team ", is the northern direction. But Βορέας, *Aquilo* (" dusky, watery " ?), a northerly direction and wind, came to be applied more exactly to the NNE wind, Ἀπαρκτίας being the true-north wind. The Greek Μέσης (" middle wind ") was presumably the NE wind, though the name Καικίας (derived maybe from the river Κάϊκος), properly the ENE wind, was sometimes given to the NE or even to the NNE wind. Any eastern direction was called in general by the Greeks Εὖρος (" parching " from εὔω? or " dawn-region " from ἔως? or " breezy " from αὔρα?), *Eurus*. From it blew the east wind (Ἀπηλιώτης or Ἀφηλιώτης " from the sun ", *Subsolanus* " under the sun "; sometimes called Εὖρος, *Eurus*). But later, the wind Εὖρος, Eurus, or *Volturnus* or *Vulturnus* (wind of what is now Monte Vulture in Apulia) was specially the ESE, though sometimes it was the

NOTE ON WINDS

SE—indeed in one old system even NE. From the SSE came the Εὐρόνοτος (" east-south "), *Phoenix*. The southern direction proper was μεσημβρία, *meridies*, " mid-day ", and the south wind was Νότος (" wet ", " damp wind "), *Auster* (" hot wind ")—names applied also to south-westerlies and their directions. To the SSW wind were applied the names Λευκόνοτος (" clear-weather damp "—it was naturally used also for a due south wind) and Λιβόνοτος (" Libyan-African damp "). The SW wind was Λίψ, *Africus*, though the name Λίψ was used not only more precisely for the SSW but also widely for the western direction and sometimes for the southern. Any west wind was for long called Ζέφυρος (" wind of the dark "), *Favonius*, " favourable wind "; but later the name Ζέφυρος was usually the due west wind. Across southern Gaul and the sea to the central Italian coast blew *Circius* from the WNW. This is the *mistral*. Another Celtic wind *Caurus* or *Corus* came from the NW; and in Greece there was Θρασκίας or Θρᾳκίας, " Thracian wind ", from the NNW. There were other winds, some locally named. In particular Ἀργέστης (Argestes in mythology was a son of Astraeus, father of the winds) was vague. In Homer ἀργεστής means " clearing ", " brightening " and is applied to a southern wind. By some later writers it was, as applied to a particular wind, held to blow like Λίψ from the south-west; but by most people perhaps like Corus from the NW.

With regard to Book V. 16.3–V. 17.2, although there are two solstices, the summer and the winter, Seneca, in accordance with common Roman custom, uses the epithet *solstitialis* with reference to summer only.

—E. H. Warmington.

WINDS

Winds at the Earth's surface, and their directional sources.
Sen. *N.Q.V.* 16.1–17.5. See also pp. 311–312.
O: observer.

ZONES

The Graeco-Roman imaginary hemisphere of heaven as if in a sense seen from outside; showing, in out-of-scale perspective, a projection of imaginary circles of heaven onto a hemisphere of the Earth (shaded).
1: arctic belt or zone. 2: north temperate zone. 3: torrid zone. 4: south temperate zone. 5: antarctic zone.
Sen. *N.Q.V.* 17.2–4.

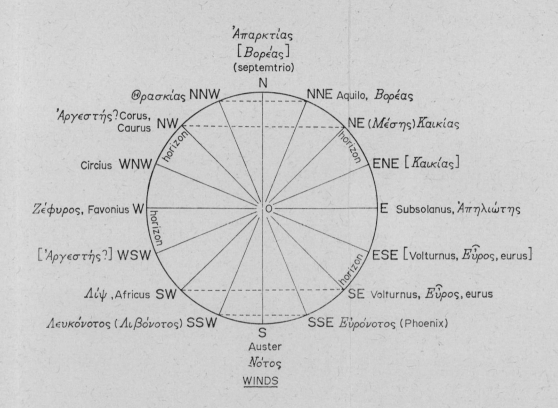

WINDS

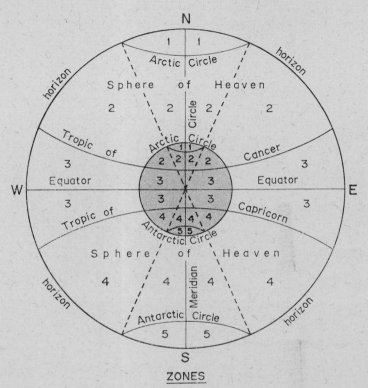

ZONES

Printed in Great Britain by
Richard Clay (The Chaucer Press), Ltd.
Bungay, Suffolk

THE LOEB CLASSICAL LIBRARY

VOLUMES ALREADY PUBLISHED

Latin Authors

AMMIANUS MARCELLINUS. Translated by J. C. Rolfe. 3 Vols.

APULEIUS: THE GOLDEN ASS (METAMORPHOSES). W. Adlington (1566). Revised by S. Gaselee.

ST. AUGUSTINE: CITY OF GOD. 7 Vols. Vol. I. G. E. McCracken. Vol. II. and VII. W. M. Green. Vol. III. D. Wiesen. Vol. IV. P. Levine. Vol. V. E. M. Sanford and W. M. Green. Vol. VI. W. C. Greene.

ST. AUGUSTINE, CONFESSIONS OF. W. Watts (1631). 2 Vols.

ST. AUGUSTINE, SELECT LETTERS. J. H. Baxter.

AUSONIUS. H. G. Evelyn White. 2 Vols.

BEDE. J. E. King. 2 Vols.

BOETHIUS: TRACTS and DE CONSOLATIONE PHILOSOPHIAE. REV. H. F. Stewart and E. K. Rand. Revised by S. J. Tester.

CAESAR: ALEXANDRIAN, AFRICAN and SPANISH WARS. A. G. Way.

CAESAR: CIVIL WARS. A. G. Peskett.

CAESAR: GALLIC WAR. H. J. Edwards.

CATO: DE RE RUSTICA; VARRO: DE RE RUSTICA. H. B. Ash and W. D. Hooper.

CATULLUS. F. W. Cornish; TIBULLUS. J. B. Postgate; PERVIGILIUM VENERIS. J. W. Mackail.

CELSUS: DE MEDICINA. W. G. Spencer. 3 Vols.

CICERO: BRUTUS, and ORATOR. G. L. Hendrickson and H. M. Hubbell.

[CICERO]: AD HERENNIUM. H. Caplan.

CICERO: DE ORATORE, etc. 2 Vols. Vol. I. DE ORATORE, Books I. and II. E. W. Sutton and H. Rackham. Vol. II. DE ORATORE, Book III. De Fato; Paradoxa Stoicorum; De Partitione Oratoria. H. Rackham.

CICERO: DE FINIBUS. H. Rackham.

CICERO: DE INVENTIONE, etc. H. M. Hubbell.

CICERO: DE NATURA DEORUM and ACADEMICA. H. Rackham.

CICERO: DE OFFICIIS. Walter Miller.

CICERO: DE REPUBLICA and DE LEGIBUS: SOMNIUM SCIPIONIS. Clinton W. Keyes.

CICERO: DE SENECTUTE, DE AMICITIA, DE DIVINATIONE. W. A. Falconer.

CICERO: IN CATILINAM, PRO FLACCO, PRO MURENA, PRO SULLA. Louis E. Lord

CICERO: LETTERS to ATTICUS. E. O. Winstedt. 3 Vols.

CICERO: LETTERS TO HIS FRIENDS. W. Glynn Williams, M. Cary, M. Henderson. 4 Vols.

CICERO: PHILIPPICS. W. C. A. Ker.

CICERO: PRO ARCHIA POST REDITUM, DE DOMO, DE HARUS-PICUM RESPONSIS, PRO PLANCIO. N. H. Watts.

CICERO: PRO CAECINA, PRO LEGE MANILIA, PRO CLUENTIO, PRO RABIRIO. H. Grose Hodge.

CICERO: PRO CAELIO, DE PROVINCIIS CONSULARIBUS, PRO BALBO. R. Gardner.

CICERO: PRO MILONE, IN PISONEM, PRO SCAURO, PRO FONTEIO, PRO RABIRIO POSTUMO, PRO MARCELLO, PRO LIGARIO, PRO REGE DEIOTARO. N. H. Watts.

CICERO: PRO QUINCTIO, PRO ROSCIO AMERINO, PRO ROSCIO COMOEDO, CONTRA RULLUM. J. H. Freese.

CICERO: PRO SESTIO, IN VATINIUM. R. Gardner.

CICERO: TUSCULAN DISPUTATIONS. J. E. King.

CICERO: VERRINE ORATIONS. L. H. G. Greenwood. 2 Vols.

CLAUDIAN. M. Platnauer. 2 Vols.

COLUMELLA: DE RE RUSTICA. DE ARBORIBUS. H. B. Ash, E. S. Forster and E. Heffner. 3 Vols.

CURTIUS, Q.: HISTORY OF ALEXANDER. J. C. Rolfe. 2 Vols.

FLORUS. E. S. Forster; and CORNELIUS NEPOS. J. C. Rolfe.

FRONTINUS: STRATAGEMS and AQUEDUCTS. C. E. Bennett and M. B. McElwain.

FRONTO: CORRESPONDENCE. C. R. Haines. 2 Vols.

GELLIUS, J. C. Rolfe. 3 Vols.

HORACE: ODES AND EPODES. C. E. Bennett.

HORACE: SATIRES, EPISTLES, ARS POETICA. H. R. Fairclough.

JEROME: SELECTED LETTERS. F. A. Wright.

JUVENAL and PERSIUS. G. G. Ramsay.

LIVY. B. O. Foster, F. G. Moore, Evan T. Sage, and A. C. Schlesinger and R. M. Geer (General Index). 14 Vols.

LUCAN. J. D. Duff.

LUCRETIUS. W. H. D. Rouse.

MARTIAL. W. C. A. Ker. 2 Vols.

MINOR LATIN POETS: from PUBLILIUS SYRUS TO RUTILIUS NAMATIANUS, including GRATTIUS, CALPURNIUS SICULUS, NEMESIANUS, AVIANUS, and others with "Aetna" and the "Phoenix." J. Wight Duff and Arnold M. Duff.

OVID: THE ART OF LOVE and OTHER POEMS. J. H. Mozley.

2

OVID: FASTI. Sir James G. Frazer.
OVID: HEROIDES and AMORES. Grant Showerman.
OVID: METAMORPHOSES. F. J. Miller. 2 Vols.
OVID: TRISTIA and EX PONTO. A. L. Wheeler.
PERSIUS. Cf. JUVENAL.
PETRONIUS. M. Heseltine; SENECA; APOCOLOCYNTOSIS. W. H. D. Rouse.
PHAEDRUS AND BABRIUS (Greek). B. E. Perry.
PLAUTUS. Paul Nixon. 5 Vols.
PLINY: LETTERS, PANEGYRICUS. Betty Radice. 2 Vols.
PLINY: NATURAL HISTORY. Vols. I.–V. and IX. H. Rackham. VI.–VIII. W. H. S. Jones. X. D. E. Eichholz. 10 Vols.
PROPERTIUS. H. E. Butler.
PRUDENTIUS. H. J. Thomson. 2 Vols.
QUINTILIAN. H. E. Butler. 4 Vols.
REMAINS OF OLD LATIN. E. H. Warmington. 4 Vols. Vol. I. (ENNIUS AND CAECILIUS.) Vol. II. (LIVIUS, NAEVIUS, PACUVIUS, ACCIUS.) Vol. III. (LUCILIUS and LAWS OF XII TABLES.) Vol. IV. (ARCHAIC INSCRIPTIONS.)
SALLUST. J. C. Rolfe.
SCRIPTORES HISTORIAE AUGUSTAE. D. Magie. 3 Vols.
SENECA: APOCOLOCYNTOSIS. Cf. PETRONIUS.
SENECA: EPISTULAE MORALES. R. M. Gummere. 3 Vols.
SENECA: MORAL ESSAYS. J. W. Basore. 3 Vols.
SENECA: TRAGEDIES. F. J. Miller. 2 Vols.
SENECA: NATURALES QUAESTIONES. T. H. Corcoran. 2 Vols.
SIDONIUS: POEMS and LETTERS. W. B. Anderson. 2 Vols.
SILIUS ITALICUS. J. D. Duff. 2 Vols.
STATIUS. J. H. Mozley. 2 Vols.
SUETONIUS. J. C. Rolfe. 2 Vols.
TACITUS: DIALOGUS. Sir Wm. Peterson. AGRICOLA and GERMANIA. Maurice Hutton. Revised by M. Winterbottom, R. M. Ogilvie, E. H. Warmington.
TACITUS: HISTORIES AND ANNALS. C. H. Moore and J. Jackson. 4 Vols.
TERENCE. John Sargeaunt. 2 Vols.
TERTULLIAN: APOLOGIA and DE SPECTACULIS. T. R. Glover. MINUCIUS FELIX. G. H. Rendall.
VALERIUS FLACCUS. J. H. Mozley.
VARRO: DE LINGUA LATINA. R. G. Kent. 2 Vols.
VELLEIUS PATERCULUS and RES GESTAE DIVI AUGUSTI. F. W. Shipley.
VIRGIL. H. R. Fairclough. 2 Vols.
VITRUVIUS: DE ARCHITECTURA. F. Granger. 2 Vols.

Greek Authors

ACHILLES TATIUS. S. Gaselee.

AELIAN: ON THE NATURE OF ANIMALS. A. F. Scholfield. 3 Vols.

AENEAS TACTICUS, ASCLEPIODOTUS and ONASANDER. The Illinois Greek Club.

AESCHINES. C. D. Adams.

AESCHYLUS. H. Weir Smyth. 2 Vols.

ALCIPHRON, AELIAN, PHILOSTRATUS: LETTERS. A. R. Benner and F. H. Fobes.

ANDOCIDES, ANTIPHON, Cf. MINOR ATTIC ORATORS.

APOLLODORUS. Sir James G. Frazer. 2 Vols.

APOLLONIUS RHODIUS. R. C. Seaton.

THE APOSTOLIC FATHERS. Kirsopp Lake. 2 Vols.

APPIAN: ROMAN HISTORY. Horace White. 4 Vols.

ARATUS. Cf. CALLIMACHUS.

ARISTOPHANES. Benjamin Bickley Rogers. 3 Vols. Verse trans.

ARISTOTLE: ART OF RHETORIC. J. H. Freese.

ARISTOTLE: ATHENIAN CONSTITUTION, EUDEMIAN ETHICS, VICES AND VIRTUES. H. Rackham.

ARISTOTLE: GENERATION OF ANIMALS. A. L. Peck.

ARISTOTLE: HISTORIA ANIMALIUM. A. L. Peck. Vols. I.–II.

ARISTOTLE: METAPHYSICS. H. Tredennick. 2 Vols.

ARISTOTLE: METEOROLOGICA. H. D. P. Lee.

ARISTOTLE: MINOR WORKS. W. S. Hett. On Colours, On Things Heard, On Physiognomies, On Plants, On Marvellous Things Heard, Mechanical Problems, On Indivisible Lines, On Situations and Names of Winds, On Melissus, Xenophanes, and Gorgias.

ARISTOTLE: NICOMACHEAN ETHICS. H. Rackham.

ARISTOTLE: OECONOMICA and MAGNA MORALIA. G. C. Armstrong; (with METAPHYSICS, Vol. II.).

ARISTOTLE: ON THE HEAVENS. W. K. C. Guthrie.

ARISTOTLE: ON THE SOUL. PARVA NATURALIA. ON BREATH. W. S. Hett.

ARISTOTLE: CATEGORIES, ON INTERPRETATION, PRIOR ANALYTICS. H. P. Cooke and H. Tredennick.

ARISTOTLE: POSTERIOR ANALYTICS, TOPICS. H. Tredennick and E. S. Forster.

ARISTOTLE: ON SOPHISTICAL REFUTATIONS.
On Coming to be and Passing Away, On the Cosmos. E. S. Forster and D. J. Furley.

ARISTOTLE: PARTS OF ANIMALS. A. L. Peck; MOTION AND PROGRESSION OF ANIMALS. E. S. Forster.

ARISTOTLE: PHYSICS. Rev. P. Wicksteed and F. M. Cornford. 2 Vols.

ARISTOTLE: POETICS and LONGINUS. W. Hamilton Fyfe; DEMETRIUS ON STYLE. W. Rhys Roberts.

ARISTOTLE: POLITICS. H. Rackham.

ARISTOTLE: PROBLEMS. W. S. Hett. 2 Vols.

ARISTOTLE: RHETORICA AD ALEXANDRUM (with PROBLEMS. Vol. II). H. Rackham.

ARRIAN: HISTORY OF ALEXANDER and INDICA. Rev. E. Iliffe Robson. 2 Vols.

ATHENAEUS: DEIPNOSOPHISTAE. C. B. Gulick. 7 Vols.

BABRIUS AND PHAEDRUS (Latin). B. E. Perry.

ST. BASIL: LETTERS. R. J. Deferrari. 4 Vols.

CALLIMACHUS: FRAGMENTS. C. A. Trypanis.

CALLIMACHUS, Hymns and Epigrams, and LYCOPHRON. A. W. Mair; ARATUS. G. R. Mair.

CLEMENT OF ALEXANDRIA. Rev. G. W. Butterworth.

COLLUTHUS. Cf. OPPIAN.

DAPHNIS AND CHLOE. Thornley's Translation revised by J. M. Edmonds: and PARTHENIUS. S. Gaselee.

DEMOSTHENES I.: OLYNTHIACS, PHILIPPICS and MINOR ORATIONS. I.-XVII. AND XX. J. H. Vince.

DEMOSTHENES II.: DE CORONA and DE FALSA LEGATIONE. C. A. Vince and J. H. Vince.

DEMOSTHENES III.: MEIDIAS, ANDROTION, ARISTOCRATES, TIMOCRATES and ARISTOGEITON, I. AND II. J. H. Vince.

DEMOSTHENES IV.-VI.: PRIVATE ORATIONS and IN NEAERAM. A. T. Murray.

DEMOSTHENES VII.: FUNERAL SPEECH, EROTIC ESSAY, EXORDIA and LETTERS. N. W. and N. J. DeWitt.

DIO CASSIUS: ROMAN HISTORY. E. Cary. 9 Vols.

DIO CHRYSOSTOM. J. W. Cohoon and H. Lamar Crosby. 5 Vols.

DIODORUS SICULUS. 12 Vols. Vols. I.-VI. C. H. Oldfather. Vol. VII. C. L. Sherman. Vol. VIII. C. B. Welles. Vols. IX. and X. R. M. Geer. Vol. XI. F. Walton. Vol. XII. F. Walton. General Index. R. M. Geer.

DIOGENES LAERTIUS. R. D. Hicks. 2 Vols. New Introduction by H. S. Long.

DIONYSIUS OF HALICARNASSUS: ROMAN ANTIQUITIES. Spelman's translation revised by E. Cary. 7 Vols.

EPICTETUS. W. A. Oldfather. 2 Vols.

EURIPIDES. A. S. Way. 4 Vols. Verse trans.

EUSEBIUS: ECCLESIASTICAL HISTORY. Kirsopp Lake and J. E. L. Oulton. 2 Vols.

GALEN: ON THE NATURAL FACULTIES. A. J. Brock.

THE GREEK ANTHOLOGY. W. R. Paton. 5 Vols.

GREEK ELEGY AND IAMBUS with the ANACREONTEA. J. M. Edmonds. 2 Vols.

THE GREEK BUCOLIC POETS (THEOCRITUS, BION, MOSCHUS). J. M. Edmonds.

GREEK MATHEMATICAL WORKS. Ivor Thomas. 2 Vols.

HERODES. Cf. THEOPHRASTUS: CHARACTERS.

HERODIAN. C. R. Whittaker. 2 Vols.

HERODOTUS. A. D. Godley. 4 Vols.

HESIOD AND THE HOMERIC HYMNS. H. G. Evelyn White.

HIPPOCRATES and the FRAGMENTS OF HERACLEITUS. W. H. S. Jones and E. T. Withington. 4 Vols.

HOMER: ILIAD. A. T. Murray. 2 Vols.

HOMER: ODYSSEY. A. T. Murray. 2 Vols.

ISAEUS. E. W. Forster.

ISOCRATES. George Norlin and LaRue Van Hook. 3 Vols.

[ST. JOHN DAMASCENE]: BARLAAM AND IOASAPH. Rev. G. R. Woodward, Harold Mattingly and D. M. Lang.

JOSEPHUS. 9 Vols. Vols. I.–IV. H. Thackeray. Vol. V. H. Thackeray and R. Marcus. Vols. VI.–VII. R. Marcus. Vol. VIII. R. Marcus and Allen Wikgren. Vol. IX. L. H. Feldman.

JULIAN. Wilmer Cave Wright. 3 Vols.

LIBANIUS. A. F. Norman. Vol. I.

LUCIAN. 8 Vols. Vols. I.–V. A. M. Harmon. Vol. VI. K. Kilburn. Vols. VII.–VIII. M. D. Macleod.

LYCOPHRON. Cf. CALLIMACHUS.

LYRA GRAECA. J. M. Edmonds. 3 Vols.

LYSIAS. W. R. M. Lamb.

MANETHO. W. G. Waddell: PTOLEMY: TETRABIBLOS. F. E. Robbins.

MARCUS AURELIUS. C. R. Haines.

MENANDER. F. G. Allison.

MINOR ATTIC ORATORS (ANTIPHON, ANDOCIDES, LYCURGUS, DEMADES, DINARCHUS, HYPERIDES). K. J. Maidment and J. O. Burtt. 2 Vols.

NONNOS: DIONYSIACA. W. H. D. Rouse. 3 Vols.

OPPIAN, COLLUTHUS, TRYPHIODORUS. A. W. Mair.

PAPYRI. NON-LITERARY SELECTIONS. A. S. Hunt and C. C. Edgar. 2 Vols. LITERARY SELECTIONS (Poetry). D. L. Page.

PARTHENIUS. Cf. DAPHNIS and CHLOE.

PAUSANIAS: DESCRIPTION OF GREECE. W. H. S. Jones. 4 Vols. and Companion Vol. arranged by R. E. Wycherley.

PHILO. 10 Vols. Vols. I.–V. F. H. Colson and Rev. G. H. Whitaker. Vols. VI.–IX. F. H. Colson. Vol. X. F. H. Colson and the Rev. J. W. Earp.

6

PHILO: two supplementary Vols. (*Translation only*.) Ralph Marcus.

PHILOSTRATUS: THE LIFE OF APOLLONIUS OF TYANA. F. C. Conybeare. 2 Vols.

PHILOSTRATUS: IMAGINES; CALLISTRATUS: DESCRIPTIONS. A. Fairbanks.

PHILOSTRATUS and EUNAPIUS: LIVES OF THE SOPHISTS. Wilmer Cave Wright.

PINDAR. Sir J. E. Sandys.

PLATO: CHARMIDES, ALCIBIADES, HIPPARCHUS, THE LOVERS, THEAGES, MINOS and EPINOMIS. W. R. M. Lamb.

PLATO: CRATYLUS, ZARMENIDES, GREATER HIPPIAS, LESSER HIPPIAS. H. N. Fowler.

PLATO: EUTHYPHRO, APOLOGY, CRITO, PHAEDO, PHAEDRUS. H. N. Fowler.

PLATO: LACHES, PROTAGORAS, MENO, EUTHYDEMUS. W. R. M. Lamb.

PLATO: LAWS. Rev. R. G. Bury. 2 Vols.

PLATO: LYSIS, SYMPOSIUM, GORGIAS. W. R. M. Lamb.

PLATO: REPUBLIC. Paul Shorey. 2 Vols.

PLATO: STATESMAN, PHILEBUS. H. N. Fowler; Ion. W. R. M. Lamb.

PLATO: THEAETETUS and SOPHIST. H. N. Fowler.

PLATO: TIMAEUS, CRITIAS, CLITOPHO, MENEXENUS, EPISTULAE. Rev. R. G. Bury.

PLOTINUS: A. H. Armstrong. Vols. I.–III.

PLUTARCH: MORALIA. 16 Vols. Vols. I.–V. F. C. Babbitt. Vol. VI. W. C. Helmbold. Vols. VII. and XIV. P. H. De Lacy and B. Einarson. Vol. VIII. P. A. Clement and H. B. Hoffleit. Vol. IX. E. L. Minar, Jr., F. H. Sandbach, W. C. Helmbold. Vol. X. H. N. Fowler. Vol. XI. L. Pearson and F. H. Sandbach. Vol. XII. H. Cherniss and W. C. Helmbold. Vol. XV. F. H. Sandbach.

PLUTARCH: THE PARALLEL LIVES. B. Perrin. 11 Vols.

POLYBIUS. W. R. Paton. 6 Vols.

PROCOPIUS: HISTORY OF THE WARS. H. B. Dewing. 7 Vols.

PTOLEMY: TETRABIBLOS. Cf. MANETHO.

QUINTUS SMYRNAEUS. A. S. Way. Verse trans.

SEXTUS EMPIRICUS. Rev. R. G. Bury. 4 Vols.

SOPHOCLES. F. Storr. 2 Vols. Verse trans.

STRABO: GEOGRAPHY. Horace L. Jones. 8 Vols.

THEOPHRASTUS: CHARACTERS. J. M. Edmonds. HERODES, etc. A. D. Knox

THEOPHRASTUS: ENQUIRY INTO PLANTS. Sir Arthur Hort, Bart. 2 Vols.

THUCYDIDES. C. F. Smith. 4 Vols.

TRYPHIODORUS. Cf. OPPIAN.
XENOPHON: CYROPAEDIA. Walter Miller. 2 Vols.
XENOPHON: HELLENICA. C. L. Brownson. 2 Vols.
XENOPHON: ANABASIS. C. L. Brownson.
XENOPHON: MEMORABILIA AND OECONOMICUS. E. C. Marchant.
  SYMPOSIUM AND APOLOGY. O. J. Todd.
XENOPHON: SCRIPTA MINORA. E. C. Marchant and G. W.
  Bowersock.

IN PREPARATION

Greek Authors

ARISTIDES: ORATIONS. C. A. Behr.
MUSAEUS: HERO AND LEANDER. T. Gelzer and C. H.
  Whitman.
THEOPHRASTUS: DE CAUSIS PLANTARUM. G. K. K. Link and
  B. Einarson.

Latin Authors

ASCONIUS: COMMENTARIES ON CICERO'S ORATIONS.
  G. W. Bowersock.
BENEDICT: THE RULE. P. Meyvaert.
JUSTIN–TROGUS. R. Moss.
MANILIUS. G. P. Goold.

DESCRIPTIVE PROSPECTUS ON APPLICATION

LONDON   WILLIAM HEINEMANN LTD
Cambridge, Mass.   HARVARD UNIVERSITY PRESS

Date Due

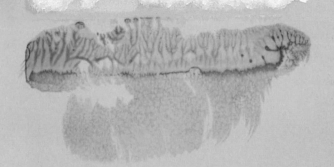